END

MW01614910

"Aptly named, Light on the Frin̲ rupted by the common cold of human suffering; depression. In this book, Drs. Lovejoy and Knopf provide biblical, theological, psychological and medical counsel that is both sound and practical. It is a valuable resource for those who suffer with depression, as well as the clinicians who work with them."

Gene Harker M.D. Ph.D.
Physician, Psychologist and Professor
Indianapolis, Indiana

"Depression is a significant road block to being conformed to the image of Christ. It is time we gave people permission and skills needed to embark upon a holistic journey of healing in Christ in this crucial area. I believe this book can play a significant part in that journey."

Dr. Rick McKinley
Pastor of Imago Dei Community
Author of *This Beautiful Mess* and *Jesus in the Margins*
Portland, Oregon

"The complex interactions of spiritual, psychological and physical factors that contribute to depression need real and understandable answers. Good news! Here is hope and insight. This book is a guide, not down a road of guilt and shame, but provides a path into freedom and wholeness."

Marcus "Goodie" Goodloe
Catalyst, Mosaic Church
Los Angeles, California

"Finally a biblical view of depression that makes sense! All of us have visited the dark hole of despair and depression—some of us have lived there too long. This book is a must-read for anyone who wants to climb out of that hole or help someone else out. Drs. Lovejoy and Knopf in Light on the Fringe: Finding Hope in the Darkness of Depression not only focus a biblical and informed professional light on depression, but chart the biblical course out of the storm into the calm."

Dr. Rich Rollins
Co-author of *Redeeming Relationships*
Hercules, California

"Too often there is misunderstanding in the Christian community regarding mental illness, its meaning and interpretation—with harsh consequences for those lacking understanding. This book presents a wonderful integration of psychological and spiritual insight offering real HOPE to those suffering from depression. Highly recommended."

Jon Messinger, M.D.
Psychiatrist
Portland, Oregon

"I highly recommend the book Light on the Fringe: Finding Hope in the Darkness of Depression by Dr. Gary Lovejoy and Dr. Gregory Knopf. It is a must-read for counselors, pastors and those struggling with depression to help them find a greater understanding of the struggles of depression. It also explains that we do not have to live in despair but can live with joy if we understand what depression is telling us and don't ignore it. I am looking forward to referring the book to many to find incredible healing."

Julie Woodley
Founder/Director of Restoring the Heart Ministry
East Setuaket, New York

"What a great book! I couldn't put it down until I reached the final page. Drs. Lovejoy and Knopf combine a solid biblical worldview with a medical and psychological insight to create one of the best books on the human struggle I've read in years. If you care about people, you must read Light on the Fringe. This is a book about faith and hope and health. It's a book that will help you help others and help yourself."

Dr. Steve Stephens
Author of *Worn out Woman,*
20 Rules and Tools for a Great Marriage* and *Risking Faith
Portland, Oregon

"In the past 35 years, I have witnessed too many pastors who have lost their passion for ministry due to depression. I strongly recommend this book for all leaders who want to maintain their zeal for ministry in their 40s, 50s and 60s. What's more, I highly recommend it for everyone in their congregations, especially those who are hurting and wondering how their faith relates to their pain."

John Bradley
President, IDAK Group
Portland, Oregon

"Where was this book when I hit the wall? Drs. Lovejoy and Knopf open the door to understanding and walking through the real pain of depression. It's clear, practical and points to the source of all hope. If you or someone you care about is experiencing depression, read this book."

Randy Shaw
Director, Northwest Church Planting
Founding Pastor, Mosaic
Portland OR

"Drs. Lovejoy and Knopf have written an easy to approach book that will help us better understand the nature of depression and exercise our spiritual circuits to help restore wellness. The authors explain how there is a hope present, not only from the illness, but from self-imposed guilt, doubt, shame and uncertainty. They illuminate a clear path for the believer to regain hope. Light on the Fringe: Finding Hope in the Darkness of Depression *is precisely on target. This is a book I will want all of my patients of faith who struggle with depression to read. Indeed, I am pleased to recommend it to everyone, including family members, pastors and*

counselors as an excellent study of the path to recovery from depression through a spiritual journey from legalism to grace through faith. This uplifting guide will help many back onto the path of healing of both mind and spirit."

Warner B. Swarner, M.D.
Medical Director, Cornerstone Clinical Services
Portland, Oregon

"This book is impressive! Clearly thought out and researched. It is a study in depression that will help those who read it better understand themselves and how God will cause growth in the worst of times (when it really doesn't feel like He is). It is also the best biochemical interpretation of depression that I have read and the appendix information is very helpful as well."

Reg P. Marto, Ph.D.
Clinical Psychologist
Portland, Oregon

"After pastoring for over 30 years, I have come to the conclusion that many followers of Christ struggle with this problem. Dr. Lovejoy and Dr. Knopf have recognized the important balance of integrating the roots of depression and the important principles and tools (backed by sound biblical doctrine) which people can use to respond more effectively in overcoming their depression. This book is long overdue and I know it will have a profound impact on the many people who desire to be free of the emotional battle that haunts their daily lives."

Dale E. Ebel
Senior Pastor, Rolling Hills Community Church
Tualatin, Oregon

"Knowing Gary Lovejoy and Greg Knopf, I expected their book to be filled with deep psychological and medical wisdom backed by years of clinical experience. I was not disappointed! But I hadn't quite expected the depth and breadth of biblical and theological insights. Now I don't know how to categorize the book. Is it a fine theology text, an excellent commentary on the whole Bible or the best Christian book on depression I've ever read? Perhaps all of the above!"

Gerry Breshears, Ph.D.
Professor of Theology, Western Seminary
Co-author *Vintage Jesus, Death by Love, Vintage Church, Doctrine*
Portland, OR

"This book, like the Psalms of Lament from which it draws in part, presents real issues that affect many, many people. It addresses the problem of those who would challenge the spirituality, even the salvation, of people who are beset with depression. But depression has ranged through time barriers (b.c. and a.d.) and is no respecter of persons (Christian or not). In Light on the Fringe, there is help for many; even for troubled critics."

Dr. Ronald B. Allen
Senior Professor of Bible Exposition
Dallas Theological Seminary
Dallas, TX

LIGHT ON THE FRINGE

finding hope in the darkness of depression

Gary H. Lovejoy, Ph.D.
and Gregory M. Knopf, M.D.

In The Light
COMMUNICATIONS
imparting wisdom & personal wholeness

Light on the Fringe: Finding Hope in the Darkness of Depression

All Scripture quotations, unless otherwise indicated, are taken from the *New American Standard Bible*, ©
1960, 1962, 1963, 1968, 1971, 1972, 1973, 1975, 1977, 1995 by The Lockman Foundation.
Used by permission.

Other versions used are:
NIV—Scripture taken from the Holy Bible, *New International Version*®. Copyright © 1973, 1978, 1984 by
International Bible Society. Used by permission of Zondervan Publishing House. All rights reserved.
NRSV—The Scripture quotations contained herein are from the *New Revised Standard Version Bible*, copy-
right 1989, by the Division of Christian Education of the National Council of the Churches of Christ in the
U.S.A. Used by permission. All rights reserved.
TLB—Scripture quotations marked (TLB) are taken from *The Living Bible*, copyright © 1971.
Used by permission of Tyndale House Publishers, Inc., Wheaton, IL 60189.
All rights reserved.

Publishing and Marketing Support Provided By:
Jeff Pederson at JPED Publishing Group
www.jpedpublishing.com

Library of Congress Cataloging-in-Publication Data
Lovejoy, Gary H.
Light on the Fringe: Finding Hope in the Darkness of Depression / Gary H. Lovejoy and Gregory Knopf.
p. cm.
Includes bibliographical references.
ISBN 978-0-9842177-0-0 (trade paper)
1. Depression, Mental—Religious aspects—Christianity. 2. Depressed persons—Religious life. I. Knopf,
Gregory. II. Title.
BV4910.34.L68 2009
248.8'625—dc22   2008032486

DEDICATIONS

We dedicate this book to our clients—once-hurting people who invited us into their lives for a short time, whose transparency helped us to see the conflicts that often exist between spiritual understanding and emotional experience—that is, between faith and adversity. We commend their courage to challenge their thinking with the truth—something that God has bid us all to do. Above all, we thank them for the ways they encouraged us to reexamine our own faith, to make it more real and relevant to the issues God's Word has addressed and to do so with compassion and tenderness.

ACKNOWLEDGMENTS

We want to thank those whose timely insights over the years have stimulated our thinking, especially the folks in our covenant group. These dear friends, whom we have known and fellowshipped with for nearly 25 years, have, throughout our professional careers, provided their unwavering emotional and spiritual support. We also want to thank our families for enduring the time-intensive responsibilities of such a project. Their interest, patience and encouragement reassured our efforts to stay the course until we completed our work.

Also deserving of our gratitude are those who have given their time and energy to review (or listen to) various parts of the book and to give us invaluable feedback about its content. These have included Cheryl Adelman, Roger Greene, Linda Streger, Dr. Don Harris, Himon and Nellie Cradduck, Betty Holmlund, Ken Aust and Kathy Ward. We are also indebted to David Sanford, who worked with us and provided unstinting support for our project.

Special thanks go to Brian Smith, whose herculean efforts to edit the manuscript will never be forgotten. His sensitive spirit and undeniable expertise uplifted the entire enterprise. We must also mention the wonderful direction we've received (and are still receiving) from our publishing, branding and marketing director, Jeff Pederson (President/CEO of JPED Consulting, LLC—JPED Publishing Group and Brand Development). His creative spirit, dynamic energy and incredible ability to see the larger picture have provided an enthusiasm for this project few could ever match. Finally, the list would not be complete without recognizing the editing work on the final draft done by Doug Schmidt. His ability to refine a manuscript and capture the voice of the author is remarkable.

Lastly, how can we ever thank enough the tireless efforts of Sue Lovejoy (Dr. Lovejoy's wife) in tackling the seemingly endless task of typing one draft of the manuscript after another? Her indefatigable spirit made possible what few volunteers could have done. We should not fail to mention, too, the assistance of professional typist Karen Weitzel, whose able hand and inspiration made the task easier for us all.

CONTENTS

FOREWORD

If you want advice about fixing your car, you seek out an experienced mechanic; if you want advice about selling your home, you seek a successful real estate agent; and if you want to know more about the weather, you seek the reports of a trained meteorologist. But if you want to understand something as deeply personal as your experience of depression, you would not merely seek a competent therapist—you would also seek one whose mature Christian faith is evident and whose values are similar to your own. In all the years I have known him (and that goes back to our college days together), Gary Lovejoy is just such a person. Indeed, his unwavering belief in God's healing power, his deep love for people, his intellectual curiosity and his understanding of the paradoxical traps others find themselves in makes him compassionate about the Christian's struggle with depression.

Always a man to thoroughly prepare himself for something, Dr. Lovejoy is well educated and trained as a therapist who systematically explores every dimension of a problem. After many years of private practice, in which he has counseled several thousand depressed people, (many of them believers), Dr. Lovejoy has come to some important conclusions about integrating spiritual and emotional insights that reframe the issues clients most often struggle with. In *Light on the Fringe: Finding Hope in the Darkness of Depression,* he answers the question that is so commonly found on the lips of his Christian clients about how to relate their depressive experience to their faith. Many of them feel guilty about being depressed or believe they have somehow failed God by not being sufficiently "happy"—and so have become even further depressed. But Dr. Lovejoy fits their struggles into the larger picture of the image of God in each one of them. He does this in an intensely engaging style, using many relevant examples that bring his ideas into the living room of our experience. By identifying how depression (like anger and fear), is a key emotional alarm system signaling that something in our life needs our attention, he has removed the stigma with which some people view emotional struggles.

Like pain in the physical body, depression is not itself the primary problem but rather a signal calling attention to that problem. To this end, Dr. Lovejoy debunks many of the myths that Christians believe (and that the church often teaches), which serve to inhibit them from even seeking the help they need in the first place. Accordingly, he accurately reveals how God has actually responded to his servants' episodes of depression, episodes that are described in detail in the Bible. He points out that most of the great characters of redemptive history suffered depression at one time or another and yet God used them mightily for His glory.

Without a doubt, *Light on the Fringe: Finding Hope in the Darkness of Depression* is a book that provides the proper basis for understanding self-acceptance, even during the most trying of times. It provides, too, an eye-opening discussion on the misguided perceptions about God that weigh many of us down, and the uplifting alternative rooted in the intimacy for which we are hardwired. Along the way, he makes many useful and practical suggestions for dealing with the various depression-generating strategies we sometimes employ to solve our problems. For this reason alone, Dr. Lovejoy has provided a much-needed volume in a critical area of emotional life. For the believer, it especially addresses those troubling questions that create as much distress for the spiritual life as they do for our emotional health.

Included in this meaningful integration of psychological and theological concepts is a thorough discussion by coauthor Dr. Gregory Knopf concerning the current scene of antidepressant medications. He helpfully points out how each of these medications are used and when they may be contraindicated. As a medical professional, he gives us a peek into the physiology of depression that puts our mind at rest about the conditions under which antidepressant medication is most needed and effective.

All in all, this book should be available for reference in every Christian home. Besides being a good read, it is an invaluable aid in keeping our heads straight about God's view of our struggles. I could not recommend it more highly for our depressed brethren and for those who work with them.

—Dr. Gary Smalley
Author and Speaker on Family Relationships

PREFACE

We were doing a series on the Psalms in our church and I was due to speak on Sunday. As I looked over the psalm chosen for that week, Psalm 22, I could only think of the folks I had counseled just the week before who struggled with the emotional pain conveyed in this Psalm. As they poured out stories of hurt, I could see the psalmist nodding his head in empathy. Indeed, his feelings of abandonment are all too familiar: "My God, my God, why have you forsaken me? Why are you so far from saving me, so far from the words of my groaning? O my God, I cry out by day, but you do not answer, by night and am not silent...But I am a worm and not a man, scorned by men and despised by the people"(vv. 1-2, 6).

Many of us have felt something like this at some point in our lives. Some of these words were even uttered by our Lord in His agony on the cross. But they were originally King David's deeply felt words of despair.

Low points. We all have them. The trouble is, we usually don't know what to do when we're there or how to make sense of them in light our faith. In fact, we tend to think they indicate that we're spiritual failures.

One day, some time ago, Dr. Knopf and I were caught up in a conversation about the frequency of this kind of thinking among our Christian patients. We had both come to the same conclusion: what makes depression difficult for many Christians is their confusion over what it reflects about their spiritual life. Over the years, we have watched countless believers wrestle with self-hatred and self-blame, convinced they are useless to God and a burden to others. They struggle with the idea that God actually wants them to treat themselves with grace and to see themselves for what they are: the marvelous result of His compassionate handiwork. This is what Christian psychologists and others variously call "self-esteem" or "self-acceptance." But God calls it simply knowing the truth.

As Psalm 139 points out in beautiful poetic terms, if anyone knows us, God does. He created us with strengths in order to testify of His glory and honor. He has designed everything about us down to the smallest detail. Nothing was left to chance.

It should not surprise us that depression is part of that design.

What?! How is that possible? Because depression exposes the ways we are thinking and behaving that are unhealthy for us. It dramatizes how far we have drifted in our faulty processing of the past. Depression is unpleasant because it is a purposefully uncomfortable alarm system designed to get our attention. We don't need to be afraid of it or use it as a weapon to dump judgment on ourselves. These reactions only undermine the real purpose of the experience.

Understanding what God has to say about depression and how He responds to us when we are going through a dark period tells us a lot about the God we serve. It also tells us how we can use the experience of depression as a means of growth that will, in time, strengthen our relationships with others and deepen our faith in God. Looking at depression from this perspective gives us a way of seeing that it has, indeed, a divinely designed purpose.

This book is the result of ongoing discussions about these things over many years. We hope that it enlightens and lightens you. Our journey through life is meant to be shared in community—so we warmly invite you into the conversation.

Gary H. Lovejoy, Ph.D.
Gregory Knopf, M.D.

THE LANDSCAPE OF DEPRESSION

I am poured out like water,
And all my bones are out of joint;
My heart is like wax;
It is melted within me.
My strength is dried up like a potsherd...

—PSALM 22:14-15—

Jeff was a financial advisor who had to take a medical leave from his job. He was no longer emotionally functional. In fact, he had been hospitalized just weeks before with severe depression. As he sat in my office, fidgeting with his coat buttons, he rambled on in disjointed sentences about how miserable life had become. "Life seems like one meaningless routine after another," he complained. "It's a dog-eat-dog world out there where people are out there looking for ways to sucker-punch someone. What's the point? Is that all there is to life?" Jeff was normally quite affable—indeed, "the life of the party" at times. But now he had become quiet and withdrawn, even shutting out his wife of 25 years.

As the session progressed, he said that his company, where he had become a vice president several years earlier, had recently demoted him. His closest friend in the company—another vice president—had turned on him and falsely reported to the president that Jeff was courting offers from a rival company. Jeff felt betrayed by someone he had fully trusted. And that's when the bottom fell out. He said, "My father betrayed me when he ran off with another woman, my roommate in college got caught cheating in a class and blamed me for writing his paper, which almost got me kicked out of school and my best friend in high school stole

1

my girlfriend. I could go on, but you get the idea. You can't trust anybody." For the first time in his life, he started drinking heavily, alarming his wife. As she described it, he was becoming a stranger in their house, pulling away from the entire family. Depression was clearly an unwelcome guest in their household—posing a threat to Jeff's job, his marriage and his relationships with his children.

Many depressed people follow a similar pattern. They become paralyzed by lethargy and isolation. Few of them are aware that many others share their dark experience, the meaningless montage of bitter disappointments. In their despair, most are convinced that no one else could understand what they're feeling.

To make matters worse, they often have no clue as to their real problems—or if they do, what to do about them. Their emotional or physical withdrawal only deepens their desperation and feelings of helplessness. They retreat into apathy and emotional numbness to insulate themselves from more pain. Getting out of bed is often a major accomplishment. They just can't generate enthusiasm for anything, least of all for any activity that requires even a little effort.

Friends and family become distressed by the depressed person's growing irritability. Their compulsive overeating or disinterest in food altogether only compounds their concern. The family is often frustrated by having to live under a dark cloud that hangs ambiguously over their heads. They want their depressed loved one to "do something." But depression's tightening grip seems to rob the depressed of the initiative to do anything. Yet taking some sort of initiative is *exactly* what their emotional alarm is telling them to do.

Still, they persist in their passivity as their paralysis becomes increasingly self-inflicted. They avoid taking responsibility for the solutions to their problems—partly because they truly believe that a solution, if it exists at all, is beyond their control. They blame their fatigue and insomnia on some undefined physical illness and often seek a diagnosis from their physician. But when the doctor rules out any medical cause—which is frequently the case—their mounting emotional pain becomes even more intolerable. What they want, more than anything else, is some kind of relief. This doesn't mean, however, that they are necessarily looking for personal change. They just don't want to hurt anymore. In the meantime, their behavior may become so disturbing that it literally forces others to intervene on their behalf. If no one heeds the warning signals and takes some kind of action, the unthinkable can happen: suicide.

Whether we like it or not, everyone is involved when depression occurs—the depressed person and those who care about him or her. Depression is a call to action, even if avoidance or denial is the usual choice of action. Nonetheless, it always presents the opportunity to find new ways of thinking and behaving that will ultimately free a depressed person to recapture his enthusiasm for living.

CAPITALIZING ON THE ELEMENT OF SURPRISE

Some people become so completely adapted to their soul's emptiness that they fail to realize they're depressed. They've resigned themselves to the meager existence they believe is about as good as it's going to get. Some life circumstances, such as a physical disability, are beyond anyone's control, but believing this limits potential satisfaction in life is an assumption that ignores the power of *choosing one's perspective*. Death camp survivor, Viktor Frankl, showed us through his experience that our *interpretations* of events determine how we react to difficult situations. He argued that the attitude we take, even toward a circumstance we cannot change, is critical to our ability to not just survive these situations, but to grow through them.

We are wired to find meaning in every situation. We prefer order, understanding and predictability to uncertainty and all the anxiety created by the unknown. When we can't readily identify purpose in our circumstances, we're likely to impose a meaning of our own. We may try to reduce our anxiety by assuming (usually wrongly) the motives of others around us. These assumptions, especially when they are distorted by our own projections, can cause us to respond inappropriately to others.

On the other hand, we might explain our circumstances in just as distorted assumptions about ourselves. We may explain negative events in terms of internal causes ("I never do anything right" or, "I'm worthless"), ones that will never change ("I'm hopeless") or ones that will affect everything else in our life ("My whole life is ruined"). It's easy to see how this pessimism and self-blame can become the foundation for depression. In fact, it's one of the most common ways depressed people interpret life's many disappointments. Jeff, our distressed financial advisor, certainly felt this way. In time, however, he began to see how his fatalism produced a false, almost hypnotic, train of thought that was dismantling his every chance for happiness.

We all live with some uncertainty in life. But as our anxiety over uncertainty reaches higher and higher levels, we increase our risk for depression. We end up believing we are powerless and as a result, we respond in ways that reinforce these feelings.

The good news is that *at any point in this cycle* we retain full autonomy over our beliefs. Though we are free to choose hopelessness, we are just as free to believe that a situation can and will change for the better. An optimistic outlook may, in fact, enable us to see actions we can take to alter our difficult circumstances. Optimism reduces anxiety—responding positively is an exercise in empowerment. As we become less anxious and more empowered, we significantly reduce our chances of becoming depressed.

So, if we observe that our usual responses to difficult circumstances aren't working—*which is what depression is telling us*— then why not heed the warning signal? Look on the upside. Do something different—something surprising. Consider the alternatives. Try something new. Rediscover your creativity.

EXPLAINING THE COMPULSION TO EXPLAIN

Why are so many people obsessed with knowing the meaning behind every event? Because, for the sake of feeling secure, they want to control their circumstances—and understanding something is the first step toward controlling them. But as useful as control is, this powerful drive can lead to unintended and counterproductive consequences. Trying to control something that's not in our control leads to frustration and exhaustion. We don't have the power to make others more pleasant or less obnoxious. We do, however, have the power to change our response to them.

We must learn to distinguish between what we can and cannot control. We can make change in ourselves, but we can only inspire change in others. Many people who are chronically depressed haven't learned this distinction. Their depression often results from a twofold mistake: First, the futility in trying to micromanage everything and everyone around them and second, their reluctance to acknowledge responsibility for what belongs to them and them alone.

> **When we live a life of resignation, we come to believe that trouble is not only unavoidable, but also deserved...**

Is it any wonder so many people give up hope?

Though we can choose how to interpret our experiences, the idea rarely occurs to us. Instead, we rely on a familiar grid—one comprised of our emotional survival myths...like the rule that says we must protect ourselves at all times from a hostile world. These myths usually grow out of early formative experiences in our families. New healing experiences in the present can challenge and alter these myths, but only if we give them a chance.

When we live a life of resignation, we come to believe that trouble is not only unavoidable, but also deserved—all the more reason to deny to ourselves any possible strategy for a better life, and all the more reason for perpetuating our own dreadful, self-fulfilling prophecies. Protection then, becomes our only option. We are left to hope that others will take pity on us; that taking action on our own behalf is not even an option. Inside, we grow puzzled, resentful and defensive toward a world that doesn't seem to care enough to help. In fact, at times it seems only to favor those who've hurt us. A. W. Tozer described this fortress mentality: "The heart's fierce effort to protect itself from every slight, to shield its touchy honor from the bad opinion of friend and enemy will never let the mind have rest. Continue this fight through the years and the burden will become intolerable."[1]

It's not hard to understand why people who feel this way are caught off guard when their doctor suggests professional help. After all, doesn't he know that they are already doing the best they can under the circumstances? Does he think they're just too "stupid" or "weak" or "crazy" to survive on their own? However, if they can get past this resistance and consider the idea that they can do something about their depression, they've taken a critical step toward a life-altering shift in their thinking.

Though they may still fear change, they will come to see the link between their inner conflicts and their outward fatigue, insomnia, headaches and other symptoms. In fact, as their problems are reframed in terms that suggest *solutions*, they will become more hopeful. And when they do, they will finally see their depression as the constructive, growth-directing signal that it is.

Recognizing depression as depression and viewing it as a useful guide is a good beginning. But it's only the beginning. Its resolution requires an exploration of what's underneath and coming up with a practical plan of action.

BIOLOGY OR ENVIRONMENT?

There has long been an argument over whether depression is the result of a problem in physiology (a "disease") or whether it is largely due to specific experiences (a psychological problem)—the so-called "chicken and egg" controversy. This has led us to clarify causal factors as either "endogenous"(pronounced, "en-daj-eh-nes") or "exogenous"(pronounced, "ek-saj-eh-nes"). If it is an *endogenous depression* (such as bipolar affective disorder, postpartum depression, peri-menopausal depression or certain psychotic depressions), it means that there are no clear external reasons why someone should become depressed. In other words, there are no apparent harmful experiences that we can point to which would explain the depression. Instead, the sharp emotional downturn is usually attributable to *internal* physiological or hormonal factors.

This type of depression is more likely the result of any number of problems within the body—some of which are not always easy to identify with certainty. But what we do know is that certain genetic conditions, hormonal imbalances, hypoglycemic reactions, medication side effects and biochemical deficiencies in the brain are all examples of organic factors that can play a significant role in depression. The important point is that these depressions have largely internal origins and are primarily biological in nature.

That doesn't mean , however, that psychological issues cannot be involved in such depressions. For example, in post-partum depressions, in addition to the rapid hormonal changes taking place, the new mother can also be overwhelmed with the responsibilities of caring for a baby, by the lack of free time and sometimes, by negative changes in the marital relationship.

In a similar fashion, external influences can also affect someone with bipolar affective disorder—a complex disorder with many different symptoms and several different types, which can be generally characterized by extreme changes in mood from mania to depression. In this disorder, when the person is experiencing a manic state, he or she is usually elevated or agitated in mood often with inflated feelings of power or importance. They seem to require little sleep, engage in risky or impulsive behavior and have racing thoughts, which are often expressed by talking too fast or too much. Then, quickly and unpredictably, they can swing to a deep depressive state, where they suffer extreme fatigue or loss of energy, dark moods involving intense feelings of worthlessness and guilt, indecisiveness and recurrent thoughts of death and suicide. This disorder often runs in families and is widely understood to have a strong genetic component. Yet it, too, can be affected by significant stressors—such as a major transition in life, like an unexpected career change, having children or going off to college.

I saw a young woman in her 20's suffering from bipolar disorder (as did her aunt and grandmother before her). When she left home and started college in another city, she began going on wild escapades of drinking and sexual promiscuity, all-night parties and working herself into large debt with uncontrollable spending sprees. She had been close to her family and, in some ways, dreaded leaving for college where the demands of class work did not come easily for her. This stress appeared to prepare the ground for a manic episode that had led to academic probation at school and turmoil at home. This kind of upheaval is common among bipolar clients.

There is another type of depression that is not primarily biological in origin. This type, which we most frequently encounter in our clients, is of the *exogenous* variety. This is depression that *does* involve clearly identifiable causes from outside stress—either past, present or both. Factors considered important here may include family upheaval; loss of loved ones, frustrated goals, loss of job or job promotion, marital discord, identity issues, a history of sexual or physical abuse and a host of other possibilities. In every case, it's important to understand how much each stressful event has uniquely contributed to the person's emotional state.

In general, *exogenous* depressions have a better long-term prognosis and often are easier to treat—like John's, a recent client of mine, whose profound depression was linked to the sudden loss of his beloved father some 20 years earlier, a loss he had never properly grieved. When at last given that chance, he finally began to see his depression lift. Meeting his father's death with stoicism had not worked. Only by visiting his gravesite and saying good-bye (that is, by acknowledging his feelings of devastation) was he released from the depressive weight of long-stifled emotions. When he returned he remarked, "I completely surprised myself by almost impulsively falling on my father's grave and sobbing for two hours! Can you believe it? I never knew that was in me, or that something could stay with you like that. I just thought you move on and if you don't look at it, that takes care of it."

This type of depression can be triggered rapidly—a response known as "reactive depression"—by sudden stressors like divorce, an occupational setback or almost any traumatizing incident. Conditions for this kind of depression can also develop slowly as with the accumulated damage from a parent's verbal abuse, over-protection, over-dominance or neglect. Such emotional injuries can leave us susceptible to stressors later in life.

As a case in point, several years ago a couple came to see me after the husband had been in a prolonged state of sullen depression. He had been raised in a highly critical home where he was blamed for everything that went wrong in the family. When his parents finally got a divorce, he internalized responsibility for that too. When he got married, he was unprepared to deal with a wife who had a critical bent and tended to be pessimistic. As a result he withdrew from her, which only made things worse since she was hurt by his isolation and apparent rejection.

He became so depressed that at one point, he attempted suicide. He was saved by a neighbor who happened to hear his car running in the garage. Several years of therapy with a couple of different therapists followed, but it didn't seem to help much. It was not until he could see the connection between his response to his wife and his history of absorbing criticism that he understood why he could not pull out of his tailspin. It also opened his wife's eyes to the role her critical behavior played in perpetuating a marital dance neither of them wanted.

As powerful as these experiences of depression can be, it's not always easy to trace such a clean line between biological and environmental causes. The complexity of the mind-body relationship can make precise identification of a symptom's source difficult. Are there changes in the body (especially the brain) that determine what goes on in the mind—or is it the other way around? Or is it both? It's because of this complexity that we no longer limit ourselves to such either-or questions—much less make predictions based on them.

We do know however, that depression, whether caused by nature or by (the absence of) nurture has a profound effect on brain chemistry. There is now compelling evidence that depression exerts an inhibitory effect on the production of "brain-derived neurotrophic factor"(BDNF), a brain protein which stimulates nerve cell growth and repair in the areas of the brain vital to learning, memory and higher thinking. What this means is that over time, atrophy of specific brain structures can occur in people suffering from chronic depression. Since untreated depression has the potential to damage the brain by suppressing BDNF, this becomes a strong argument for addressing our problems sooner rather later. The good news is that the beneficial changes that arise from psychotherapy and other treatments for depression (like the use of antidepressant medication) also affect brain chemistry, but in good ways. They do this among other things, by increasing that same BDNF in the brain.

So what happens in our bodies when we experience helpful change is as significant as what happens in our bodies when we experience depression. One counteracts the effects of the other (providing that treatment is timely) and they both affect the function of the brain. Fortunately, you don't have to understand this complexity of mind-body interaction to know that getting early help for your depression is as important as any other step you would take to safeguard your health.

Because depression is the result of mind and body working together, you may be asking yourself by now why we even bother to distinguish between endogenous and exogenous depression. The main reason is that by determining depression's *predominant* origins, it helps us choose the best treatment options; in other words, the most appropriate medications and the most effective therapeutic methods. That's why the all-too-common description of depression as just a "chemical imbalance" is misleading and far too limiting. Unfortunately, it often results in prescriptions for medication without considering the additional usefulness of psychotherapy, and we know that when both are working together, the result is considerably better than either one working alone.

But treatment must not stop there, for we can't forget the role of our spiritual nature. It's important to understand how faulty coping strategies can affect our relationship with God. There aren't only psychological and biological factors at work in depression, there are spiritual factors involved as well. Depression is an alarm system of the *whole person*—body, mind and spirit. How we struggle with adversity can either stir up hidden doubts about God's faithfulness or it can prompt us to act out in sinful ways. How we respond to our pain can affect our concept of God and our Christian walk. Humans are fully integrated beings so that what happens in one area of our lives affects every other area. Nothing is left untouched by our experience. The sooner we realize this truth, the sooner we will understand that becoming whole again requires attention to every facet of the problem. Most importantly, viewing things through the prism of our faith can help us actually see the optimism tucked away in the experience of depression.

A PURPOSE TO THE LOSS OF PURPOSE

Depression is an alarm system designed to get our attention and warn us of danger to both our psychological and physical well-being. Like smoke detectors and security alarms that call for a quick response to a problem, depression is an alarm that was never intended to be ringing indefinitely without action to address the problem. Damage results when any danger signal is ignored or simply endured. This is important to realize because most depression will not entirely disappear (at least, not permanently) simply with the passage of time.

Only changing how we think and act will accomplish that.

Some therapists believe that depression purposefully slows a person's life down to a lethargic crawl, conserving energy for the changes he or she needs to make. While that may not be depression's primary function, it provides another argument for the value of depression. One thing is certain: Anything that originates in the mind of God is not just an intelligent design, but a merciful one as well. Underlying every emotional experience, even a mystifying one such as depression, is a helpful purpose to be discovered.

Sometimes this purpose is played out in a family system. We see this when a person's depression influences other relationships in the home—usually creating further stress in their environment. However, even one strategic, positive change can set off a cascade of adjustments and a corresponding chain of emotional payoffs.

I witnessed this in dramatic fashion with one family I recently counseled. While the dad sought to rescue the mother from her chronic depression, the children forfeited playtime and time with their dad to compensate for putting all their energy into household chores. Everyone tiptoed around the house. Then Mom entered counseling and began to improve—in fact, she improved so much that she could resume her responsibilities in the home. But as a consequence, Dad lost his sense of purpose and withdrew while the kids left the chores and the house to Mom, spending all their time with friends.

Dad eventually learned that rescuing his wife was a means of avoiding conflict with her. He was petrified about their differences. Through counseling, he found better ways to invest himself in his marriage and more effectively resolve conflict. As a result, the children reconnected with both of them. In the end, the treatment of Mom's depression led to improved relationships throughout the entire family. One of the children said, "At first I was scared that mom was going to leave us. Then later I thought Dad was going to leave us. But after they got help, they told me that they loved us too much to ever do that so I finally realized we were going to stay a family."

As unpredictable and tumultuous as these changes may seem, they're vital to healthier patterns of interaction. These extraordinary outcomes remind us just how interdependent with one another we all really are.

THE WAR INSIDE

We've now become familiar with the various symptoms of depression: Feelings of sadness and emptiness, helplessness and hopelessness, loss of interest or pleasure in life activities, loss of energy or constant fatigue, insomnia (difficulty getting to sleep or staying asleep), feelings of intense anxiety, changes in appetite and weight, decreased energy, excessive or misplaced guilt, feelings of worthlessness, physical symptoms such as bodily aches and pains, sometimes increased agitation including outbursts of anger and irritability, difficulties thinking and concentrating and recurrent thoughts of death or suicide. However, it's important to know that you don't have to have all of these symptoms at once to be diagnosed as depressed. All you need is four or more of them to confirm the diagnosis. Such symptoms can, of course, vary widely in intensity and duration.

When these symptoms are disabling to where even routine tasks seem impossible and this lasts for at least two consecutive weeks, you're probably suffering a major depressive episode. It's with these episodes that suicidal thoughts (and attempts) are most likely. One woman I saw spent almost her entire time in bed. She lost her job because she couldn't handle it anymore so she went on state disability. Not knowing what to do, her family simply left her alone most of the time. Between periods of sobbing, she would merely stare into empty space. "I was consumed with thoughts of ending my miserable life—taking a bottle of sleeping pills or something," she said. Suffering from major depression, she required medication and intensive therapy over a period of time.

On the other hand, if such symptoms in much less severe form endure chronically for at least two years you're more likely experiencing what we call *dysthymia*. Dysthymic people continue with their responsibilities despite persistent unhappiness and hopelessness. They will often slug it out with life on their own, sometimes refusing to seek professional help. Even though they are despondent, they are not in danger of hospitalization. Instead, they often rely on friends or family or maybe a compassionate pastor to help them through. When they do come in for counseling, they are usually more ready to take on the work of sorting through their issues.

Childhood depression is described somewhat differently in that it is more likely to be manifested in agitation and acting out behavior than in sadness or apathy. Extreme cases may involve addictions or conduct disorders evidenced by repeated defiance of authority. Young people's symptoms more often land them in a correctional institution than a mental health clinic. We don't usually connect depression with contempt and defiance, so it's harder to recognize the problem in teenagers. That's why troubled teens are less likely to get help in a timely fashion—sometimes not until their desperation leads them to suicidal behavior.

In both adults and children, the undercurrent of self-hatred is often the first issue to address as it can otherwise undermine a person's motivation to change. Why pursue personal transformation if you think you're incapable or even undeserving? Without rekindled hope, therapy is unlikely to be productive. Insecure people typically feel humiliated, ashamed, worthless and incompetent at every setback in their initial attempts to change. So we must reframe what successes and failures mean in order for them to grow toward healthy self-respect. They must reach a point where such setbacks only leave them disappointed or dismayed, but not ready to give up. They must start being at least as good a friend to themselves as they are to others. That usually means treating themselves differently from the way they were treated growing up. How they were treated in the past is the primary reason they don't respect themselves now.

The self-rejecting person generally reads setbacks not as an *act* of failing but as *being* a failure. They view themselves as incapable of success. Conversely, those who respect themselves allow failures to teach them how to behave differently, or how to live with their strengths and weaknesses so they can fine-tune their strategies to get the most out of life. Notice that both experience setbacks and failures—no one is immune to adversity. They just respond quite differently to the same situations.

When we cannot accept ourselves, we avoid attempting anything new or doing things in a new way. Consequently, taking *small steps* of change is important in slowly desensitizing ourselves to the risk we fear. Even small successes can empower us to significantly alter our world and our perspective of what's happening.

> **God's direction *always follows* our decision to step out and test the waters**

Many emotionally incapacitated Christians overlook the strength that faith can give them—which is why they typically respond to Jesus' teachings on discipleship with guilt and pessimism. For example, the phrase, "Take up your cross" is a terrifying proposition and yet the believer's failure to do this only leads to more anxiety and self-condemnation.

A LIFESTYLE OF SELF-SABOTAGE

The apostle Paul once wrote that he knew the secret of being content in every situation (see Phil. 4:12-13). He realized that regardless of his circumstances, he could respond to them with courage and optimism. While we can't always avoid negative circumstances or the sins of others, we can be empowered to overcome them. It's the lure of resignation that the Holy Spirit empowers us to resist. The apostle learned the joy of mindfulness in God's presence. It stirred him to be proactive, *willing to experiment with his options.* This is what Jesus bids us to do when He told us "to seek" and "to knock"(Matt. 7:7). God's direction always follows our decision to step out and test the waters. This was what the apostle Peter discovered so dramatically one stormy night on the Sea of Galilee (see Matt. 14:22-32).

God has an adventure in store for each one of us if only we take up His offer. He knows we are far better off when we are willing to take a risk. Nowhere does He suggest that we greet life with silence or retaliation. Instead, He tells us to take the initiative to make a difference. Unfortunately, this offer of hope is too often lost on us because we are too busy fearfully running away from life.

The common refrain, "I will never measure up" echoes our deep sense of personal defeat when we are depressed—and underlying it is our resentment toward the criticism we've received from others. When we feel inadequate, we withdraw from situations involving the slightest risk of failure. Or we may purposefully under-perform to keep from testing our true limits. A clinical professor of mine called this "studied incompetence," to describe people who do this as avoidance of responsibility and who push tasks onto other "more capable" shoulders. In effect, they want to be shielded from every potential failure.

When we make "avoiding risk" a lifestyle, it sabotages every relationship and every goal. In marriage it creates distance and loneliness because one spouse fears he might be unable to provide something the other asks. Intimacy problems are addressed only indirectly or not at all and so the relationship gradually dies of neglect—one partner feeling incapable of giving and the other no longer interested in responding.

Many families train their members to deny their needs and feelings and to alter reality to protect the family secrets. Above all else, they are trained never to trust themselves. The resulting paralysis destroys any chance for fulfilling relationships. This kind of life is governed by robotic perfectionism, methodical discipline and rigid convictions. Gone are spontaneity, interpersonal honesty, honest dissent and mercy—either toward themselves or others. Under these conditions, they have no convincing reason to pursue intimacy. It's not surprising that their marriages become little more than empty, loveless gestures in the name of social (or perhaps biblical) obligations.

Others are trained to see themselves as victims, unfairly martyred by everyone else. Awash in a sea of self-pity and paranoia, they unwittingly poison every relationship they enter—especially those that could be the most healing for them. Another reaction to this perceived persecution from the world is to take on a more aggressively negative attitude, a posture of gloom and doom. Here we see people retaliating angrily against everyone they think is making them feel badly about themselves. They exhaust the stamina of their most loyal friends, deepening their own despair and further ravaging their self-image. All they succeed in doing is compounding their self-hatred. As author Theodore Rubin puts it, they hate themselves for hating themselves.[2]

Some of us have the ability to cover up our unhealthy thinking so well that we come to believe our own propaganda. We project confidence at one level, but exactly the opposite at another, sending conflicting and confusing messages to others. If you've ever felt lost in a conversation with someone who's hurting, it's probably because they have mixed feelings about letting you know what's going on. Double messages, delivered through verbal and nonverbal cues, keep peoples' heads constantly spinning. Such double-speak may be the mind's last-ditch effort to rescue the remaining shreds of identity from self-destruction.

Sometimes people assert, "I *can't* change, so you'll just have to accept me the way I am." Their refusal to even discuss any kind of change nearly always destroys the spirit of a relationship. By placing responsibility for growth entirely on the other person's shoulders, they are in effect saying that facing one's own pain is far worse than facing another's angry withdrawal.

We may trace the roots of this fear to certain, sometimes traumatizing, experiences early in life. This is understandable, but the attitude of helplessness hinders learning and action that can reverse the legacy of the past. These individuals remain stuck in their histories becoming perpetual children in adult bodies. Because they couldn't control the painful events that happened to them as children, they find it difficult to accept the fact that they *can* control their reactions to life events now. They may become easy prey to addictions, which only further entrap them or they may simply give up all ambition and wait passively to be rescued. One client's story illustrates this phenomenon:

> *"When I was a little boy, I used to lock myself in the bathroom, away from my brothers and parents and bawl my eyes out. I'd cry because no one understood me. No one seemed to really care how I felt. I waited and waited for someone to knock on the door and ask me if I was okay. What I really wanted was someone to break down the door and rescue me from my aloneness. But no one came. In many ways, I never really left that bathroom. I've been waiting and waiting for someone to rescue me—to give me direction. To save me. But no one is coming."*

For years he had been living the pointless existence of lost dreams and dreary expectations, oblivious to the truth that fulfillment was indeed within his reach.

My client, Jeff, whom we introduced at the beginning of this chapter, took a different path—a path not unlike that of many who have proved to be resilient in the face of adversity. He realized that his current response to betrayal was conditioned by his experience with a father who had abandoned the family when he was a boy. *In response,* he chose to let go of the resentments that were eating away at his insides and to retool his life. He discovered, like the apostles Paul and Peter, that he could venture into new territory and thrive. He "knocked" and new opportunities were opened to him. He no longer created a self-defeating rut by using his history to excuse his inappropriate behavior today. As Jeff put it, "I'm tired of letting my father determine my life. He had his own problems to struggle with and I understand that, but those problems don't have to be mine. I'm ready to try something new." Instead of investing his energy in constant ruminations about the past and in seeking attention and sympathy in the present, he threw off the legacy of his father and took up the challenge of personal change.

In a life of faith, we don't have to bear this challenge alone. What's more, we can freely acknowledge our failures along the way and know that our value never changes. God's love is never relative, just as His truth never wavers—including His truth about the objects of His affection. Nothing can change this truth—neither our rebellious behavior nor our accusations against God and His goodness. Not even the spiritual inertia of our self-pity. That's because the constancy of His affection is rooted in His unchanging nature.

AN ALLY TO TRUST, A MESSENGER OF HOPE

Emotional pain, like physical pain, can dominate our attention and cause tunnel vision reducing our ability to interpret events accurately. Part of the strategy for change then, is to widen our focus to uncover patterns that have escaped our notice. We sometimes find it hard to accept the fact that change is more often incremental than exponential, involving small but steady steps rather than dramatic insights and instant solutions. True, some clients' problems are relatively straightforward requiring perhaps only one or two sessions to resolve. But the great majority of clients present complex issues that take much longer. That's why the work of therapy requires steadfast resolve, even when it's sometimes uncomfortable. The payoffs however, are more than worth it.

The resolution of old, often festering, problems finally releases emotional energy for tackling issues in the present—energy that has long been used to push down feelings from the past. Until counseling, we have been merely compounding our stress, building a backlog of issues demanding our attention. If things were to remain that way, the entire dam holding back our emotions would collapse from the accumulated pressure behind it. That's why it's so important that depression is there, to push us to address our unfinished business.

It takes great courage to confront the skeletons in our closet. The God who urged Joshua to be of good courage when taking the field of battle or who spurred on David to defeat the Philistines, is the same God who invites us to heroic change in our own lives. Heroism can be found on the emotional battlefield just as surely as it can be found in a military warzone. The goal is always the same: A sweeping triumph over the enemy.

Any honest effort leads to gain. Each new choice we make provides more evidence of God's loving hand, quietly orchestrating our gradual release from bondage. A step here, a step there; like pieces of a puzzle, they all work together for our good. For it is God who calls us to tap into the freedom of our spiritual heritage, to allow the freedom of His love to awaken our slumbering spirits.

Hurting people are seldom impressed by sermons on gratitude for adversity. Many wonder if God even cares. It's good to realize that He does. Yes, adversity *does* provide evidence of His interest and compassion—but we first must be attuned to it. We must know His voice in the darkness of our pain, like scared sheep recognizing the voice of their shepherd. For our destiny is not to go it alone, but to meld our faith into His unswerving faithfulness.

God's thinking is radically different from ours. Thankfully, we don't have to understand His thinking to be transformed by it (in the same way that we don't have to know how medications work to be physically restored by them). We can simply come to appreciate

His compassionate and creative work in us—and that includes the work of our ally, depression.

Therein lies our hope.

FINDING HOPE

1. It's important to distinguish between what you can control (changing yourself) and cannot control (changing others) to *free yourself from frustration and emotional exhaustion.*

2. Consider challenging your distorted thinking (irrational beliefs) as *an invitation God has given you to experience the world in new, more useful ways.*

3. With each setback or disappointment ask yourself, "What would I say to my closest friend if he/she were in this situation?" Then *determine to say those same things to yourself.*

4. If you think it's unfair to not get what you want, *consider experimenting with new ways to work with what you have.*

5. Observe how people with healthy coping skills talk to themselves about setbacks and try to incorporate that thinking into your own. *Become more solution-focused.*

PURPOSE IN DEPRESSION: OUR BUILT-IN ALARM SYSTEM

*Our problems are not here for us to solve them
but for them to solve us.*

—SALVADOR DE MADARIAGA, SPANISH WRITER—

A couple I counseled had just watched their new 5,000 square-foot home burn to the ground. A shrieking smoke alarm startled them awake that night. They jumped out of bed and ran into the hallway to find the entire back of the house ablaze. Fighting a choking cloud of smoke, the wife rushed to their son's bedroom, scooped him up and ran out the front door. Her husband called the fire department, grabbed what possessions he could and raced out after his family. Dazed, they watched the flames destroy their dream home.

They'd lost so much. But they were grateful that their smoke alarm worked. It saved their lives! They still had their son. They realized, as never before, the importance of warning signals. We may dislike the shock associated with warning signals, but they push us into action, sometimes preventing the unthinkable. This experience was a turning point for this couple. Afterwards, they reordered their priorities.

The world is filled with alarms—fire alarms, theft alarms, intruder alarms, maintenance alarms and a host of others. Our car dashboards sport an array of warning lights signaling trouble with oil pressure, water temperature or battery. We have gauges telling us when to get gas, when we're pushing the engine's rpms too high or even when a door is ajar. We can hardly take a step without some alarm system protecting our best interests. Should it surprise us that a powerful, wise God would equip our bodies in a similar way? We're wired with alarm systems that prepare us for a myriad of things that menace our well-being.

THE VALUE OF OUR INNER ALARM SYSTEM

Depression is one of these protective systems—which is what makes it so purposeful. Its amber light of discontent signals problems that have, until now, escaped our notice. If we do nothing about these problems our defenses will disintegrate. Depression alerts us to do something about the problems before they destroy our chances for meaningful living. In one way or another, these problems reflect our longing for love, significance and appreciation. Depression warns us that our emotional attachments are damaging. Depression is, in fact, one of four emotional alarm systems we have. The other three are fear, guilt and anger. These signals tell us something is amiss in our relationships with others or ourselves.

Fear is the alarm system that alerts us to physical or psychological danger, calling for immediate defense. Guilt is geared to issues of moral compromise, warning us of spiritual injury if alternative action isn't taken. Anger is a common reaction to someone who has hurt us or has created some sort of loss in our lives.

Anger is one of the most frequently triggered alarm systems and it's also the least well managed. Quite often we become angry because we are reciting internalized messages about ourselves— messages that originated with our parents or other significant childhood figures. These messages are just as mistaken now as they were then. This anger comes out of the self-hatred of those who, in the past, endured a dysfunctional family.

Anger can reveal our frustration when we don't get what we want. It can also be a secondary reaction to another signal, such as guilt or fear. Whatever the source, anger can prompt us to reevaluate and change our communication patterns or change something in ourselves. Indeed, without periodic expressions of legitimate anger, our relationships would not likely change much. Instead, they would become stagnant and sterile, unfulfilling to everyone. Many people wish they handled anger differently. The apostle Paul taught that, while anger *itself* isn't sinful, many things we *say or do* when we're angry are (see Eph. 4:26ff). He distinguished between anger as an emotional state and the rage which is at the root of most destructive attitudes.

Understanding anger is important because it's an early warning system that tells us our emotional state may descend into depression if things remain unchanged. Anger tends to be immediate. Depression develops more slowly and usually manifests its warnings more persistently over time. Depression is usually triggered by chronic, unresolved issues, which may go under-

Depression is really meant to be our ally, not our enemy.

ground because they're too threatening to deal with openly. Maybe someone hurts you, so you become angry. Then you feel guilty about your anger, so you bury the feeling (and the guilt)—and the slow inner burn turns to the self-hatred of depression. These kinds of interactions between emotions can become quite complex.

One thing is certain: Depression, like all emotional alarm systems, can create such discomfort that it *demands* our attention. We're forced to acknowledge that a problem exists or the havoc will persist until we confront and resolve it.

Depending on our personal histories and response patterns, depression may inhibit appropriate action. In fact, it might inhibit all action. But its purpose is to point to the value of change. When it succeeds in prompting change and producing growth, we discover the reason for viewing depression *optimistically*. Depression is really meant to be our ally, not our enemy.

This may be contrary to all you've been taught, but it's the inescapable conclusion about every emotional alarm—including this one.

WITH FRIENDS LIKE THIS...

The positive potential of depression can be seen in a recent book by Andrew Solomon in which he describes his own despair. Solomon concluded from the drama of his experience that depressive episodes can lead to better choices and beneficial change:

> *The long pause that a depression forces...often causes people to change their lives in useful ways, especially after a loss...There really are up sides to depression; it's just hard to see them when you're in it...I am now able to understand things that I just could not understand before; and the things I don't understand now, I will in time, if they matter...Almost every day I feel momentary flashes of hopelessness...I hate those feelings, but know that they have driven me to look deeper at life, to find and cling to reasons for living...Every day, I choose to be alive. Is that not a rare joy?*[1]

Mr. Solomon's experience forced him to understand his own freedom more fully, to exercise the "rare joy" of making life-changing choices. It has provided him wisdom and new meaning, as well as reasons for celebrating the challenge of adversity. We can make our choices any way we want—wisely or poorly—but no one can take away our opportunity to make them. Even when facing conditions we cannot change, the choice of attitude is ours—no one else's.

Even though depression can be beneficial, of course, nobody ever wishes for it. We're not saying anyone should. But when depression does strike, we gain more from life by learning its lessons—as when James encouraged us to welcome the testing of our faith, because such experiences can strengthen our stamina for hard times (see Jas. 1:2-8). Testing can give us wisdom to recognize the dangerous instability of "double-mindedness," by which

James meant the habit of vacillating between doubt and faith, between conviction and ambivalence or clarity and confusion. This instability allows fatalism to creep in and so depression follows.

God's ways will, at times, be difficult to discern, especially when our experience goes off course from our expectations. Responding with cynicism blinds us to seeing God's presence and purpose in our hardship. Faith however, calls us to depend on a God who cares about His creation. Some people put God on trial for their suffering, attacking His character—a tendency that Paul confronts in Romans 9. And yet we are surrounded by evidence of God's goodness. Without a righteous God, nothing about faith or hope makes sense. Indeed, the existence of *any* goodness in the world is attributed to God's righteous presence and sovereign purpose. Evil will not prevail because God refuses to abandon us to the shipwreck of our own sinfulness.

Author Francis Schaeffer once noted that, if we argue for an impersonal universe—one without a personal God—then the very existence of human personality would be tragically, logically absurd.[2] It would be futile to understand why we enjoy reflecting on the human condition, why we engage in interpersonal communication or even why we love one another. These pursuits would be as meaningless as the sense of smell in an odorless environment. Our deepest longings would be reduced to illusion.

But if we attribute our universe to a personal God, then our experience becomes intelligible—and purposeful. Our desires and behaviors can fit into a sensible pattern. Life is complex. It can't always be reduced to simple, predictable terms. But God has equipped us with emotional signals to help us adapt to the world's complexity.

These signals, difficult though they may be to manage, are necessary for healthy functioning. That's why the alerting role of depression can be likened to the biological alarm system of pain. For *depression is to the psychological self as pain is to the physical self.*

Almost no one enjoys pain. (Few of us are true masochists!) Many would prefer to be completely numb to it. But that rare individual, born partially or wholly unable to feel pain, holds a different opinion. As unpleasant as it is, pain is perhaps the most valuable sensory system we have. It prevents untold damage, even fatal damage to our bodies by alerting us to take preventative action. When we turn an ankle, the pain drives us to take weight off the injured foot, so we limp. If the pain continues, we seek medical diagnosis and care. Otherwise, we might further injure the ankle, maybe severely.

The great missionary physician, Dr. Paul Brand, has described what happens to leprosy patients who lose the sense of pain in their extremities.[3] He watched in horror as an African man reached his pain-deadened hand into a fire pit to retrieve a fallen piece of meat from the red-hot coals. This failure of the pain warning system explains why leprosy often leads to disfiguring damage to hands, feet and other body parts. Pain is necessary to call attention to disease and injury—it helps guard our long-term physical health.

Depression performs a similar function, preserving our emotional well-being. Its troubling persistence bears testimony to its significance. Like pain, we can't merely will it away. It's there to tell us something. Ignoring it naturally leads to worse consequences. Heeding it leads to valuable insight, healing and prevention of further injury.

Why then, do we resist allowing depression to serve its purpose? One reason is that contributing factors often lie deep within us, involving issues we've avoided for a long time. In our efforts to survive painful past events, we insulate ourselves from their impact by denying them to awareness.

Sometimes, acknowledging the sources of our despair may seem to endanger relationships or threaten to shatter our sense of identity. What's more, our depression may come out of events that seem unrelated, but which we associate with earlier wounds.

We see this pattern in Barbara's struggle with depression. Coming from a turbulent alcoholic home, she couldn't wait to escape from her family. So barely out of high school, she married an older man whom she thought understood and cared for her—quite unlike her father. She dismissed his history of repeated job firings and two divorces. She accepted this man's explanations about tyrannical bosses and controlling women, which portrayed him as a victim.

Within weeks of their wedding however, she found out the lies behind the explanations. He became increasingly abusive. She feared for her life. His drinking, which she hadn't known about before they married, only made things worse. She sometimes cowered before him, praying to survive his verbal attack, praying that he wouldn't hurt her...or kill her. Her desperate attempts to placate him did nothing to quell his rage. "When he starts drinking, it doesn't matter if I'm nice to him," she said. "I think he just wants to attack me. I think he gets a kick out of seeing me scared to death...and I'm afraid that one of these times, he's not gonna stop with just words. I don't know what to do."

She became anxious and depressed because she found herself in the same never-ending nightmare, this time with a reincarnation of her defiant father. Here was yet another destructive relationship with a man. She felt as trapped as she did when she was a child.

She sought help from her church but said nothing about her husband's behavior, fearing that the leaders would confront him, making things worse in the prison she called home. When the pastoral staff finally learned about the pathetic state of her marriage, they counseled submission rather than seeing abuse as the source of her depression and taking immediate action. The consequences were devastating.

Barbara accepted the labels "rebellious" and "selfish"—after all, she already believed she was worthless. She errantly assumed responsibility, resigning herself to bear her burden alone bolstered only by the tenacity of her commitment to the institution of marriage. No joint counseling with her husband. No accountability for him. She was abandoned to fear of injury and despair for the future.

She needed to listen to her depression and its message.

OF LEMONS AND LEMONADE

It's often useful to draw upon the depressed person's own natural strengths—resources to which they have ready access for making a difference. Using existing abilities makes the change process feel more familiar and more doable.

I'm reminded of psychiatrist Milton Erickson's "African violet therapy." Visiting a depressed and suicidal woman who had withdrawn from everyone, he noted her interest in African violets. These delicate flowers are difficult to grow, but the woman had a knack for nurturing them. Erickson suggested that she use her talent by giving violets to the principals of her church's weddings, funerals, baptisms and the like. She followed his suggestion and it changed her life. When she died years later, more than a thousand people attended her memorial—people who had been moved by her quiet, generous spirit.

> **The past may shape the present, but so does a healthy anticipation of the future.**

She thought depression meant that her life was worthless. But her depression was, in fact, a window of discovery. She had a gift perfectly matched to the world of need. The poet Robert Frost wrote, "Something we were withholding made us weak until we found it was ourselves."[4] Our unique gift, freely given, opens up unforeseen possibilities for ourselves and those we touch. The past may shape the present, but so also does a healthy anticipation of the future. Optimism transforms a pedestrian life into a creative, adventurous one.

Depression represents the challenges of our feelings of help-lessness, our sense of shame and our burden of guilt. It forces us to rethink our perceptions of a world that seems to demand more than we can give. It pushes us to consider new insights about ourselves, changes that will help us cope more effectively with adversity. Depression can prompt us to discover how to grow, not in spite of, but *because of* our pain. If we can learn a more meaningful way to live and to *give,* our depression will have served its purpose.

The Bible describes many of God's mightiest acts as carried out through men who were prone to depression. Likewise, some of the great luminaries of Church history, such as Martin Luther, Charles Spurgeon and D. L. Moody suffered major depressive episodes. Depression is no stranger to God's people. We shouldn't pretend that it is. Far better to be honest about our struggles as believers, bringing a refreshing transparency to the Christian community before a culture who already constantly questions our credibility.

But most believers share a powerful fear of shedding their facades. We're terrified of being judged, especially by our churches. So we go on living our people-pleasing, sanitized lives, calling it Christian love and believing it pleases God.

AN INVITATION FOR ALL SEASONS

While suffering can defeat us, we can also answer it heroically. Some people find within themselves an added reserve to overcome even the greatest calamity, drawing upon something all bold responses to pain share in common. It has to do with a deeper sense of purpose that gives meaning in the face of apparent meaninglessness. Viktor Frankl revealed this as the secret of his survival through the horrors of the Nazi death camp at Auschwitz. The apostle Paul, too, alluded to it as the enigma of strength through weakness in the midst of his persecution (see 2 Cor. 12:9). He found unusual strength, not in himself, but in his dependency upon God; a dependency made necessary by the persistence of his own failures. The success of the Gospel—*despite* Paul's obvious imperfections—made the Lord's victorious hand more visible to the early Church.

Similarly, we tend to attribute our own success to God when it happens in spite of our weakness. In the same way, contrary to our praise of a well-delivered sermon by a great preacher, we tend to give the glory to God when an inexperienced speaker gives a testimony that spiritually moves the audience. It's not his performance but God's power that makes the difference. It's neither eloquence nor sacrificial service that wins hearts and minds. Not even martyrdom provides the triumph. Rather, the love only God can supply drives home the message of hope.

God stands ready to transform our lives, but we often can't see His hand through the veil of our pain. Sometimes our impatience with limitations frustrates our understanding of the bigger picture. In any case, rarely do we experience the kind of relationship God desires with us because we are too bogged down by memories of failed relationships that have diminished our aspirations. Yet God is patient, continuing to invite us into intimacy, a banquet of love that often seems too good to be true. Those who have experienced this true intimacy will testify to its reality, capacity for contentment and ability to nurture the soul.

A gifted client of mine had long been laboring to understand the nature of such a relationship with God. She came to liken it to the intimacy between a loving father and his child. She arrived at this conclusion as she worked through her depression:

> *"It is the question of God's hand as an intervening, directive force or as something resting gently on the believer's shoulder, infusing him with the power to see the mysteries that abound...I wonder if feeling God's hand on my shoulder is like a father touching a child to get his attention so he can point out something the child would otherwise have missed. So it seems that the sense of loss I've experienced is but a part of something much bigger that is hap-*

pening to me, like a window of opportunity to understand things that the mind can never know, only the heart."

I'm convinced that God is honored when we struggle to understand Him. Faith in Him means freely admitting our ignorance and our questions—just like when the desperate father, seeking Jesus' help for his son, cried, "I do believe; help me overcome my unbelief" (Mark 9:24, NIV)! God desires our acknowledgment of fallibility and doubts, which prepares us to receive the truth. Arrogant certainty never motivates us to seek God's face, because it cannot stir the passion to look beyond the limits of our own minds.

If we persist in following God's journey of discovery, we'll be drawn into the accepting, redemptive heart of God Himself. There, surprisingly, we find our weakness is made strong by His love. Paul described this phenomenon as a strange and otherwise inexplicable peace that wells up within the soul (see Phil. 4:4-7). Contentment doesn't just happen. Contentment is learned.

INSTRUMENTS OF LOVE

Notice how we keep running again and again into the concept of connection—loving and being loved—the survival kit for the human heart. Even under the most desperate conditions, intimacy's appeal lingers in the air, luring us with its promise of healing.

Viktor Frankl described love as an important conduit of meaning—deeply loving someone is a primary reason for feeling emotionally alive.[5] As long as German death camp prisoners could attribute meaning to their experience, even if only by treasuring an imagined liberation date, they could survive the Nazis' worst. This triumph of the spirit was not possible however, without reaching beyond the suffering, lifting their eyes to a hope connected to the relational requirements of the heart. These formidable conditions—the common ground of pain—fostered some of the prisoners' deepest connections with each other.

Frankl saw prisoners at Auschwitz bond with their fellow prisoners, often giving of themselves to meet one another's survival needs. One would give his ration of bread to an ailing friend. Or he might complete a chore for a weaker comrade rather than see him beaten for "dereliction of duty." These heroic deeds, in the courageous, pain-forged bonds of intimacy, momentarily removed them from their suffering. Their suffering freed them to be vulnerable and sacrificial toward one another. It brought out the best. It endowed with nobility men who were otherwise stripped of dignity.

When people reach out of their isolation to others, seeking relief from their suffering, they tend to go beyond head knowledge and appeal to the passionate side of relationships. Our deepest needs are addressed not by intellectual answers, but by the experience of love. Notice that Jesus connected His message of redemption to the passion of His Father for His people. By His sacrifice He demonstrated that God's love cannot be vanquished. Through His pain, He revealed the power of divine intimacy that's far greater than the meager offerings of the secular world.

> **Our deepest needs are addressed, not by intellectual answers, but by the experience of love.**

If only in our most agonizing moments we could realize that we've already been invited into this kind of emotional and spiritual bond. Because our Lord has shared our earthly pain, we find in Him the healing opportunity to view our suffering through the window of a loving father's empathy. A relationship with Him fills *the spiritual void that makes suffering so much worse,* freeing us to rebuild from our losses on a new foundation.

Even with those losses, God's love inspires us to make the most of what we have left, to assemble the remaining pieces of our life into a new arrangement. Itzhak Perlman, arguably the world's finest violinist, once demonstrated this kind of triumph. His passion for music enabled him to craft a magical moment from the shards of apparent disaster. Listen to syndicated columnist Jack Riemer's account in the *Houston Chronicle:*

> *On November 18, 1995, Itzhak Perlman, the violinist, came on stage to give a concert at Avery Fisher Hall at Lincoln Center in New York City. If you have ever been to a Perlman concert, you know that getting on stage is no small achievement for him. He was stricken with polio as a child and so he has braces on both legs and walks with the aid of two crutches. To see him walk across the stage one step at a time, painfully and slowly, is an unforgettable sight. He walks painfully, yet majestically, until he reaches his chair. Then he sits down, slowly, puts his crutches on the floor, undoes the clasps on his legs, tucks one foot back and extends the other foot forward. Then he bends down and picks up the violin, puts it under his chin, nods to the conductor and proceeds to play. By now, the audience is used to this ritual. They sit quietly while he makes his way across the stage to his chair. They remain reverently silent while he undoes the clasps on his legs. They wait until he is ready to play. But this time, something went wrong. Just as he finished the first few bars, one of the strings on his violin broke. You could hear it snap—it went off like gunfire across the room. There was no mistaking what that sound meant. There was no mistaking what he had to do. People who were there that night thought to themselves: "We figured that he would have to get up, put on the clasps again, pick up the crutches and limp his way off stage—to either find another violin or else find another string for this one." But he didn't. Instead, he waited a moment, closed his eyes and then signaled the conductor to begin again. The orchestra began and he played from where he had left off. And he played with such passion and such power and such purity, as they had never heard before. Of course,*

anyone knows that it is impossible to play a symphonic work with just three strings. I know that and you know that, but that night Itzhak Perlman refused to know that.

You could see him modulating, changing and recomposing the piece in his head. At one point, it sounded like he was de-tuning the strings to get new sounds from them that they had never made before. When he finished, there was an awesome silence in the room. And then people rose and cheered. There was an extraordinary outburst of applause from every corner of the auditorium. We were all on our feet, screaming and cheering; doing everything we could to show how much we appreciated what he had done. He smiled, wiped the sweat from this brow, raised his bow to quiet us and then he said, not boastfully, but in a quiet, pensive, reverent tone, "You know, sometimes it is the artist's task to find out how much music you can still make with what you have left." *What a powerful line that is. It has stayed in my mind ever since I heard it. And who knows? Perhaps that is the [way] of life—not just for artists but also for all of us. So, perhaps our task in this shaky, fast-changing, bewildering world in which we live is to make music, at first with all that we have and then, when that is no longer possible, to make music with what we have left.*[6]

This is the artist's heroic pursuit of the finest he can produce. God, the Artist of Life, is the creator of excellence in each one of us. He lovingly sets excellence before us as our goal. Even when badly wounded, we may safely enter His sanctuary, where his concerto of compassion plays in our hearts, inspiring us to new strength. Only the music He performs on the instrument of our soul can fulfill us, because it resonates with our desire to be loved. No broken heartstring need cause us to fall silent and withdraw from the stage of life. God teaches us to play our damaged instrument with a new intensity—modulating, changing and recomposing the music of our lives. When played to the tempo of God's grace, our song inspires praise from the hosts of heaven.

THE MUSIC OF DISCOVERY

In therapy, Barbara painfully reviewed her confining relationship patterns and began to see herself in surprisingly new ways. Her healing didn't happen overnight. But in time she understood why she had willingly accepted abuse from her husband and from herself, and how that contributed to her depression. She learned a more effective, more assertive approach to dealing with her husband. She now knows that no one has to pay for someone else's sins in a kind of lifelong purgatory. She sees the distinction between real and false guilt and consequently, no longer carries the burden of misguided devotion. Freedom in Christ has a new ring to her. She accepts God's love and grace and her faith now serves to nurture, not injure, her mental health. She recognizes her power to make genuine choices. During our last session she commented, "Sometimes I'm amazed how lost I had become—I didn't think I even had a right to live, but I was also scared to die because I never felt I had done enough to get to heaven. At one point, I actually thought that God had sent my husband to punish me for what a disappointment I had been to Him. But I would never go back there in a million years. My days of being abused are over and now I know that this is what God *really* wants for my life." In pursuing professional help, Barbara courageously waded against the strong current of dysfunctional messages. Such courage is rare, but only because more people don't choose it.

It's so important to understand depression as the hope-inspiring prelude to a better life. It's a guide to help us make sense of our emotional design, leading us to self-acceptance and tapping into our hard wired longing to be loved. Without its ministry, we would not seek connections with God or people. Life would be an absurdity—an aimless drifting, cut loose from spiritual moorings, a desolate derelict on the sea of misguided reason and cruel chance.

Millions of people exist like this—directionless and without purpose. They don't have to. Nonetheless, they betray their own souls, forsaking the heart's true desire. They blame external chaos when life's randomness is often due to abandoning their own dreams. They disengage from everyone, even from that still small voice calling them to an adventure in intimacy. Only when they realize that depression is a clarion call to change do they begin mending their broken hearts. Depression may be the only way to distract us from our deadening routines long enough to consider something different.

Barbara accepted depression as an ally. It rescued her from a war between emotional exhaustion and the dictates of a legalistic faith by showing her that it's a needless war. Her depression was, in fact, a consequence of wrong thinking and misguided theology.

Returning to the music of our faith helps us live out the melody of healing. And I like to think that while God supplies the lyrics and the tune, we counselors have the rare privilege of helping to repair the instruments.

FINDING HOPE

1. The discomfort of your *depression has a positive signaling purpose* to prompt you to take action on an unattended problem.

2. God has given you the freedom to *make choices that change your world and address your pain.*

3. You are physically and psychologically *designed for a purpose.* Your *longings to be loved reflect that purpose,* a purpose that is both personal and interpersonal.

4. Depression gives you the opportunity to discover something important about life: Although the past may influence the present, *the way you anticipate the future* does so as well.

5. It's when you struggle that you discover *God's principle that strength can be found through weakness.*

6. *Depression can be the hopeful prelude to something better.* Remember, *beautiful music* can still be played on the instrument of a damaged soul.

DEPRESSION IN GOD'S LARGER DESIGN

Knowing ourselves teaches us what to ask. It helps us to identify the areas of need in our lives. It also teaches us how to approach God.

—JAMES HOUSTON—

The events of September 11, 2001 forever changed our lives. In less time than it takes to watch your favorite morning show, almost 3000 people in New York City and Washington, D. C. died. Our nation was stunned but resilient, in no small measure due to a reawakening of religious sentiments. Church attendance rose. People prayed. Politicians openly affirmed God's mercy. If only briefly, God took center stage. Our national outpouring of emotion reminded us of the void in this country's soul. For the moment at least, we put off spiritual amnesia by acknowledging God once more.

There had been warnings of an impending terrorist attack, but we failed to heed them because we were lulled into the belief that the threat did not exist. Only after a tragedy did we take action. In our crisis, we awoke from our denial and developed a network of preventive detection systems under a new Department of Homeland Security. In the course of these events, we demonstrated our uniquely human capacity for devising innovative problem-solving strategies. But as is so often the case, this capacity has proven to be a two-edged sword. While we find new and creative ways to solve our problems, we tend to regress to denial—we believe that the triumphs of our ability to reason are all that we need to live successfully. One of our greatest strengths then, becomes a weakness, creating a false sense of security in our own competency.

Our culture teaches that our accomplishments can replace our dependence on God. Our God-given rationality has become our Achilles' heel. We've trapped ourselves. What we have been given by God has never seemed enough. He made us a little lower than the angels, but we claim superiority over all. He crowned us with glory and honor, but we demand admiration. He loves us, but many have written Him off as irrelevant. Nothing short of assuming complete authority seems to satisfy us—and even that doesn't satisfy us. We have spurned the awe that creatures owe their Creator. We've edited the blueprint of our own design and the original is forgotten.

Faith in scientific inquiry as the only means of understanding the world has blinded us to eternity's landscape. To remove God from life's equation is to eliminate the only ground for human significance. Denying the spiritual world view, we fail to appreciate why we're so precisely equipped to handle threats to our well-being.

In our materialism, we have dismissed questions about the meaning of life as too religious, leaving a spiritual vacuum that the cult of science cannot fill. We are just too wedded to the tangible world of "hard data" to admit to anything else. Yet we cannot reduce emotional states to the mere activity of certain biological systems without missing God's design and purpose for our psychological makeup. A colleague of mine at the college where I taught once said to me in frustration, "This religious stuff is just superstitious nonsense that keeps getting in the way of teaching the superiority of science. Why do you persist in helping these people pursue their ignorance? Can't they *(and you)* see that life is nothing more than the accumulation of stimulus-response connections that can be traced to the evolution of our biology? Sometimes, I think I might as well give up teaching—nobody learns anything from it anyway. I'll never understand you—you're educated and you still believe that stuff. I think it's pretty hopeless."

In rejecting such reductionism, Viktor Frankl argued that rather than being "pushed" toward meaning by some biological drive, we are actually *pulled* toward meaning by something that appeals to our human spirit. From this point of view, our emotional alarm systems are designed to keep bringing us back to a purposeful life—which of course, is the life God intended—a view my colleague could never accept.

We have no difficulty explaining short-range physiological events such as the "flight or fight" response preparing the body for action. But longer-term emotional states, like depression, require a broader explanation that incorporates the divine logic behind the system. All emotional signals were originally meant to arouse our repugnance to evil and to stimulate joy in response to goodness. But after the Fall, these signals were needed for damage control. The hardships of a fallen world required a design that steered us back to the purpose of loving—back to God Himself.

Our emotional signals are therefore, part of the divine image. Any warning system, such as depression, though unpleasant to experience, is meant to guard that image. Depression is not merely a disease to treat, but an experience that leads us to something better. It may prompt us to clear away the baggage of a difficult past or to process a significant loss.

Clinical practice tells us that in most cases, depression has a far more useful role than we think. It's not simply a matter of chance errors in the function of enzymes. Author Andrew Solomon, who experienced depression himself, agrees. "Anyone who lives through [depression] knows that it is never as simple as complicated chemistry."[1]

Now, we are by no means dismissing the biological factors or genetic predispositions to depression. They certainly occur and in such instances, depression signals the onset of measurable brain dysfunction. That calls for a specific, mainly medical, course of treatment. But the majority of depression cases can be traced back to relational causes. Depression can prompt us to examine conflicts that we were previously too distracting or more likely, too fearful to face. When this signal intrudes and pries open our tightly-held irrational beliefs, it can open up an entirely new way of thinking.

Nothing less than the trauma of depression is likely to stimulate such change.

IN THE BEGINNING: A LIVING PARADOX

Man was originally created in the *perfect* image of God—perfectly in His likeness. But Adam, denying his inferiority to God, chose the path of moral independence. And so man's soul was marked and his moral senses permanently dulled. In love, God warned Adam against this spiritually fatal step. But Adam proceeded to damage his divine image and developed a tendency to sin. As amazing as it may seem, even though Adam freely rejected his natural spiritual inheritance, God never put a single condition on His love.

We know that God is wholly righteous with no capacity for evil (cf. Jas. 1:13). Man however, lacks God's power to resist evil by himself, so he is reliant on God to sustain purity. Apparently though, Adam and Eve weren't convinced. They held fantasies of moral indignation, cultivated by Satan when he openly questioned God's goodness. As a result, they took matters into their own hands. Today's secular humanism is only the most recent expression of this ancient theme.

The consequences for Adam and Eve were disastrous, ending their tenure in the Garden and staining their divine image. Most tragic of all was the fact that they were cut off from their Creator's presence. They were powerless to regain any of this on their own. But God, in His mercy, took the initiative to restore this intimacy and to offer healing for a damaged divine image.

This is the story of the Gospel: an incorruptible love brought to bear on a sin-corrupted need to be loved. It's just like God to create a people who need intimate fellowship so that we might serve God and minister in love to the hearts of people. But we are able to love like this *only* because He loved us first! (See 1 John 4:19.)

That love transforms people. It allowed Stephen, the first Christian martyr, to forgive his killers. It took Saul's zealous pursuit of religious legalism and turned it into a white-hot fire for God. And it calls out to us in our meaninglessness and offers us a sense of purpose. If we want to find meaning to our lives, we must first ask ourselves, "What's the point?" The point is that the good life can never be found on our terms, but only in God's design.

When Jesus was asked to identify the greatest commandment in the Torah, He gave a two-part answer: Love God and love your neighbor (see Matt. 22:35-40). How can these two be included in the same response? It's a matter of authenticity. Just as faith without works is dead (see Jas.

...love's existence depends on God's presence in the world.

2:26), so the profession of love is hollow without corresponding behaviors. To say we love God and yet harbor ill will toward others is a deception (see 1 John 4:20-21). On the other hand, even unbelievers can love one another. The truth is that even when misdirected by a secular culture, love's existence depends on God's presence in the world. It's part of the divine image in man—an image that is essentially relational in character.

This brings us to one of the Bible's most puzzling observations. Before he sinned, Adam experienced complete, unhindered communion with God. And yet, the Lord said, "It is *not* good for the man to be alone" (Gen. 2:18, NIV, emphasis added). Why wasn't God enough for Adam?

I believe it's because Adam—who could never be self-sufficient, whose sociability was limited by a finite mind—needed interpersonal interaction with someone similarly finite. We are created with the relational character of our Creator. And we can fellowship with God. But finite man needs something that an infinite God doesn't need. Unlike a triune God, who is whole within the intimacy of His own three-part being, man must find wholeness by connecting with someone outside of himself. God finds perfect completion within Himself and doesn't need us to complete Him. We, however, need other finite humans to complete our powerful aspiration to love. Just as we must intimately connect with our Creator to fill our spiritual hunger, we must also connect with fellow created beings to fill our social hunger.

Adam's loneliness was not due therefore to an insufficiency in God's companionship, but rather to the fact of his own limits as a created being. And so God created woman as the man's "helper," which is translated from the Hebrew *ezer*. Most often, the Bible uses this word to refer to doing God's work. It never implies inferiority, but rather elevates the woman's role to one of honoring God. So God created the woman to do godly work in meeting Adam's companionship needs at the finite level. God meant intimacy between a man and a woman to serve as an earthly model for the relationship between God and His people. Human intimacy helped Adam understand the depth of relationship he also needed with God.

That's why God constantly refers to His relationship with His people in terms of marriage. He refers to the New Testament Church as His bride. He describes Old Testament Israel's sinful behavior as "harlotry" or "adultery," leading to a painful "divorce." Man's relationship with God was from the beginning intended to be one of faithful intimacy, just as we see with happily-married couples. Only a relationship like this can nourish and uplift the soul.

Here we see the creative genius of our God: Our desire for intimate relationship—part of the Creator's image in us—is ultimately responsible for the spiritual unrest that lures us back to our reason for being. We find meaning when we understand ourselves as we were intended to be.

But sin changed everything. It blurred the original splendor of our design and left us in an unnatural state—spiritually-dead and emotionally-naked. Notice that Adam and Eve suddenly became aware of their physical nakedness *after* they sinned. They had lived in selflessness, absorbed in God's and each other's companionship. But sin, by nature, involves self-centered gratification—it refocused man's attention on himself. Their new awareness of their unclothed bodies symbolized the shame of their selfishness. They were "stripped" of their natural state—union of body and soul— now hopelessly divided bodies with spiritually-dead souls. Since then, man's struggle in this broken world is, at its root, his ongoing grief over the loss of what could have been.

Now, if the first couple had become inclined toward evil, for what possible reason would God perpetuate the race, allowing the birth of children who would inherit corruption and multiply evil still further? It might seem like madness, but God's purpose was, once again, ingenious. He provided yet another relational picture to help us understand His desired relationship with us. How better to understand God's forgiveness and grace than by raising and loving our own children? Don't we love our children regardless of their grievous misbehavior? If we're good parents, of course we do.

Healthy parental love is then, the best model for understanding God's love for His children, making sense of His actions and highlighting His grace as the natural overflow of a caring Father's heart. Reflecting this idea, my daughter once said to me, "Daddy, I know you love me no matter what I do—that's like Jesus isn't it?" Though still a child, she really got it. Of course, I scooped her up in my arms and showed my love for her even more!

CREATION:
THE INTIMACY OF IMAGE MAKING

God's creation of man was itself a powerfully intimate act. He said, "Let us make man in *our* image" (Gen. 1:26, NIV, italics added). He made a personal investment in us—a spiritual and emotional likeness. Hebrew scholars draw attention to the profound implications of the grammar of Genesis 2:7. God did not give man a soul; he created him as a living soul, as a living personality interacting with his Creator. Our natural tendency to seek relationships in general and intimacy with God in particular, is not simply an added human attribute—it's who we are! We were born for love and nothing less can adequately define or justify our essence.

Most clients who walk into my office live in a world of relational pain. They talk about depression, loneliness, insecurity, never measuring up, resentments and the like. *But what they are invariably describing is a frustrated desire to be loved and to love someone in return.* Ask a client if she is lonely and she will often break down in a torrent of tears. Mention something about God's love and he will comment on the lack of it in his relationships. One woman said to me, "All I crave for is for someone to hold me and tell me I'm truly loved. I just want to feel special to someone…is that too much to ask?"

To capture the imagination and stimulate the hope of emotionally-hungry people, we have to demonstrate that human-to-human love is an obtainable reality. This tangible demonstration has always been and still is, the most powerful pathway to understanding the reality of God's love.

Time spent with a Christian counselor may be a person's first true encounter with authenticity in a relationship. One of the goals of that relationship is the client's experience of God's loving presence. But, as important as that is, it's only the beginning. Somehow, clients must also learn new ways of connecting this experience to their relationships with the important people in their life—in ways that will eventually make counseling no longer necessary.

Confronting our hidden fears, dealing directly with our anger and guilt, admitting our feelings of shame, this work is not merely cathartic—it is transforming. It takes the energy we've long used destructively and redirects it toward fulfilling relationships and productive interactions. But we don't break old patterns easily. You would think the intense pain of such patterns would stimulate us to action. Sometimes it does. But we humans have a remarkable capacity to endure pain and resist the change that would reduce it. Every time we ignore our natural warning signals, we are saying in effect, "I know a better way."

THE ILLUSIONS OF THE FALL DIE HARD

When Adam abused the privilege of the Garden and ignored the importance of his relationship with his Creator, he did so believing he was better off in charge. In spite of Adam's blatant arrogance, God's love was patient. In fact, He didn't merely endure our rejection. He lavished His sacrificial love upon us by sending His Son. It's one thing to sacrifice for your friends, quite another to die for your enemies. This is rare among humans, even though it is natural for God. Yet it's the love we hunger for (see Rom. 5:6-8).

The Gospel is the story of a sacred intimacy no other faith can duplicate. It moved the apostle Paul to claim that we become an entirely new creation when we accept our Lord's offer of redemption (see 2 Cor. 5:17). This offer is utterly unique, which is why it became the focal point of all of human history.

It's reassuring that even Hollywood, in its moral vacuum, occasionally gets something right. The script for the film *Tuck Everlasting* was written around the theme that if we fear anything, it should be the unlived life—the stagnation of so many relationships that pass for intimacy. They are filled with "busyness" but offer little meaningful interaction. Our frantic American lifestyle too often robs us of time for building relationships. And many marriages, which somehow manage to avoid divorce, nonetheless exist in a state of living death. Isn't the indiscriminate use of tranquilizers evidence of this lifestyle's emptiness? Must we exist as mere caricatures of the divine image, always searching for momentary pleasure?

Observe the woman, displaying anger toward her husband, but inwardly grieving over her loneliness—the loss of "the man she married." She turns away from him to faith and friends as her only comfort. Or the husband, depressed about a marriage that's evaporating before his eyes, believing he can never please his wife. He retreats from her and into work as his only solace.

Alarms are sounding right and left. Both are experiencing emotional crises. But the outcome depends on their responses. Will they listen to the signals and realize that their depression is pointing toward change? Or will they react defensively, resorting to blaming or stonewalling? Even in so-called stagnant relationships, depression is usually part of the mix, warning of impending relational meltdown. I remember one woman said after her divorce, "My husband and I could never get past our accusations of one another—it just seemed like we were both so depressed that we were determined to make each other equally miserable. If only we could have realized what we were doing..."

We see then, that depression can alter the relationship pattern itself. Emotional pain, like its physical counterpart, sharply narrows our focus and then turns it inward creating a variety of communication problems. For instance, self-preoccupation can impair our willingness to listen to others and to empathize with them. Without the ability to see life from the other person's perspective, we cannot connect intimately.

Relationship patterns are likely most altered when depression goes unrecognized as a warning signal. It's misused to justify retreat into silence or lashing out in defense. In such cases, we tend to talk about our depression as an overpowering "condition" with a life of its own. We become convinced that we need more understanding, more tolerance. Self-pity sets in and, in our "victim" state, our prognosis becomes even less optimistic. One man who talked this way complained, "Why can't people see that I can't help myself...it's just the way I am, so why won't they accept that?" He failed to see that while God was in charge of creating his person, he was responsible for changing his behavior.

Sometimes whole families—by their choice of words, relationships, decisions and self-imposed limitations—are organized around a single member's depression. That's because they are conditioned by the fear of triggering still another wave of negative reaction. Mother will tell the kids, "Don't make any noise; your father is not feeling well, so we all need to be quiet." Or Father may say, "it's important to obey your mother —you know how bad she feels when you misbehave." So you see, even guilt manipulations may be used in the effort to avoid another meltdown.

These destructive relational outcomes result when we fail to understand the purpose of depression. But if we see it as the signal it is, we have a better chance of discovering our core issues and resolving them. Sometimes, we need objective outside help to sort out these issues without becoming overwhelmed in the process. That's because in the midst of our own depression, our problem-solving ability is overshadowed by negativism and the temptation to surrender to helplessness. We can better resist resignation if we understand our depression not as a personal failure, but

> **We were created both for a purpose and with a purpose.**

as a context for pursuing a different course of action. This perspective however, requires a willingness to do some hard emotional work—something that many people spend their lives avoiding.

We were created both *for* a purpose and *with* a purpose. God never leaves anything to chance. We see His purposeful actions throughout redemptive history. In the events leading up to the Exodus, God targeted each of the 10 plagues at one of Egypt's false gods demonstrating His superiority over each of them. Though these were acts of judgment, they were also compassionate demonstrations (both to the Egyptians and the Hebrews) that God is the sole intervening power of the universe.

We see purpose in God's every act of creation and in His every act in history—even in our lives. He is a relational God who loves all He has created. Given that initial investment, we are assured that all His actions in our lives are directed toward the goal of healing, protecting and glorifying His image in us.

TAKING RESPONSIBILITY: A LESSON IN LOVE AND MEANING

Knowing what it means to be created in the image of God is essential for understanding the human experience. Scientific study alone will always be limited if we assume that everything is traceable to material causes. It will inevitably result in misleading conclusions and false predictions. Worse still, such errors will be attributed to the imprecision of science rather than to the unpredictability of free will and the actions of a transcendent God. We must therefore look in a different direction to find the true blueprint for human behavior.

The average person though, is not so much interested in the technical details as in the practical implications of human knowledge. He prefers to focus on what seems to make life more worthwhile, what leads to fulfilling relationships and what adds meaning to his life's work. Most people want to believe their lives matter—that there's a point to living beyond just using up space and oxygen.

Centering the universe around ourselves however, can never achieve this goal. Man cannot manufacture his own purpose, as humanists attempt to do. When he tries, he violates the divine image and robs himself of the capacity to think accurately about himself. All he is left with is his intractable denial.

> **Humility in the name of wisdom, though, is far better than ignorance in the name of vanity.**

Faith-based critical thinking, on the other hand, focuses not so much on answering the questions our culture raises, but on questioning the answers our culture gives. We can only find meaning beyond the natural order by seeking truth with eyes of faith, which is what makes the divine image so important. It's a humble endeavor to seek answers, not merely within ourselves but through the Creator's revelation. Humility in the name of wisdom, though, is far better than ignorance in the name of vanity.

Searching for purpose along the pathway of wisdom reveals the importance of our capacity for love. But those who are convinced of their unlovability often feel compelled to seek acceptance along an unwise path. In Andrew Lloyd Webber's musical, *The Phantom of the Opera,* the disfigured phantom, caught up in his self-perceived unlovability, implores his young hostage to relieve his unbearable solitude and love him genuinely. But the maiden loves another and the phantom lashes out in murderous rage. Tragically, the phantom's loneliness and "unworthiness" is self-imposed. He believes he is a victim imprisoned by the ugliness of his burn-scarred face and spurned by a society that rejects anything short of beauty. In reality, he is his own jailor thwarting his own yearning for a bond of intimacy. In the end, the strangely discordant opera he composed for his beloved reflected a life out of tune with reality and inharmonious with the music of the life he sought.

Here we see all the interacting elements of the divine image intended to form loving connections but now distorted by rejection and humiliation. The phantom's misguided efforts ended in self-destruction. Few people seek answers by means of such monstrous behavior, but most of us have used some form of self-defeating behavior in our attempts to escape loneliness, rejection and self-hatred.

In one way or another, every counterproductive attempt to find relief is a way of avoiding personal responsibility for our growth. Playing the victim produces no long-term rewards. We can blame God, people or fate—rarely, if ever, acknowledging our own poor choices—but to do so is to surrender to the deception of helplessness. Relinquishing personal control means giving up the idea of taking active steps toward a remedy.

FOLLOWING DEPRESSION'S LEAD

Louis Pasteur once observed that, "chance favors the prepared mind."[2] Everyone should understand the nature of depression, whether or not they're dealing with it now. It's never too early to learn what it really means, what to expect when this alarm system is triggered and how to follow its lead to growth.

Those who have gone through depression often experience, among other surprising benefits, a greater sensitivity to the suffering of others. Adversity strengthens not only our coping skills but our empathy as well. A client of mine, who had struggled with depression, was able to comfort his wife through a subsequent trauma of her own. With new understanding, he came alongside her as a healing companion in her despair. He was instrumental in helping her process her experience successfully. After the worst had passed, she reflected on her husband's help. "He is so different now. I have never seen him as sensitive as he is now. Though it was awful when we went through it, his depression has changed him… and I mean for the good!" It was apparent that his personal struggle had produced an empathy that strengthened their marriage.

God never wastes an experience, even a painful one. Even if we don't understand what's happening in the moment, our *anticipation of growth* can help us endure and see it through. The usefulness of this purpose-driven behavior is captured in a humorous incident during a family vacation a few years ago. We were visiting extended family on a farm near the Ozarks. On a hot, humid afternoon, we noted that their dog, which appeared old and worn-out, lay nearby breathing laboriously and moving as little as possible. My wife's cousin, Ron, grinned and told us the dog was his bird dog, capable of chasing down fallen birds with the best of them. He went into the house and soon reemerged, holding his favorite shotgun. Immediately, the slumbering dog leaped to his feet, ears erect, tail extended and began running in circles and barking like a pup, ready for bird hunting. Ron broke into hearty laughter over our startled reaction and reminded us that, "a dog with a purpose is a dog unleashed for action."

What a parable for the human scene! When we see a clear purpose—for our depression in the short run or for our life in the long run—we find new energy, new conviction and a new longing to follow our deepest desire. It unleashes a revitalized motivation to pursue the blueprint of our creation!

When we fail to grasp the purpose of this experience, it is easy to slide into despair—even suicidal despair. Either that or we resign ourselves to an emotional numbness, accepting depression as a part of life with no meaning beyond its symptoms. Depression, in that case, becomes the color of defeat washing our entire future in shades of gray. The resulting apathy cripples our ambition and fosters escapism from anything we don't want to face. Like actor Jack Nicholson's character in the film, "As Good As It Gets," he assumed that his life would never get any better than the depressing compulsive routine he had called his life.

This resignation is similar to the way we rationalize sin as moral expediency. "That's just modern life" is the common refrain of relativism. We make a pact with culture: Cede moral authority to "them," and "they" become our defense against acknowledging our own sin. Author John Eldredge laments, "Something awful has happened, something terrible, something worse even than the fall of man. With that greatest of all tragedies we merely lost paradise and with it everything that made life worth living. What has happened since is unthinkable. We have gotten used to it. We are broken into the idea that this is just the way things are."[3]

When we likewise adapt to depression, refusing to acknowledge its signal value, we slip into the abyss of lost hopes, lost dreams and lost relationships—a continuous repetition of the same unproductive thinking and behavior that triggered the alarm in the first place. God has placed within us a desire for much more than that. But when we refuse to take the necessary risks in God's love, we fall back on the principle that nothing ventured is nothing lost. By then, *everything* has been lost already.

THE VIRTUE OF HOPE AND THE HOPE OF VIRTUE

It has been said that hope, however remote, is still far better than its absence. For with hope comes the determination to change. But its absence robs us of even the willingness to try. Remember, it's the precious moments of joy in our life that gives us a glimpse of a future governed by hope.

A Samaritan woman came to the town well one fateful afternoon. She had hoped for a life of love, but her pursuit of tenuous marriages and promiscuous relationships led only to disillusionment. Jesus met her there, knowing her soul's desperate thirst and He offered her the living water of His transcendent peace. At last, her thirst was quenched and her hope for a life worth living fulfilled. With excitement, she exclaimed to her startled people, "Come, I have found the Messiah!"

Today, Jesus calls us to something greater than we can ever imagine. But we are often blind to His mercy and deaf to His words of truth. A veil of emotional trauma obscures our view of God and distorts our view of self. We often have refashioned truth according to our own "wisdom," twisting it into something unrecognizable. But God always responds in our best interests. He may choose to answer our pain with a compelling revelation of our irrational beliefs. Or maybe He will bring people into our lives as agents of change. Or, in His wisdom, He may simply choose to wait and let life's consequences do their work of teaching.

God's actions or inactions may not always make sense to us. Indeed, we may become impatient, accusatory or even cynical. Yet incredible though it may seem, God fully understands our responses. He is not fragile! He knows that we will never completely comprehend His infinite wisdom. Nor can we begin to understand the magnitude of His righteousness.

But trusting in His virtue is the choice that makes the difference between perceiving God as a righteous Father and viewing Him as a petty dictator. It is our acceptance of God's goodness that gives us the confidence to disclose the troubled contents of our depressed mind and heart, knowing that it will provoke His compassion, not His wrath and judgment.

It's this sense of safety that's necessary to pry open the closed heart of damaged people, to peel back the patches of lifeless bravado which have sealed their deep wounds. In relationship with God, a trusting heart is a healing heart. And a community of believers that speaks God's tender words of truth is a healing community.

With these loving connections, we may begin at last, to reclaim and repair the character of our divine image.

FINDING HOPE

1. Emotional signals like depression are part of a *warning system meant to guard the divine image.* As such, they are vital for preventing further damage.

2. *God's answer* to man's dilemma? *An incorruptible love* brought to bear on a need to be loved corrupted by sin.

3. You were *created by love and for love.* It is essential for understanding your *human identity and for providing personal meaning.*

4. The best antidote to the temptation to withdraw into helplessness is to recognize that *depression sets the stage for true change.*

5. *God never wastes an experience.* When you believe He will grow you through your pain or disappointment, *you are better prepared to endure it.*

6. *Trusting God's goodness* is the first step in building the *intimate connections that are healing to your divine image.*

DEPRESSION AND THE GRAND BLUEPRINT

*Every one of us is given the gift of life and what a
strange gift it is. If it is jealously preserved, it impoverishes
and saddens, but if it is spent for others it enriches and beautifies.*

—IGNAZIO SILONE, ITALIAN POLITICIAN AND EDITOR—

When depression sounds its alarm, it insists that we face the issues we've been avoiding. Examining our core beliefs and the experiences that gave rise to them is an ordeal few of us find pleasure in. However, this important process unearths the basis for most of our behavior. That's because helpful information isn't all we turn up; pain, anger, guilt and fear surface as well.

Yes, some core beliefs can arouse joy, excitement and anticipation. But many dredge up old wounds and messages that formed what we believe to be the "real me" under our façade—the helpless, inadequate, unlovable, bad, worthless "me" that we believe in but try to deny. They also shape corollary beliefs about other people ("they're all malicious," or "no one can really be trusted"). Together, such notions grossly distort our view of the world as well as ourselves, blinding us to the beauty of the divine image within.

Depression also signals the presence of the notorious companion of fear and guilt called *shame,* which tells us we shouldn't feel the way we do. False shame is a reaction of humiliation and self-criticism to pain and personal threat from the past—the origins of which are often cloaked in secret, selective and often disturbing memories. Devastating abuse, parental neglect or over-dominance by others early in life has trained us to respond with misdirected reactions in the present. So we devise protective measures—parallel lives, illusions, and denial. But these are only self-defeating measures that in the long run, cause worse pain than the truth. When our defense system begins to collapse on itself, depression is there telling us to reconstruct our coping skills. Our injury once again takes center stage, insistent and convincing us that the status quo is no longer acceptable.

Depression is a call to personal courage, a paradoxically-positive mechanism that only God could have conceived. Hard though this may be to accept, depression is designed to bring us back to the truth—to what we were originally intended to be. Shame and fear tempt us to retreat, but depression challenges us to sift through the rotting garbage—the lies that we tell ourselves, learned from our parents or others who themselves are in pain.

Courage is widely misunderstood. It doesn't mean fearlessness. Courage is doing what's right *in spite of* our fear. It's in our best interest to reverse the anxiety-driven, self-hypnotic trance of our internal monologues to confront our secrets with the power of truth. But our self-deceptions try to intimidate us, claiming the authority of people we used to trust. They survive as long as they keep us cowed—but the sooner we examine and oppose them, the sooner they will begin to crumble.

Whoever you are, at your foundation is the image of God, perfectly-designed, conceived in love and intended to be nurtured in a mutually-giving relationship. You are forever God's handiwork and no emotional damage changes this fact. The people in our life who care and can help—therapists, pastors or friends—are in reality, servants of the soul, seeking to restore to visibility what God has *already done* in us.

Depression calls us to rebuild, sometimes from the foundation up, our framework for meaningful living. This requires a new blueprint—or rather the original one derived from the divine image—the expression of God's goodness in us. The old family blueprint doesn't work. It lied about the value God places on us. It excused evil and its toxic effects. But when the old blueprint has guided our lives, the relevance of our divine image has faded from view. So let's start reconstructing our identity by focusing on the attributes of this image in us.

We'll examine each of its five dimensions, while aware that they interweave and interact with each other. Together, they form the dynamics of human personality, making human beings utterly unique among the species.

THE COGNITIVE DIMENSION: THINKING ABOUT OUR THINKING

I was playing the game of peek-a-boo with our two-year-old grandson, Jacob, and I noticed he was doing something new. Before, he would giggle when he saw me suddenly appear from behind a wall—but now he would walk around the corner, looking for me. Peek-a-boo had now become hide-and-seek.

The former game is based on the element of surprise, the latter on the thrill of discovery. Our grandson had attained what developmental specialists call "object permanence." Early on, when objects or persons would disappear, in his mind they no longer existed. But now he understood that objects continued to exist even if he couldn't see them and so he now actively hunted for them. This and subsequent benchmarks of mental growth eventually lead to abstract thinking which is what sets Jacob and all other humans apart from the rest of creation.

Perhaps foremost then among the attributes of God's image in us is this *cognitive dimension*. It gives us our self-reflective consciousness, the ability to think about the human condition, to formulate a philosophy of life and to make free choices—including tragic ones—that determine our direction in life. It was once said that we are "the only part of creation that seeks to know *all* of creation."

This distinctly human thirst to *know* is also connected to our desire for *control*.

It's a pity though, that we fail to better train our mental faculties for cultivating intimacy. We learn to solve problems in order to adapt physically to our world, but that's not enough. We must also learn to live with one another, with God and with ourselves. Our thinking cannot be separated from our freedom of will. Such thinking shapes our choices just as our choices shape our thinking. Healthy thinking about relationships helps us choose to accept God's love, to love others and to love ourselves.

Our cognitive capacity allows us to discover significance in what we do to optimistically plan a future with specific objectives.

> **Our cognitive capacity allows us to discover significance in what we do...**

When we misuse or misrepresent this part of the divine image, we end up disconnected from our Creator, confined to our own island of self-inflicted misery. God however, refuses to leave us stranded there. Instead, He allows depression's clamor to reawaken our capacity to reconsider our choices.

The Bible is by no means silent concerning the importance of our thought life. In Proverbs 23:7 we read, "As [a man] thinks within himself, so he is." Our thinking habits shape the person we eventually become, determining whether we become optimistic or pessimistic, rage-filled or peaceful, victimized or victorious. In Jeremiah 17:9-10, we're reminded that our thought life is naturally deceitful and self-serving, which is why we need the Holy Spirit's reality checks.

We put our thinking to the test by submitting it to the light of God's Word. This is a difficult personal discipline that requires a humble admission of weakness, ignorance and sin.

But our thought life also represents the central avenue to our heart. In Philippians 4:6-9, the apostle Paul taught that right thinking can help us replace our anxiety with the peace of God. By monitoring the content of our thought life—meditating on whatever things are good and true, things that nurture truth and courage—we can remain centered in the reality of God's presence and avoid the paralyzing effects of obsessive negative rumination.

Paul was not a first-century Norman Vincent Peale, preaching the power of positive thinking, but rather a first-century enthusiast for preaching the power of *godly* thinking. We're not talking about spiritualizing every problem and flinging verses in every direction at the slightest provocation. Those who do so may seem pious, but underneath they tend to be critical and insensitive to other people's needs. They're often insecure, attempting to live within an insulated, compulsive world they control. They hide behind their faith, intimidating others to prevent them from getting too close. This is clearly *not* what the apostle meant.

Paul's version of godly thinking focuses on priorities such as reconciliation rather than destructive conflict, emotional freedom instead of burdensome restrictions; grace over legalism, progressing toward clearer, sometimes uncomfortable reality, rather than regressing back to comfortable but dysfunctional ways of thinking.

I know the effects of a legalistic thought life first hand. I was raised in a church where playing cards was seen as corrupting, dancing of any sort was seductive and attending public school rather than private Christian school fell short of the mark. These things were communicated, not so much by formal teaching, but by judgmental attitudes or behavioral codes. I became quite familiar with the experience of guilt and all the distorted thinking that comes with it. I also know however, how freeing it is to be unburdened from false sanctions by having a truer understanding of genuine faith.

Fear of humiliation can cause many of us to seek conformity by engaging in emotional compromises. So we must be careful not to sacrifice truth by letting others do our thinking for us, even if we consider them important to us. But we also must not act out of vanity. When a husband and wife accuse each other of a "lack of submission" or "un-Christlike headship," they're often being intellectually dishonest, assuming a self-righteous position that makes a mockery of faith. While both spouses hold stubbornly to their version of "the truth," each puts most or all of the blame on the other. At the same time, they avoid any reality testing for their own point of view. Their marriage suffers the consequences and, if they're already depressed, so does their state of mind. I saw a couple who were emotionally exhausted from being on trial all the time. "He never listens to me and when he does, he dismisses everything I say," the wife said with exasperation. "She never gives my arguments the time of day," the husband countered. The two were locked into a perpetual battle for the truth, completely unaware that their respective views were little more than subjective evaluations.

The content of our thinking determines our feelings and behaviors in all of our relationships. Like modern cognitive therapy, the New Testament teaches that our thoughts influence the quality of our emotional lives. But we can't make long-term positive changes by simply resolving to think well. Here's where the intellectual component of the divine image must lean heavily on the spiritual component—without faith in God to guide and strengthen us, we have no moral compass to chart a new mental path. On our own, we can easily use our "beliefs" to justify a sinful lifestyle.

We've inherited our capacity for self-reflection from our Creator. It puts us in touch with our built-in desire to connect with someone beyond ourselves. It convinces us of our God-given value and helps us understand His compassionate heart. Finally, it prompts us to sift through the evidence of His love, and discover the intimacy that fulfills our purpose for living.

THE EMOTIONAL CONNECTION: THE DEPTH OF PASSION

Another attribute of the divine image in us is the *emotional*. This dimension makes sense only in relationships, where our feelings deepen our interactions and give communication its richness and complexity. It's also where we find most of the important alarm systems that warn us of relational trouble.

In the Gospels, we read that it was Jesus' emotional life that bridged His divine nature and His humanity (e.g., Matt. 9:36, 15:32, 26:36-38; Mark 3:5, 11:12-17; Luke 7:13, 19:41; John 11:33-35). It's a major reason why we connect so deeply with Him. Having been transformed by the power of the cross, we have unlimited access to His boundless compassion. What's more, Jesus' free expression of emotion gives us the freedom to admit to our own. This is what allows us to blend our hearts with His. It is part of the "here and now" experience of redemption that complements and fills out our intellectual contemplation of it. And it paves the way for giving ourselves fully to passion in every truly intimate relationship.

In our connections with each other however, passion can become a two-edged sword. While it enriches our experience of intimacy, if uncontrolled it can be destructive. We can find both sides of passion in marriages where the spouses tend to have opposite traits (which is common). One partner may be more impulsive and expressive and the other more routine driven and cautious. Each sees in the other some quality they intuitively know they need in order to experience a healthy balance—but that same quality can also be a source of significant irritation.

If a socially gregarious, emotional woman marries a quiet, introverted man because she is drawn to the fact that he seems to have his feet on the ground, she will often find later that she is irritated by his "stick in the mud" attitudes about getting together with others. He, on the other hand, may become irritated by the sense that he is always being dragged to one social function after another, even though he was initially attracted to the way she seemed so active and "full of life."

One way that a relationship can go wrong is when one or both partners try to change the other to be more like themselves. Usually, the extroverted person does this by means of overt aggression and the introvert by means of passive aggression. This only puts the marriage under stress, often leading to depression in both spouses.

Most of us have learned our more troublesome emotional reactions in our homes of origin. When we grow up in emotionally-repressive families, we're likely to be much less spontaneous in our adult relationships, less emotionally open and on guard against an intimacy that feels unfamiliar and threatening. This was the plight of a man who came into my office grieving the loss of his 25-year marriage. He said he loved his wife but found it nearly impossible, for some reason, to voice this love to her. Underneath, he yearned to be loved, but his wife felt deprived and eventually left him. The last thing she said to him was, "I can't take the silence anymore; I don't know how you can go day after day without showing any affection or demonstrating any interest in talking about our relationship. Apparently you'd just as soon be alone; but for me, I want something more, a lot more." With that, she walked away.

Similar results have occurred in personal friendships and even work relationships, which have suffered from a lack of adequate interaction. Whether due to insufficient social skills or to controlling manipulation or whether it is simply a smoke screen for anger, continual silence is destructive. Even though silence may feel safe to some, too much of it tends to kill relationships. The crisis of depression in situations like these might be telling us that our feelings are not as dangerous as they seem and that we will find the fulfillment we seek when we set free the emotional characteristics of God's image in us.

Any practicing therapist will tell you that these are the kinds of issues that motivate people to seek help. It's rarely about intellectual differences. That's why it's the *process* of conflict rather than its content that usually arouses pain and anger. It's feeling invalidated—not experiencing disagreement—which destroys a relationship. In other words, feeling like your opinions or preferences don't count. It's not surprising then that the emotional dimension of the divine image, which is the source of many critical alarm systems, is so important in diagnosing and solving problems with relational intimacy. Once a person regains hope and sees that these alarms, once activated, are urging him or her to take ownership of the solution, that person is able to become more constructive in relationships.

Our thinking abilities help us develop our belief systems, but our emotional capacities invest our beliefs with priority and intensity. Blocked feelings invariably empty life of its depth and richness. The chronic deprivation that results makes us vulnerable to seeking stimulation in all the wrong places. The temptation of that promiscuous glance or that risky indulgence only reveals

> **Paradoxically, the same emotional capacities that add richness to our experience can also become a highway for our most destructive impulses.**

the arid state of our emotional life. Terrible damage awaits us down this path—sometimes irrevocable damage. Paradoxically, the same emotional capacities that add richness to our experience can also become a highway for our most destructive impulses.

Almost without exception, when we abuse our freedom by crossing the line, we have already lost the innocence of intimacy. Even so, restoration is available. Hopeless as we might feel at times, Jesus stands ready to heal us by bringing back the Father's image in us. In Him we find grace, not condemnation, with a future of freedom to replace the imprisonment of our past.

THE MORAL CONNECTION: THE CHARACTER OF CONVICTION

Our intellect is necessary for understanding the significance of truth. Our emotional capacity is necessary for experiencing the significance of love. However, it is our moral character that's necessary for seeing the significance of sin and the beauty of righteousness. Our moral sense allows us to be convicted by God's still small voice and cheered by the murmurs of His pleasure. This *moral dimension* of the divine image provides us with the awareness of what is holy, just and virtuous. It's the source of our ability to discern right from wrong, to distinguish between good and evil.

In the beginning, man encountered only good in fellowship with the Father. But after the Fall, he discovered the destructiveness of evil. That's why every human society has followed some code of ethics, which reflects the collective conscience of its people.

But because of our cravings for sin, we experience healthy guilt to guide us back to our moral bearings and to the joy of honoring God. It's our compass in times of temptation, confusion and compromise. Perhaps more than any other aspect of the divine image, we seek to neutralize or neglect the moral dimension. We silence the voice of integrity, the claims of conscience within. We underestimate the seduction of evil and minimize the dangers of vice. We ease our discomfort over ethical lapses with rationalizations like, "Everybody does it" or, "It doesn't harm anyone." Yet we often pay a price for such mental gymnastics—a type of depression that won't go away until we come to terms with our moral compromises.

Our self-defeating behavior demonstrates how easy it is to subvert the original intention of our alarm systems. Sometimes we carelessly exercise our free will to short-circuit God's design for our safekeeping. The truth is that we cannot think well, love well or live well if we haven't chosen well. We can act with moral honor or we can deceive ourselves into accepting the unthinkable. Either way we're defining the self. As Andrew Solomon puts it, "We can never escape from choice itself. One's self lies in the choosing, every choice, every day."[1]

Without the morality of the divine image, we would be unable to appreciate God's view of our choices. Moral conviction may seem pitiless in its assessment of our foolishness, but it also affirms our godly intentions. That's the point of our heavenly Father's correction.

THE SPIRITUAL CONNECTION: CHANNEL OF DIVINE GRACE

Our moral sense interacts with and is informed by the *spiritual dimension* of God's image within us. This dimension makes us aware of a reality that exists beyond our experience. Since the dawn of time, man has been aware of something or someone greater than himself. Although this awareness has often been expressed in idolatry and superstition, its existence is the unmistakable product of natural revelation.

This has been demonstrated time and again when missionaries have reported wholesale conversions of certain tribes in remote regions—conversions that occurred immediately upon first presentation of the Gospel message. Long before any missionary arrived, these people acknowledged a divine power behind nature and sought a greater revelation. When they heard the Gospel, they rejoiced that God had answered their petitions.

A missionary friend of mine once shared that he had such an experience in the remote mountains of Mexico. From the first day he had arrived in one village after another, the tribes' people fell down and worshipped Jesus, exclaiming with tears streaming down their faces that, "Our God has not failed us…at last, we have His name!"

Long ago the writer of Ecclesiastes taught that God had placed eternity in man's heart (see Eccles. 3:11). The seventeenth-century philosopher Blaise Pascal called it a "God-shaped vacuum." Yet despite man's consciousness of the supernatural, he still resists turning his heart to the God of creation (see Rom. 1:20-23). He invents his own gods or worships the created order itself. In essence, he worships himself.

In one way or another, every religion except Christianity makes good works the source of man's salvation. In other words, it's what man *does* that counts, so that people define their importance chiefly by the authority they assume for themselves—not by the grace God extends to them through the Cross. This self-focus closes their eyes to God's eternal power in creation and leaves them vulnerable to their own finite thinking.

Much of human philosophy is a rational attempt to explain away our mysterious spiritual impulses. Most modern intellectuals refuse to accept the idea that spirituality is even an aspect of the self—let alone that it responds to God's voice. In psychology, this antipathy toward God began with Sigmund Freud, who struggled most of his life to come to terms with the "irrationality" of the spiritual world view. His brilliant colleagues, part of a faith-sensitive intellectual community of the time, tended to dismiss his reasoning about God by raising questions that he couldn't adequately answer.

Harvard psychiatrist, Armand Nicholi, Jr., compares Freud's thinking with that of Oxford professor C. S. Lewis. He points out that Freud's private ambivalence fueled his public determination to prove his case for atheism. Lewis converted from atheism to Christianity because of the faith's inherent logic, but Freud never acknowledged the Scriptures' historicity or consistency. Instead, Freud constructed a model that explained away human spirituality with such terms as "universal obsessional neurosis," "projected wish fulfillment," "ignorance" and "superstition."

Freud himself was raised in an orthodox Jewish home. Yet his rejection of his father's faith led him not to "enlightenment," but to a lifelong bout with depression. He could have heeded this warning signal and acknowledged the relevance of the spiritual domain. But instead he tried to numb his despair through a variety of sedatives, leading eventually to a cocaine addiction.

Our God-given alarm systems work not only in individuals, but on the societal level as well. Throughout history, we have seen cultural upheavals spawned by the denial of the spiritual, which led to degradation, violence and downfall. The French Revolution, springing out of the distinctly antireligious bias of the Enlightenment, led to one of the most brutal and bloody periods of French history. It didn't help that the corruption of the church leadership left the people with an insufficient cultivation of their spiritual character. So without spiritual guidance, there was nothing to moderate or redirect the rage unleashed by the revolution. What began as a noble effort to give a voice to the peasant ended in the chaos of naked revenge.

The mayhem of the Bolshevik Revolution—and the ensuing nine decades of "national depression" in the Soviet Union—is but another tale of disaster that arose out of a spiritual void. It was sparked by the atheistic writings of Karl Marx, who inspired such despots as Vladimir Lenin and Joseph Stalin. Much the same can be said of the influence of Friedrich Nietzsche's godless thinking on Adolph Hitler's brutal Third Reich. As history shows, where divine revelation is denied, where God becomes merely an asterisk of a former culture, life disintegrates into human tragedy. "The fool has said in his heart 'There is no God,' they are corrupt and have committed abominable injustice"(Ps. 53:1). A spiritual world view is important for building a meaningful society where good will is honored and the individual is valued.

It's interesting that those who most oppose spiritual things often come from strong religious backgrounds. They also tend to show clear signs of angry depression. When I was a psychology student in the 1960s and 1970s, I learned that one of my professors who was hostile to Christianity had a strong (albeit legalistic), evangelical background. At the college where I taught, I discovered the same about colleagues who enjoyed dismantling a student's biblical arguments. I've concluded that many, like Freud, who are hostile to issues of faith, may be trying to silence an underlying insecurity about their own spirituality.

Over the years, I have counseled depressed clients who have had a long history of struggling with the idea of God. Typically, they were annoyed by Christians who seemed confident in their faith. Depressed as they were, they could never bring themselves to believe that a Christian's spirituality was, in fact, real. They were convinced that it must be some sort of false front. Only when some of these clients became Christians did they understand why faith had appeared to be so disingenuous to them.

In a different way, this is what happened to Saul (who became the apostle Paul) after he witnessed Stephen's martyrdom. Saul didn't deny the reality of the spiritual realm, but he had spent his young adult life attempting to force it into a legalistic framework rather than the true model of God's grace. Saul's doubts about Pharisaical Judaism were probably raised by Stephen's great defense of the Gospel, his heroic death, his peaceful confidence and his incomprehensible forgiveness of those who stoned him. At some level, Saul must have known that Stephen had experienced something the rabbinical teachers had failed to discover. He embarked on a violent crusade to wipe out the Christian community, but God brought him to a point of crisis in which he submitted and allowed God to speak and work through him, the way God had always intended.

Despite the continuous assault on the spiritual world view— by governments and individuals—God refuses to abandon man to his own misgivings about faith. Many of those who so abuse God's image in themselves eventually encounter a spiritual restlessness and despair that can only be remedied when they become sensitive to His gospel of grace. Many who encounter depression are, in reality, being urged by their emotional pain to take another look at the divine image they've suppressed. Depression may even be the tool that awakens our God-ward impulse, rekindles our hope and allows us to respond to God's incomprehensibly sacrificial, utterly supernatural story.

THE SOCIAL CONNECTION: INVITATION TO INTIMACY

The *social* part of the image of God is what gives us the ability connect with other people. We were conceived in the mind of God who in His essence is relational. And so our primary purpose in life is to love, to taste of the greatest intimacy ever known. Adam's greatest loss was his continuous, joyful *connection* with God. That's why God's redemptive plan is, at its core, to reconnect with man.

The indisputable truth that God is deeply relational is reflected in the fact that people, made in His image, cannot feel fulfilled without belonging to a community. Studies have shown that the chronic recluse eventually experiences debilitating emotions, including prolonged periods of depression and sometimes even psychotic behavior. After spending most of a winter alone in Antarctica, Admiral Byrd realized that, "the [mere] absence of conversation makes it difficult for [a man] to think in words. 'I talk to myself and listen to the words, but they sound hollow and unfamiliar.'"[2] As the fullness of ordinary conversation fades, so does the brain's ability to process something as simple as a loving touch.

> **Our social connecting points, though they seem random, always reveal a hunger, if not a passionate desire, for acceptance.**

As babies, we start out life seeking caring, intimate touch, attaching ourselves to our Mom for love and affection. These social connections give us the ability to trust and feel secure, which in turn, determine how well we adjust later in life. Babies deprived of these bonding experiences suffer emotionally and even have higher mortality rates. Because of God's image in us, we as adults continue to seek this sense of connection throughout our lifetimes.

One of the goals of therapy is to clarify the importance of genuine intimacy and how its absence has hurt us. Our social connecting points, though they seem random, always reveal a hunger, if not a passionate desire, for acceptance. When we avoid authentic intimacy, it usually means we fear rejection—not that we have a preference for solitude.

Hebrews 10:24-26 tells us not to avoid getting together with other believers because our faith requires the nurture of a loving community. When we miss out on Christian fellowship, our faith becomes vulnerable and we become weaker in our beliefs. We're wired to spend time with people—it's absolutely necessary to preserve our spiritual health. When we acknowledge our need to connect with others, we reflect what James described as a living faith (see Jas. 1:26-27).

When a church becomes marked by resentment, we can see the wear and tear on its emotional fabric. These kinds of challenges should remind us that healthy fellowship is critical to the emotional needs of the local body. People who leave their churches seldom do so because of theological differences. They leave because they're lonely. They didn't meaningfully connect with other people and so became restless. Their sense of isolation and sometimes deep depression tells us about the importance of bonding. We are born to be in relationship and our deep longing to be in community only highlights that unchanging truth. One woman told me, "The church has become, for me, the loneliest place on earth. Church members walk past you as if you are invisible; they seem to talk only to their friends and to be their friend, you must have to pass some kind of litmus test I guess, one I obviously failed."

This law of engagement governs virtually every social setting. The more intimate the setting, the more intensely we feel its significance. That's why there's nothing more wrenching than loneliness within a marriage.

Randy and Becky entered my office in a state of depression. Each felt let down by the other. Their conflicts fed a growing alienation. Randy escaped to his workshop and Becky spent hours watching TV. They misunderstood each other's response as rejection, though in reality they were merely protecting themselves from further pain. Randy moaned, "I just can't compete with that stupid TV—I think she's married to that thing!" Frustrated, she replied, "The only reason I watch so much TV is because you abandoned me to your work ages ago. Do you really think I would just sit on the couch in the dark waiting for you to talk with me?" Ironically, they both longed to restore the friendship they once loved. Eventually they did just that, but not before they suffered many needless wounds.

Our deepest longing is for a *shared* love. You hunger for this kind of affection, but may have found it elusive. Perhaps you think such experience is nothing more than the stuff of movies and novels. I assure you—we've witnessed it as clinicians and experienced it in our private lives. It's achievable, but it takes effort.

In 2 Peter 1:5-7, we're reminded that love, like all other virtues, involves hard work. In this age of instant gratification where the quick fix is the remedy of choice, the necessity of working at relationship seems foreign. We tend to define love by what's in it for us. But relationships are fundamentally about others and ultimately about God. Only when we accept this will we discover what love has to offer.

Our Christian faith enables us to join hands with brothers and sisters in God's family and draw close to a God who views His creation with limitless affection. In the end, it is this reality that answers the need of man made in the image of a social God. Yet one of the greatest enemies to this freeing truth is the scourge of self-rejection. When a depressed person is caught in the grip of low self-esteem, hopelessness takes over and isolation often becomes the goal. An ally (depression) has now been turned into an enemy. So, for the sake of renewing the hope of the divine image, we will now turn our attention to this pivotal struggle.

FINDING HOPE

1. *You are forever God's handiwork and* no amount of emotional damage changes this fact. What starts with His affirmation will end with it.

2. *Your inherited capacity for self-reflective thought* gives you the ability to consider a purpose beyond yourself. It also provides you with the ability to *recognize the importance of intimacy.*

3. *Jesus' free expression of emotion is a model* for admitting freely to your own. Stoicism is not a part of the godly life, but passion is.

4. *You love well when you choose well.* It's your *moral sense* that allows you to appreciate God's view of your choices.

5. Your *spiritual longings* make clear the unmistakable character of natural revelation and confirm your need for a Redeemer who *gives you a purpose for living.*

6. As a social being, you find *fulfillment in relationships* and discover *belongingness in community.* Depression highlights your need of these things.

THE STRUGGLE WITH SELF-ESTEEM: FRIEND OR FOE OF HUMILITY?

> *Self-rejection is the greatest enemy of the spiritual life because it contradicts the sacred voice that calls us the "Beloved." Being the Beloved expresses the core truth of our existence.*
>
> —HENRI J. M. NOUWEN—

Several years ago, Denise[1] walked into my office troubled about the emptiness of her life and her sense of failure as a Christian. Her feelings of worthlessness, inadequacy and helplessness poured out in sobs. "I'm the biggest disappointment to God on the planet" she cried. "I've tried everything I thought a Christian is supposed to do, but I still feel hopeless and depressed. I can barely get out of bed each day. It's pathetic, isn't it?" She buried her face in her hands for a long moment before again looking at me. "All my life, I've been told that Christians are supposed to ignore themselves, that it was wrong to care about your own needs, even if you're in despair." Denise's legalistic understanding of her faith had encouraged her to believe that self-reproach was essential to pleasing God. "I'm worthless; I don't matter," she said softly. "Why don't I just accept that?"

Denise was exhausted from trying to alleviate her suffering. At her point of deepest depression, she sought out her pastor, who had prayed with her and gave her some Bible verses to comfort her. She continued her tailspin, so the church elders laid hands on her and prayed for her recovery.

When her depression deepened, an older woman was assigned to "mentor" her and give her reassurance from God's Word. Meanwhile, some of her friends in her home Bible study group suggested that she might be oppressed by an evil spirit. So they anointed her with oil and prayed for release.

Nothing brought relief. Denise began to believe she was beyond help and that God had abandoned her. She thought that her depression must be due to some hidden sin—sin that, like quicksand, would drag her deeper down if left concealed. So she repented of any sin she could think of, searched the Scriptures and prayed. Still, depression kept its grip. In fact, by now, she was depressed about being depressed because she believed that Christians, at least ones in good standing, were never supposed to suffer through these kinds of dark periods. This belief, of course, made matters even worse.

Finally, a co-worker recommended a therapist. She resisted this suggestion because her pastor opposed psychology as a corruption of God's truth. But, eventually, her searing pain convinced her to give therapy a try. *"Besides,"* she thought, *"he's a Christian therapist—so he can't be entirely a tool of the devil!"*

So there Denise sat, trembling, certain she had failed God and her friends. Because she had no clue to the nature of her problem or how to solve it, she was looking for a miracle that would transform her into the "right kind of Christian,"—happy and content. In her thinking, her depression meant that she was somehow untrusting toward God. What she didn't realize was how much her mistaken beliefs had laid the groundwork for self-rejection.

THE QUESTION OF SELF-ESTEEM

Some people might brand Denise's agonizing search as "spiritually misguided"—if for no other reason than because she had begun to question God's interest in her. God had seemed just like everyone else in her life. *"If He's really unconditionally loving,"* she reasoned, *"shouldn't even a reprehensible soul like me receive a little mercy?"*

She just wanted to feel that she was worth something—that she somehow mattered to others—a desire that she had been told was the work of vanity. The legalism she embraced, which focused on repaying God with good works, which considered self-reproach as a virtue, was seen as part of proper submission to Him. She had been taught that the idea of valuing yourself was part of a worldly, feel-good philosophy that ignored man's sinful nature.

This unbiblical belief system is common among Christians. It's well intentioned, but flawed. It equates self-esteem with conceit and self-worship, the offspring of a narcissistic culture and the opposite of biblical humility. It describes self-esteem as "self-importance," an attitude encouraged by what some have called "seductive atheistic psychology." I've counseled many pastors who believed this way. But in the midst of their own personal crisis, they came to realize just how much such ideas had sabotaged their walk with God. One pastor put it this way, "It took me awhile and not without a lot of pain and anguish, but I finally understand that God actually *wants* us to feel good about who we are. I only wish that I had understood this for all those years I told my congregation that desiring higher self-esteem was a selfish goal that ignored God's greater purpose."

So what does healthy self-esteem mean? Is it, as opponents argue, just a rationalization for a selfish lifestyle? Is it the enemy of humility?

Certainly no one would deny that humility is a hallmark of Christian teaching. But at the heart of the self-esteem controversy is a question:

Can a believer live in true humility without a genuine sense of personal worth?

HUMILITY VS. HISTORY

The question of self-esteem's validity is central to our understanding of depression. Virtually everyone with depression experiences low self-esteem. There is no question that self-preoccupation is one of the most common reasons people have difficulty express-ing biblical humility. This is because *low* self-esteem—not high self-esteem—is the enemy of humility.

How can I say this? Well, to start, the Bible defines humility as giving ourselves to one another in love. It is an *attitude of ser-vice*. A humble person is one who reaches out toward people out of gratitude for what God has already done for him. However, people who have a crumbling sense of worth tend to withdraw from oth-ers. This self-preserving strategy is meant to salvage what is left of their sense of worth by protecting themselves from rejection or other injury. It's a strategy that avoids taking personal responsibil-ity in a relationship by seeking healing—or at least relief—*in iso-lation*. But withdrawal is rarely a useful solution. It doesn't help with feeling better about yourself. But that doesn't stop someone who is hurting, someone who is motivated almost solely by the avoidance of pain, from pursuing it anyway.

As Christ-followers, we seek a lifestyle that is honoring to God. To that end, we want to remove every barrier to effective Christian living. To many people's surprise, depression serves precisely such a purpose because it is, first and foremost, a signal that something must change. Since low self-esteem causes us to walk *away* from others (or at least to emotionally distance ourselves from them), rather than walking humbly, lovingly and unselfishly *toward* others, then the depression it triggers tells us to examine what's wrong and experiment with new behaviors to find a remedy.

Sometimes our suffering is the result of our sin, a sign that we've drifted from God. But more often such suffering is the collat-eral damage of life in a sinful world, which leaves its mark on vir-tually every human relationship. Depression often results when we experience betrayal or abuse, particularly by someone close to us.

So indeed, depression is often related to sin—at times our own, but commonly the sin of others who have wounded us. Nonetheless, it's important to understand that depression itself is not sinful—nor should it be seen as the central problem. Rather, it's a symptom of something else and its purpose is to alert us to take a closer look at the real problem.

Sometimes examining our histories leads us back to our families of origin and uncovers the sin of the people who were entrusted with our safety as children. We can begin to see with adult eyes the warped perspectives we developed in response to our parents' damaging behaviors. We start to recognize how our childhood grid still interprets the behavior of others—inaccurately—as threatening or demeaning, thus sending us into a nosedive. Although childhood experiences and environmental stressors are not the only factors in depression, they are perhaps the most important ones in identifying core issues.

Regardless of its source however, one thing is certain: Depression is a reliable indicator of emotional injury. It's a helpful diagnostic tool. Indeed, it is a gift of a loving God and an important guide toward healing the wounds of our past.

LOVE AND SELF-ESTEEM

When Jesus was asked about the greatest of God's commandments, He offered a profound assessment of the Old Testament Law: "You shall love the Lord your God with all your heart and with all your soul and with all your mind…You shall love your neighbor as yourself. On these two commandments depend the *whole Law* and the Prophets" (Matt. 22:37,39-40, italics mine). In other words, we are obedient to God's commandments whenever we are loving God and loving others. We are to love God with passion (with all your heart), with conviction (with all your soul) and with clarity (with all your mind). And we are to love others in the same committed way we would want to be loved.

Together, these commandments flesh out in real-life terms the law of love—the law that Jesus came to fulfill both in the life He lived and in the death He endured. The Pharisees believed the Law of Moses to be a standard of outward conduct, but Jesus showed them that it was so much more. The Law is the template for imitating God's love. Christians read these commandments but often miss their point. They have difficulty understanding, at least in practical terms, how lovingly God has called us and how He welcomes self-acceptance as part of His plan. The Law was never meant to serve as a rod with which to beat ourselves over the head. Rather, it was meant to acknowledge the righteousness of His love and the power of loving others. It reminds us that we are God's special creation in whom He delights.

Today we love God by giving to Him in service and in worship. Similarly, we love others by giving to them in service and honor. *It may be possible to give without loving, but it's impossible to love without giving.* In fact, giving by means of a servant's attitude is the focus of the humble heart—humility is an attitude of service founded on a sense of personal worth affirmed in Christ and a sense of adequacy empowered by the Holy Spirit.

As Paul wrote to Timothy (see 2 Tim. 1:7), God has not given us the spirit of fear (which characterizes low self-esteem). Instead, he has given us the spirit of love, of power and of a sound mind (which characterizes high self-esteem). The spirit of fear—that underlying anxiety that frequently accompanies depression—is what undermines our self-esteem and cripples ambition. Ultimately, it can cause us to abandon the dreams God intended for us.

This is what happened to a young pastor named John. He came to me, paralyzed by a fear so disabling that he was no longer able to carry out his normal preaching responsibilities. He had always doubted that he had the right gifts, even though his friends and congregation routinely confirmed them. He was convinced that he was a fraud and considered resigning from the pastorate.

John had struggled with low self-esteem all of his life, pressing on only because he didn't want to let people down. Now he felt it was only a matter of time before everyone else recognized him as a failure. He'd grown up with a father who criticized him mercilessly. What's more, he was told daily that he was stupid and would never amount to anything.

Believing that he was worthless, he joined other disaffected young people experimenting with drugs and alcohol resulting in an addiction that almost killed him before age 20. He finally gave up this self-destructive lifestyle when a Christian college professor helped him rediscover his roots in the faith. Turning his energies to serving God, he became a protégé of his pastor who recognized John's people skills and preaching gifts. But underneath it all, the low self-esteem from a rejecting father never let up. When he took his own pastorate, John expected from the start that he would eventually fall apart and disappoint everyone around him.

> **Who we are and who we are destined to become, are determined by the choices we make.**

But in counseling, John learned to challenge these beliefs and discovered that God engineered his life as a pastor because He loved him and had gifted him for it. In time, John was "re-fathered" in a new kind of intimacy, a spiritual one. The voice of the critical parent was replaced with the kinder, gentler voice of his Heavenly Father, building his confidence and joy.

John realized that *he himself had perpetuated his victimization.* He had chosen to allow the echoes of his father's criticism to control his adult life. John thought he was emancipated, but in reality he continued to believe the messages of his father's earlier abuse. This was the message his depression was signaling, but he hadn't been able to see it until then.

CHOOSING INTIMACY

Who we are and who we are destined to become, are determined by the choices we make. These choices can be destructive or they can produce growth. Our choice of friends is important because they either encourage us to pursue selfish ends or they inspire us to give of ourselves to others. But the choice of Jesus Christ as our *best* friend will do far more than that: He will transform us entirely from the inside out. Our heart's deepest longing is intimacy with

God. In Him is a limitless storehouse of delights. "Delight yourself in the LORD," invites the psalmist, "and he will give you the desires of your heart"(Ps. 37:4). A client asked me, "Does that mean we get everything we want?" Knowing she meant even our momentary wishes, I answered her by emphasizing that we were created with a natural appetite for uncorrupted love and that only an inclination toward God can satisfy that hunger. She leaned back in her chair acknowledging her own desire for that kind of love.

Intimacy with God requires a courageous investment. As the psalmist explains, "Commit your way to the Lord, trust also in him and he will [satisfy your desires]"(Ps. 37:5). *Commitment* and *trust* are the essential pillars of any healthy, loving connection. But these twin pillars are quickly dismantled—abandoned as too dangerous—in a history of unhealthy, painful family interactions.

That's why people who've been hurt rarely seek what they want most; intimate connections that mean something. Though they've heard about it, they don't honestly know what intimacy looks like. Just ask their spouses. You will discover how empty they are, how resigned they've become to despair and loneliness.

That's the reason depression is a critically important signpost urging us to interrupt this pattern, to revitalize the life that's dying inside. Depression gives us the opportunity to listen to our heart's longing for relationship—especially a relationship with God.

SELF-ACCEPTANCE AND HUMILITY

From the beginning, our own lovability has been linked to being created in the image of God. To deny our own lovability is to deny this truth. To repudiate our own person is to reject the nature of His. *A God who IS love cannot create anything in His image that is not lovable.* That would be an act against His own character. When we insist on believing ourselves to be unlovable, we have been seduced by a lie. Caught in this trap, we reject even logic because personal experience has convinced us that nothing outside our own subjective reality can be trusted.

Persuasion alone can't change a person's view of himself. A new, more charitable concept of self emerges only from the ability to distinguish who we are from what we do. The value God puts on us as His creation is far more accurate than the value we put on ourselves as a product of our performance. Only when God's view of our worth becomes our own self-view are we able to experience unconditional love. It's this godly self-love that finds its expression in humble acts of selfless giving—giving that is prompted by the joy of God's grace rather than by the expectation of something in return.

One of the reasons some Christian leaders devalue the concept of self-esteem is because they're unable to understand this connection between self-attitude and a servant's heart. They confuse self-esteem with arrogant, presumptuous self-importance apart from God. They cannot accept the paradox of grace. We're valuable by divine estimation and yet we participate in a sin nature from which we will not be fully free until Christ's return. We're in the process of being sanctified, but we still seem to sin with regularity. These two conflicting worlds coexist within each believer. Is it any wonder we've encountered so much confusion over explanations of Christian behavior?

To accept and respect our own person is to submit to the glory of God's creative power. This is no excuse for conceit—life is not merely about us. We should be inspired by our intimacy with God to view ourselves more through His eyes and less through the distorted lenses of our own. Only when the old evaluation has been replaced can our eyes be opened to the wonder of His redemptive work in us. Only then can we understand self-worth as recognition of God's goodness poured out in our person.

That changes everything. "I could never really understand when people talked about feeling God's love," said a client of mine recently. "All I ever really felt was fear—fear that He would come down on me if I made the slightest mistake. When I would blow it I would then cringe, waiting to be struck down with a sickness of some kind or be involved in a car crash or something. But now I see that God isn't like that after all, that He actually wants good things for me. I can't begin to tell you how mind-blowing these ideas are to me!" This is the freedom that comes from knowing who we are in Christ and realizing that if we humble ourselves before Him, He will raise us up in His warm embrace. He will not grumble something to us about our response being long overdue.

> **It's important to remember that self-esteem is unknowable apart from its' most important characteristic: humility.**

It's important to remember that self-esteem is unknowable apart from its most important characteristic: humility. In fact, *self-esteem and humility are so intertwined that the true expression of one cannot occur without the other.*

It's only when these two are separated that attitudes toward self become a problem. Favorable self-evaluation without humility is indeed what many Christians suspect it to be—another expression of arrogance. But the opposite error, a "servant's attitude" without self-acceptance is problematic as well, for it is an unrelenting search for social approval. It's a lifestyle of placating others out of fear of rejection, out of an insatiable hunger for affirmation. It's nearly impossible for such people to believe they're God's *beloved* children. A. W. Tozer insisted that, "God never thinks any bad thoughts about anybody and He never had any bad thoughts about anybody."[2] Tozer was talking about God's thoughts about the person, not his sinful behavior. Nevertheless, these Christians cannot imagine that God doesn't feel negatively about them. They're convinced that, even if God's benevolence is true in principle, they are the exception.

In contrast to this pessimism, those who are humble accept not only God's loving attitude toward us, but also the fact that we are "fearfully and wonderfully made" (Ps. 139:14). Among other things, that means we're endowed with strengths and abilities to be exercised for His glory.

To experience personal worth then, we don't have to advertise ourselves to get others to notice us. Nor must we devalue ourselves to get them to compliment us. Instead, a sense of personal worth means that we accept who we are and honor God's invitation to enjoy the strengths He's given us. It means that we're free to acknowledge our mistakes as the result of human weaknesses and our failures as the result of our sin nature. This humble honesty is not destroyed by self-esteem, but activated by it.

When asked why he ran competitive racing events instead of leaving for the mission field, the lead character in the film *Chariots of Fire,* Olympic runner, Eric Liddell, shared this memorable line, "I feel God's pleasure when I run because God made me to run fast."[3] Now that's divinely-inspired insight into the purpose for God's gifting! Never did Liddell languish in self-reproach for his passion. He understood that God enjoys our triumphs, much as an inventor enjoys the success of what he creates. In time, Liddell went on to other victories laboring and dying on the mission field in China.

The close connection between self-acceptance and humility is at the core of God's desire for us. We find no greater statement of our personal worth than in the sacrifice of God's only Son. *To God, we are worth that ultimate sacrifice.* So when Jesus commanded us to love our neighbor as ourselves, He was assuming that any acceptance and respect toward others had to be undergirded by our divinely-determined self-worth. He taught this almost two thousand years before psychologists recognized the connection between self-attitudes and attitudes toward others and incorporated it into the canon of clinical principles.

Every novice therapist now understands that self-accep-tance—not self-centeredness or self-repudiation—is a necessary precondition to open, natural and non-manipulative relationships with others. It has been widely observed that when we are truly self-accepting, we are liberated from preoccupation with how others see us. As one writer put it, "Instead of thinking less of ourselves, we simply think of ourselves less."[4] This frees us to reach out to our neighbors, not self-consciously, as if to impress them, but humbly, so as to serve them.

FREEDOM IN THE CROSSHAIRS

Our faith in Christ creates a tension between the forces of good and evil. The struggle between the new nature and the old is always a turbulent battle. But we have the assurance that such inner conflict comes with the territory of redemption and is evidence of it. The apostle Paul knew this struggle well. He came to terms with it by resting in the hope of his salvation (see Rom. 7:15-25). He realized that the compulsions of his sinful nature only underscored God's mercy, which is what prompted him to break out in a song of praise rather than send him into a spiral of despair. He was saying that our struggle with sin is a reminder of the magnitude of God's grace.

The purpose of redemption is to reconnect us with the Source of all intimacy. Redemption accomplishes this purpose when we have allowed it to sweep away the debris of our sin and the sins committed against us. In this way, we fine-tune our souls to the same frequency as God's voice.

Genuine free will gives people the unhindered ability to choose evil. That's what makes the choice to love meaningful. That's why we can have among us both a Hitler and a Florence Nightingale. Eliminating freedom would eliminate any possibility of a truly loving relationship, even though it would also remove the risk of terrifying evil.

As long as believers keep on sinning—and they will—there will always be corruption in the Church. Church splits, religious wars and the presence of hypocrisy have done untold damage to the cause of Christ. We've all heard non-Christians argue that religion in general (and Christianity in particular) is responsible for more wars and unnecessary deaths than any other single cause in history. This over-generalization paints a false picture of faithful believers. It also ignores a central belief of Christianity, that redemption from sin is an invitation to peace, not a free ticket to sin even more. The apostle Paul said it best, "What shall we say then? Shall we go on sinning so that grace may increase? By no means!"(Rom. 6:1-2, NIV). So, we can never excuse our sin against others as somehow serving a higher purpose.

Nonetheless, our freedom can seem like a dark force tinkering with the dials of our souls. Sometimes, as wounded believers, we initiate one conflict after another to distract us from the emotional emptiness inside. At other times, we may simply drown ourselves in a sea of self-pity. But we can't silence the lie of worthlessness within, nor can we solve the riddle of an unwelcome world outside.

To cope, many of us cloak ourselves in a superficial piety, unhesitant to judge others for their sin. Having become brethren of intolerance, we destroy freedom and creativity, joy and productivity. Even when we become a cause for outside criticism of the Church, we dismiss it as evidence of the world's spiritual ignorance. We need to rein in this judgmental attitude, recognizing its harm to our witness as well as its damage to our own spiritual lives. *We cannot dishonor others without also dishonoring ourselves.*

Yes, like everyone else, we sin daily. But that's not a reason for self-rejection. If behavior alone determined our destiny, divine justice could never be averted. We would get what we deserved. But God's infinite grace has always seen beyond the outward behavior to the person—His handcrafted creation. We don't stop loving our children because they misbehave—neither does God stop loving us because we sin. His compassion is greater and so is our value to Him.

SELF-DENIAL VS. DENIAL OF SELF

During our early years, we come to believe self-messages from our friends and family. In adulthood, these messages speak so loudly that we have difficulty hearing, let alone accepting, the new messages of faith. This is true in cases of childhood abuse or neglect. As children, we can't tell the difference between truth and lies, dysfunction and health. But even in adulthood, when capacities for discernment are in place, we rarely revisit our distorted belief systems. Consequently, our old falsehoods continue to damage our self-esteem. That's why the call of our faith is in part to do the healing, world view-changing work of reevaluating our assumptions.

Replacing our self-messages isn't easy, but it can be done. We must learn how these early messages had little to do with us, and much to do with the dysfunction of our families. We must try to understand too, how these old rules of engagement now sabotage our current relationships so we can experiment with new ways of engaging others. We'll definitely go outside our comfort zone for a while; but how else can divine grace do its healing work in our wounded souls?

My client Denise was one of these wounded souls, raised in a rigid, perfectionistic home under an autocratic, emotionally-cold father. Her dad's unrealistic expectations left her with the enduring belief that she failed all the time and deserved little. With this belief, she ended up in the same kind of relationship in her marriage. She never understood grace, nor did she question her role as a whipping post for those who were important in her life. Frequently during the course of therapy, Denise returned the conversation to matters of faith. "I'm so afraid I'm going to be guilty of heresy if I start thinking that feeling better about myself is what God wants." She couldn't begin to fathom God's assessment of her worth to Him or believe that He was interested in her. The best she could hope for is that she could slide quietly under heaven's door—maybe no one would notice she wasn't supposed to be there.

Like Denise, many people suffer under legalism, striving for acceptability by substituting imagined merit for God's standing offer of divine grace. The result is reliably the same—an enduring sense of insecurity before God.

Denise insisted on equating self-rejection with humility. She quoted Jesus, "If anyone wishes to come after Me, he must deny himself and take up his cross and follow Me" (Matt. 16:24). However, Jesus wasn't saying to deny our identity or our worth and dignity before God, but to deny selfish desire and self-centeredness. He pictured the Pharisees' displays of righteous posturing, motivated by self-promotion in the eyes of men.

There is a crucial difference between *denial of self*—the humility Jesus taught—and *self-denial*—an emotional and physical deprivation of the kind promoted in Eastern religions. It's the difference between divine grace and man's works. Denial of self, by grace, defeats selfish desire—but self-denial is little more than a ritualized system of deprivation, including the rejection of various personal comforts in the pursuit of some kind of mystical spirituality. The importance of works has been the bedrock of Eastern philosophy for more than 3,000 years. In fact, in many Buddhist and Hindu sects you don't even need a concept of God to reach spiritual freedom—man is capable of attaining spiritual perfection entirely on his own. What a contrast to the kind of humility to which Jesus invites us!

Of course, Denise had no idea of this distinction between grace in the denial of self and works in the practice of self-denial. Instead, her self-hatred had blocked her understanding of God's grace toward her. She replaced the freedom of the Christian ideal with the deprivation of the abstinence ideal. She attributed her pain to God's silence rather than to her misguided thinking about herself and her faith. Ignoring the warning signal of her depression, she ran aground on the shoals of self-inflicted rejection. That's the tragedy of a faith so distorted by legalism that it no longer serves the emotional needs of the wounded believer.

We need to dispel the notion that self-rejection is the price of discipleship. The true challenge of faith is to regard the suffering in our personal histories as *human* grace denied, not as divine judgment delivered. If the truth really sets us free, then we don't have to repeat these painful histories as adults. We're invited by *divine* grace to leave behind the baggage of our past to release resentments, fears and self-hatred and to discover for the first time what freedom in Christ truly means—a satisfying life of unobstructed love. God provides the power, but it's up to us to make different choices with what we're given in life.

It takes courage to accept God's offer. We can gain strength from the display of Jesus' mercy when He intervened with the woman caught in adultery (see John 8:1-11). The Pharisees insisted that she deserved stoning according to the Law. But Jesus challenged her accusers, inviting anyone who had not sinned to step forward and cast the first stone. The crowd quietly, reluctantly dispersed. Jesus then turned to the woman and declared, "I do not condemn you, either. Go. From now on sin no more."

Jesus is speaking those words to each of us who are caught in the web of our own delusions. He's telling us, in effect, that others *can't* condemn us because they're sinners, too. And He *won't* condemn us. He then bids us to live our lives differently. What an incredible promise—freedom from condemnation and consequently, freedom from the life of perpetual victimization. In short, the prospect of a new life unburdened by an endless cycle of the same sin and by constant ruminations about the past!

I often give my clients the analogy of a cross-country runner running while looking backward. What would happen? He would crash into signposts and trees, trip over curbs and potholes, doing himself untold damage because he wasn't looking forward. That's what we do to ourselves emotionally when we review our past without looking ahead to deal with the present and change the future. We doom ourselves to a world of self-condemning rumination and endless self-pity, a world bereft of any option to do something differently to bring about a better tomorrow.

This doesn't mean that we take a Pollyanna approach to life. Neither does it mean we're supposed to ignore our pain and redefine evil. It means that we inspire one another to the kind of change that recognizes and rejects evil altogether. How can we deny ourselves and others what God has so freely given to us all? Nonetheless, if we try, depression will be there telling us that self-rejection is a delusion, one that sentences us to the same emotional imprisonment Jesus saw in the adulteress.

Faith in God was never intended to be religious ritual; it was meant to embrace all that we are and all that we do. That includes our choices in life. And we do have a choice: Either we rally our resources to alter our course and restructure how we live or we submit to the lure of resignation and give up. Our decisions can make our faith powerfully relevant or ineffectually irrelevant. It all depends on what kind of life we choose to pursue and what kind of faith we choose to embrace.

FINDING HOPE

1. Depression is neither sinful nor the central problem. Instead it is a *signal, often pointing to a long-standing issue that is solvable if given appropriate attention.*

2. Putting the emphasis on *loving others is the engine of self-esteem and the antidote to personal fear.*

3. *Personal growth* is the direct result of our *choices and healthy choices* are the direct result of exercising *humility.*

4. To fully experience your worth, recognize God's invitation *to take pleasure in the strengths He has given you.*

5. Self-denial leads to emotional imprisonment, but *denial of self leads to emotional and spiritual freedom.*

6. *Our past does not condemn us, because our future is determined by God's grace* through the presence of our faith.

THE LEGACY OF SELF-REJECTION

The courage to be is rooted in the God who appears when God has disappeared in the anxiety of doubt.

—PAUL TILLICH—

Your body is subject to attack by countless viruses, bacteria and toxins. That's why your physical immune system needs to be strengthened by good nutrition, rest and exercise in order to fight off these invaders. Likewise, your spirit needs to be strengthened to resist dangers like hopelessness and self-victimization. This means you need to be adequately prepared for injustice, misfortune and that common pitfall for believers, the perception of unanswered prayer.

Nothing energizes a person for these tests of courage like love does—especially the presence of God's selfless, unfailing love. Love is central to all healing. It enables us to examine our insides and accept what we see. That's why the most powerful vehicle of restoration has always been the warmth and safety of a caring relationship. Once we are secure in a place of

> **It's important that we understand that our very being is a *joy* to God.**

acceptance—most secure of all in God's acceptance—we find the strength to keep going and not give up when life's troubles strike.

It's important that we understand our very being is a *joy* to God. And when there is a consensus of wills—His and ours—it becomes the cause for mutual pleasure. As A. W. Tozer once observed, "God is pleased by his handiwork: God did what he did joyfully. Enthusiasm is seen in his creation."[1] We are part of that handiwork (see Eph. 2:10), which is why our creation so perfectly fulfilled His joy.

We often hear talk that receiving love is therapeutic and, indeed, that is true. But we also heal and grow when we give love to others. Just as our Lord unconditionally loved us despite our rejection of Him, so we find emotional freedom in passing that love on to others.

Michael Reagan, son of former president, Ronald Reagan, revealed in a moving interview the power of this avenue of healing. As a Christian, he became convinced that his bitterness concerning his father's failure over the years to tell him that he loved him was preventing his full recovery from a sad and turbulent childhood. So, as a middle-aged man, he decided to tell his father that *he* loved him. It didn't matter whether his father reciprocated. Michael just knew that he needed to do it for his own healing. To his great surprise, his father returned his affection. And they continued to exchange hugs and expressions of love up to the end of his father's life. He even recounted, "One time I had forgotten to hug my father before I started to leave. I quickly turned around to go back and, when I did, I looked up and saw my dad standing on the porch with his arms outstretched, waiting for my hug!" Michael's—and his father's—emotional healing came in the giving. It released the hidden, positive feelings that became the source of their reconciliation.

Our self-preoccupation can be difficult to abandon, especially when it is compelled by the powerful force of self-rejection. That's when we know that in those hidden places of the heart, we've lost contact with our soul's identity. This secret betrayal of the self is revealed in our toxic treatment of others by the way we lash out in reaction to our enduring sense of alienation.

Though we are usually unaware of it, the what's-in-it-for-me mind set is destructive to everyone, including ourselves. Only when we come to realize this are we in a position to do something about it and find the freedom we've been looking for. But first, we must admit to our limits and then look for ways to act beyond our own self-interest. When we do, we will find a deep satisfaction in reaching out to others who are struggling and doing so with a love that focuses on *their* needs, not merely our own.

When we learn to give of ourselves, we discover the practical meaning of our faith as it was meant in Jesus' command to love one another. We come to understand, too, our Lord's promise of peace—a peace that settles our unrest inside and dissolves our heart-hardening bitterness.

Liberating ourselves from the domination of self-interest and responding humbly toward others leads us to discover a life of meaningful impact for God; something we say we want. The apostle Paul said, "Do nothing from selfishness or empty conceit, but with humility of mind regarding one another as more important than yourselves—do not merely look out for your own personal interests, but also for the interests of others" (Phil. 2:3-4).

He wasn't telling us to consider ourselves unimportant. To the contrary, self-acceptance is necessary for selfless service to others. Neither was he saying to ignore our own personal interests—he was simply saying that we should regard others' interests as worthy of our attention as well. You see, recognizing our own value in God's eyes enables us also to recognize the value God puts on others. Our security in His acceptance frees us to get outside of ourselves long enough to understand another's pain. And, to our surprise, when we reach out with compassion like that, we discover that some of our own emotional needs are met in the process. It is a marvelous thing that our Creator has designed us in such a way that we receive the greatest satisfaction when we look beyond self-interest.

While we know that selfless loving and giving are central to a meaningful life, it's still difficult for many of us to grasp. Instead, we seem almost compelled to raise any number of barriers against experiencing God's grace. That's why we also know that our self-rejection—which is the principal enemy of love—is pitiless in its efforts to sustain itself!

THE SEARCH FOR INTELLIGENT LOVE

One way our self-rejection keeps us cut off from love is by refusing to believe that it's real, by dismissing the idea that there is a God who loves like that. Or, if He exists, that His grace could possibly be granted to those who are as unworthy as we are.

Since the dawn of Israel's history, God has repeatedly demonstrated that He does not qualify the exercise of His compassion and mercy. He repeatedly forgave Israel's persistent idolatry. He displayed grace toward a people who only turned to Him in times of crisis (c.f., the book of Judges). To be honest, His grace is counter intuitive. His actions defy human analysis mainly because they do not follow any of our models of predictability. History is filled with His surprises.

Most of us live by the principle that you don't get something for nothing. Yet grace is precisely that—receiving something we don't deserve. Author, Paul Tournier, once observed, "The notion that everything has to be paid for is deep-seated…So the people who long most for grace have the greatest difficulty in accepting it."[2] In our experience, grudges more often take precedence over forgiveness. Pure grace is foreign to our relational vocabulary. So too, is the kind of love that sets no conditions and understands no limits.

There are those who think that a God who provides grace that easily and loves that completely must be the figment of someone's imagination or the product of an irrational mind. But look for yourself. He's right there in the biblical record—the convicted adulteress Jesus refused to condemn (see John 8:1-11), the promiscuous Samaritan woman at the well who was offered living water for her thirsty soul (see John 4:5-26), a hypocritical Pharisee given an opportunity to explore his disbelief (see John 3:1-21), a thief granted mercy in his final hour (see Luke 23:39-43). They all defy the logic of human justice. But sooner or later we have to come to terms with the reality of God's unparalleled benevolence.

In human experience, authority and power are usually wielded for personal advantage. But when we encounter God, the ultimate authority with absolute power, we find it exercised toward merciful ends with great empathy toward others. Such an encounter is likely to so shift our thinking that spiritual change becomes inevitable.

This God offers us a place of true belonging in a family. He's a Father who seeks companionship with His children, providing nurturance and protection in every situation. With confidence, we even anticipate Judgment Day as a family matter: For the Judge is our adopted Father and our defense attorney, Jesus Christ, is His Son (see 1 John 2:1-2). That's one time nepotism really works! In spotless purity, we will enter heaven as those who are welcomed home amid great celebration.

So when we stand naked in the cold winter of our distrust, we who belong to Him must remember that we're never alone. We're never without His interest and commitment. When self-doubt and loneliness sweep over us, God is still there. Like the father's tender response to his prodigal son, God never tires of retrieving His children from their own misguided thinking. Nor does He stop confronting the misconceptions they bring with them from their dysfunctional families.

The New Testament beckons us to this new, healing family with love coursing through its members—brothers and sisters born from the same spiritual womb, drawing life from the same source of God's grace. In the very place where we have been hurt so much in the past, God provides the meaningful connections for which we have so long yearned.

Because Jesus endured extraordinary loneliness and rejection on the cross, we are offered this new life. He suffered that agony during history's darkest moment, that epic moment at Calvary in which He bore our sin. We were lost, with no chance of finding our way back on our own. But He experienced abandonment so that we might experience inclusion in His Father's love. He chose death that we might choose life. By His sacrifice, Jesus told you that you matter.

This message is your invitation to freedom. In the final analysis, it's the answer to the emotional baggage that has weighed you down and interfered with every meaningful relationship you've ever had. True personal change may not come in a day, a month or even in a year. But it will come if you accept the invitation and work through the secrets and conflicts that have held you back. Abraham Lincoln, in the darkest days of his presidency, once observed that the most optimistic characteristic of the future is that it comes one day at a time. That's about the pace you can expect it will take to trade your old self-rejection for the growing experience of God's love.

The only other option is the secret life of compromise, the closet pursuit of careless indulgence. It can take many forms, but they all lead to a pattern of anxious compulsion and clinical depression. Whether the counterfeit emotional savior we seek is pornography, food, escapist fantasy or alcohol, the cycle of momentary comfort followed by still deeper emptiness corrupts every attempt we make to find the true meaning of pleasure. Subtly it corrupts our ideals, our virtue and our honesty. Yet we become blind to the price that indulgence demands of us and of others around us. Above all, it weakens our ambition for good, our desire for godly pleasure. C.S. Lewis recognized the trap we set for ourselves:

> *"We are told to deny ourselves and to take up our crosses in order that we may follow Christ; and nearly every description of what we shall ultimately find if we do so contains an appeal to desire. If there lurks in most modern minds the notion that to desire our own good and earnestly to hope for the enjoyment of it is a bad thing, I submit that this notion has crept in from Kant and the*

stoics and is not part of the Christian faith. Indeed, if we consider the unblushing promises of reward and the staggering nature of the rewards promised in the Gospels it would seem that Our Lord finds our desires not too strong, but too weak. We are half-hearted creatures, fooling about with drink and sex and ambition when infinite joy is offered us, like an ignorant child who wants to go on making mud pies in a slum because he cannot imagine what is meant by the offer of a holiday at the sea. We are far too easily pleased."[3]

When we separate healthy desire from its spiritual meaning, we neutralize the power of virtue in our life. We settle for so little because we see unselfishness as deprivation. We see intimacy as a threat to our dishonesty. We run from the standard of God's law, where we would find the freedom to love. As the psalmist declares, "I shall run the way of Your commandments, For You will *enlarge my heart*...So I will keep Your law continually, forever and ever. And I will walk at *liberty,* For I seek Your precepts"(Ps. 119:32, 44-45, italics mine).

When God's pleasure and our pleasure are one, where His desires and ours are indistinguishable, there will, at last, be complete fulfillment.

THE DEPENDENCY TRAP

Another situation in which self-rejection trumps love is when we seek validation in the wrong place—in an excessive dependency on other people. This is a common pattern for chronically depressed people. Many are terrified of being alone and will do almost anything to keep others aware of their pain and feeling obligated to meet their needs, sometimes even by threatening suicide. One of the family members of a client I saw did this. Every time people mentioned to him that they thought he was doing better and indicated that their concerns about him had eased, he would do something dramatic like making suicidal gestures, often landing him in the hospital.

Just as the north and south poles of two magnets are drawn to each other, depressed people most often develop a mutual attraction with others who have strong rescuer tendencies. Rescuers seem driven to help depressed people find happier lives—an effort that fails, leaving their emotional resources exhausted. The obvious futility of the effort persuades them to give up the struggle. But these self-appointed saviors want to feel needed and dread letting others down so they remain trapped in relationships they no longer seek to change. When rescuers attempt to create some distance for their own sanity, the dependent person first panics and then feels victimized all over again. He cries foul and accuses the well-intentioned helper of apathy and hypocrisy. Everyone loses— no one wins.

Physicians (already seen as "saviors" to some of their patients) are often the first professionals to encounter those who are depressed. This is because of the patient's demand for attention to their "disease," not because of any conscious awareness of depression. With the repeated refrain, "There's nothing wrong with you" still ringing in their ears after visits to numerous "incompetent" doctors, such patients may seek alternative medicine or anything that will provide them the sympathy they're looking for. But in the end, they only forestall the diagnosis of their depression and the day they come to actually realize the self-sabotaging nature of their behavior.

BEYOND COMPARE

You may have begun to notice a pattern by now. Each love-rejecting strategy underlying our struggle for emotional survival in some way allows us to deny the real problems triggering the distress signal of depression. But if we keep the problems from our awareness, we will fail to make the life changes that would solve them. True, we may find momentary relief from the anxiety those problems arouse; but in the long run, we end up suffering far more and far longer. That's the paradox: Our strategies not only tend to be more protective than constructive in nature, they also are more likely to make things worse overall. Living in the grip of fear is indeed a sad thing.

We see this self-defeating characteristic in the mental habit of making unfavorable comparisons. When we compare ourselves with others—our performance, our appearance or any other quality—we're trying to confirm the inferior self-assessment we already believe. It's not difficult to find someone who appears superior in some way—ignoring, of course, our own areas of special strength and skill. This justifies our illusion of inadequacy and removes us from responsibility to change (a perceived "impossibility" anyway) and we withdraw. As we sink into deeper despair, we are more certain than ever that we're worthless and deserving of rejection. We tell ourselves that we always do the wrong thing at the wrong time. We're boring and stupid. We're certain to fail. The only point to our life is mere existence—our only purpose in relationships is to be a bother to others.

Though Brad was, by all accounts, a successful engineer, he would emerge from regional business meetings with other engineers in a state of depression. He claimed that he met so many engineers who were better than he. "When I go to those meetings, it's discouraging to see how much more effectively the other engineers solve the problems presented in the workshops. I may have the bosses fooled in my own company, but I'm telling you I'm nowhere near the best. After these meetings, I feel like such a fraud. Sometimes, I feel I should save my company the money and resign. But then I wouldn't have a job." He just couldn't get past his own inferiority feelings to appreciate the strengths he brought to the table.

The comparison game is, of course, rigged from the start, designed to guarantee our isolation, maintain our perception of incompetence and perpetuate our conviction that no one is coming to relieve us. It's an irrational mind game driven by self-fulfilling prophecies. It's an irrational stance because it overlooks every basic reality check. For instance, each of us has strengths in some areas in which others are weak. But these are usually dismissed as irrelevant. Yet if our one-sided self-evaluation is seen in the light of reality, we discover that the unique talents and positive traits God has given us are complemented, not devalued, by the talents and traits of others.

Once again, this reveals that the yardstick of our worth and adequacy is found not in our performance or any quality inherent in us, but in the absolute, unchanging character and opinion of God. The true basis for all self-evaluation has been established by a sacrificial love that is impartially offered to everyone. To God, we are on a level playing field. In spite of our sin nature—our common starting point—God has created us as objects of His affection with *infinite value.*

> **In spite of our sin nature... God has created us as objects of His affection with *infinite value.***

Just as God never intended that we use our strengths to lord it over everyone else, neither did he intend that we use our weaknesses as a battering ram against ourselves. God has gifted us individually because we belong to Him and each of us serves a unique purpose. Between one person and the next, there's no comparison.

CONFRONTING THE FAIRNESS QUESTION

Perhaps the most debilitating way that our self-rejection pushes away love is the tactic of playing victim to an unjust world. Of all our self-defeating strategies that sustain our self-hatred, this is one of the hardest to recognize for what it is, *because the world is indeed unfair.*

Referring to the inevitable fate of death, the writer of Ecclesiastes intones, "There is one fate for the righteous and for the wicked... As the good man is, so is the sinner...This is an evil in all that is done under the sun, that there is one fate for all men" (Eccles. 9:2-3). The writer was arguing that, if justice were served, the righteous would live long and prosper and the wicked would suffer and die. That of course, is not how it happens. In fact, the beginnings can be just as unfair as the ends. Some people start life in destructive homes and others don't—and some start in poverty while others in wealth. What's more, misfortune strikes believers and unbelievers alike. The list of inequities seems endless. Is it unreasonable then to ask where God is in all of this?

Injustice is a part of life, a fact that makes faith difficult at times. King David, for instance, struggled to live with oppressive circumstances, especially when God seemed to be silent, "My God, my God, why have You forsaken me? Far from my deliverance are the words of my groaning. O my God, I cry by day, but You do not answer. And by night, but I have no rest" (Ps. 22:1-2).

As Christians, we grapple with the incompatibility of two worlds—one sin-poisoned, the other righteous. Our confusion is understandable. Experience leads some to conclude that God is either too disinterested or too distracted to help or that they are not important enough to be on His radar at all. But to deny our faith is to deny all meaning in life, robbing ourselves of every motivation to think great thoughts and accomplish great things. We reduce our purpose to mere momentary gratification and consider our desperation for happiness as the only goal. Any larger purpose seems like empty fantasy, so we abandon our dreams as immaterial and "God's call" as mistaken.

But we didn't join the human race to sit it out. So how do we find the inspiration to run for the prize of his high calling (see Phil. 3:14)? The answer is found in realizing that earthly life is *meant to be* a challenge, to stimulate the best that we can give. Only if we take God at His word and accept the summons to experiment with change can we avoid the numbing resignation of fatalism.

C. S. Lewis points out that if we seek happiness before we seek our Creator, we will in the end, be denied both. He recognized how easy it is to confuse our priorities. In his words, "The best thing about happiness itself is that it liberates you from thinking about happiness."[4] Happiness is an effect, not a cause, dependent on the situation and limited in duration. When we seek the answer to meaning in the fleeting state of happiness, our path leads only to emptiness, depression and hatred of life itself.

In contrast, Jesus taught that meaning is found not in tenuous earthly pursuits but in seeking first the enduring kingdom of God (see Matt. 6:33). What He meant was nothing less than the quest to know God's heart. This is the goal for which our seeking ensures the certainty of its fulfillment. Happiness, on the other hand, is better understood to be the *result* of a life well lived, rather than the *reason* for living. And so it is that, as C. S. Lewis concluded, the quality of our relationship to God only enlarges the quality of our earthly happiness.

So what do faithful believers do with the inequities of life? Do we just chalk them up to living in a fallen world? That's not very comforting in the midst of our pain. We need to believe our suffering has a greater purpose. That's why the growth we often see coming out of our hardships is so important. We need to understand God's promise that He "causes all things to work together for good to those who love God" (Rom. 8:28) as meaning that the eventual outcome will be beneficial in some way, even if not always comfortable. Sometimes it may be quite unexpected.

Several years ago, I was involved in a serious bicycle accident in which I broke my hip and my wrist, requiring surgery and extensive physical therapy. Initially, I asked God why. But soon I began asking God to use the experience to teach me more about Him or about myself. He did both. Those months of recovery were among the richest of my spiritual life. I grew to know God far better. But there was more. The severity of my injuries prompted tests that revealed a silent hormonal condition that was slowly weakening my bones. Thankfully, the condition was treatable, but it would have remained hidden if not for the accident. True to His promise,

God used this painful, confining experience for my physical and spiritual good.

Our response to injustice depends on our concept of God. If we believe that God desires our good, then we know that He can use even traumatizing events to further His purpose in us. Singer, Michael Card, affirms in his concerts that his painful childhood with a severely depressed father taught him to better empathize with other people's pain and, by contrast, to be a healthy father for his own children. He said, "I have a picture of me when I was a small child leaning down trying to speak to my father through the crack under the closed door of the den where he spent almost every waking hour when he was home. In large part, that was the extent of my relationship with my father." But he chose to use that experience to define the difference in his own fathering.

Faith helps us put aside the contradiction of justice in a fallen world and shows us that the continuance of our sinful existence is unfair. If the impartiality of divine justice were to prevail, no one would survive. The corrupt world would be destroyed. We have the Old Testament account of the flood as evidence of that (see Gen. 6–8). But God, in His mercy and forbearance, has forestalled the final day: "The Lord is not slow in keeping his promise, as some understand slowness. He is patient with you, not wanting anyone to perish, but everyone to come to repentance" (2 Pet. 3:9, NIV).

God has never stopped loving His creation. That's why His mercy calls us to endure the suffering of this world while He stays His hand of justice, so that more people can respond to His grace and enter into the kingdom of heaven. So suffering does have meaning after all. But the Day of Judgment will most surely come—and when it does, it will end once and for all man's opportunity to accept redemption.

Until Christ's return, we can rest in the promise that God will one day answer our cry for justice. Meanwhile, we find peace not in the fairness of earthly life but in our relationship with a patient, purposeful God. Sometimes though, after painful events in our life, we doubt that we'll ever be safe again or that life will ever return to normal. Indeed, life will never return to what *was* normal, but rather to a different, more adaptive life from the growth and wisdom that can only come through hardship.

Contrary to our fears, putting the pieces of our life back together can be a creative and stimulating learning experience. Poet Lindsay Johnson likened this process to mending broken plates, "What you get is not an old mended plate trying to look the same as it was, but a whole new thing you never saw before...when things come apart, it's your chance to rearrange the pieces."[5]

Mending our lives gives us the chance to begin something entirely new, something beautiful—the chance to craft a new mosaic of attitudes and behaviors—to more fully understand God and His will. To start trusting intimacy again. To discover ourselves and the true fulfillment of our natural desires in God and His love.

THE SPIRITUAL BUSINESS OF LOVING

Depression often signals, as we have said, a tenacious self-hatred. When much of our past experience of so-called "love" is associated in our thinking with betrayal, abandonment, abuse and a host of other wounds, there's not a lot to encourage a more charitable view. Self-rejection becomes both a conclusion from experience and a shield against any further injury from the expected attacks of others.

The good news is that our healing starts at the spiritual level, for the foundation of all healing love is God's unique, unconditional love that is independent of anyone's response and, therefore complete in itself. Though our love may be limited and variable, His is unlimited and constant. That's why any stable intimacy—and the healing that it nurtures—can always be traced back to a spiritual beginning, whether those involved are Christians or not. And in some way or another, every broken relationship is related to a lack of spiritual understanding.

In the beginning, God fellowshipped with Adam and Eve. And after time has ended, God will once again dwell among His people, enjoying eternal fellowship with them. It's no accident that we are reconciled to our heavenly Father by a *personal relationship* with His Son, not merely by obedience to a commandment. Relational intimacy is a central spiritual reality in life, now and for eternity. It's not hard to see then why people who struggle to be close to anyone most likely do so with an impaired spiritual world view.

To find ourselves, we must not look inward, but outward to people who need our love. We must look outward to be accepted and to accept others, to receive service and to serve God and one another. Opening ourselves up to this kind of experience allows us to see an optimistic, three-dimensional reality, one that reveals meaning below the surface of life's painful events. Indeed, we discover the triumph of redemption over sin, of life over death, and with that discovery we become confident that everything will be determined by God's goodness.

As King David concluded, "Surely goodness and love will follow me all the days of my life" (Ps. 23:6, NIV). This cheerful expression of trust came from a man who knew long years of loneliness, rejection and failure, who lost three sons to violence. Perhaps we, too, can trust our Shepherd to lead us through those dark valleys of turmoil to the still waters of His peace.

Depression's alarm signal sometimes awakens us from a deceptive world view based on false assumptions about the true nature of love. Several years ago, I saw a client who had been adopted at birth. From her teen years onward, she developed a deep, resentful depression because of her "abandonment" by her biological mother. She only later discovered that her mother, when she was an unwed teenager, had agonized over the decision to give her up, choosing to protect her from a life of poverty. It was one of the few selfless things her mother had done during that period of her life. When my client learned that she had not, after all, been considered as "unacceptable baggage," she began to see the love of both her biological and adoptive mothers and was empowered to live a healthier life, one they had both wanted for her. She said, "I'll never forget the excitement in my mother's eyes when she saw me for the first time since I was a baby. I thought to myself, 'She *does want to see me!'* Then when she spoke about the pain of having to give me up for adoption, I saw the deep sadness flood into her eyes. I felt for the first time that she loved me all those years, even though she had no idea where I lived. It's been such a cleansing experience for both of us." She shifted perspective and was able to enjoy the experience of the love that had been there all along.

When God appears to be silent or even cruel, we feel betrayed and may question His love. But when we come to know God intimately, we see things differently. We come to understand the experiences of pain that blindside us in the larger context of God's grief over sin. While the signal of depression alerts us to a landscape of failed intentions and broken promises, God is there, quietly providing us with new opportunities to heal.

God has made us, as believers, privy to secrets that only an intimate friend would know (see Ps. 25:14). With this confidence, perhaps now we can take the risk to open ourselves to His restorative love.

FINDING HOPE

1. When you give of yourself, not only do you *discover the practical meaning of your faith,* but also the *purpose of life* itself. It's how we're designed.

2. Where many of you have been hurt in the past, God has provided a *new healing family.* To God, *you matter most.*

3. If you are prone to the comparison game, *identify the strengths you have that the other person doesn't and then thank God for giving both of you strengths* that each can enjoy.

4. Consider the difficulties you are experiencing in life as *a path to new understanding.* Ask God to *teach you something about yourself or about Him* through this experience.

5. The presence of suffering in the world confirms that God has stayed His hand of justice to *give man more time to respond to His grace and enter the kingdom of heaven.* In this way, *your suffering points to God's mercy.*

6. The ultimate criterion for measuring life experience is *God's goodness.*

A PRIMER FOR REALITY DISTORTION

As strange as it may seem, hope has its roots in despair...Indeed, if reality did not give us grounds for despair, it would never give us reason for hope.

—ROBERT VENINGA—

Jennifer and Steve were high-school sweethearts, but after nearly 20 relatively good years of marriage, their relationship was deteriorating. Jennifer became irritable and fatigued. Steve started working longer hours to avoid facing his wife's unpredictable moods. In their initial counseling session, both were depressed— he quiet and withdrawn, she puzzled and frightened by her chaotic emotional state. The couple felt the loss of the fulfillment they'd once found with each other, as well as the mounting frustration with the lack of change. Steve was confused. "I don't know what happened to the woman I married...is it something I've done? I can't for the life of me figure out what's making her upset all of the time. All I know is I don't want to be around anymore...but then again, I do. I just don't know." Jennifer was equally adrift. "I don't know why I'm crying or why I'm mad so much, but Steve has made it a lot worse. He has no patience at all with me—he just walks away with a disgusted look and finds something else to do...I'm so lonely!"

With a physician's help, we soon discovered that Jennifer suffered from severe hypoglycemia—a disorder of the body's ability to regulate blood sugar that in turn, can affect emotional stability. Once she gained control of this disorder through dietary changes, we were able to identify additional factors that added to her depression.

For his own part, Steve began to see a pattern from his childhood. During his early years, he had learned to stay out of his depressed mother's way to "reduce her stress." That's why he withdrew from Jennifer. She, in response, felt abandoned and became critical of him. As a result, Steve felt inadequate as a husband.

Realizing what he was doing, Steve began to reengage Jennifer, erasing the isolation she felt. Both of them prepared for future challenges by developing better coping skills so that the struggles of one did not have to destabilize the other. They learned that emotional pain and confusion could bring them together in the spirit of resolution rather than drive them apart and create anxiety about their future.

We see in this couple some of the many factors at work that contribute to the experience of depression. This dynamic interaction is commonplace whenever we work with troubled relationships marked by depression. It can be a dissonant symphony of conditions within each person as well as their reactions to each other. Fortunately, these responses often follow identifiable patterns.

The interplay of family of origin problems and physical conditions with the crossfire of marital conflict is but one of many patterns that can give rise to depression. With the increasing number of broken or dysfunctional families, it's not surprising that as much as 12 to 13 percent of the U. S.

> **...depression has sometimes been called the 'common cold' of emotional struggles.**

population is, at any given time, experiencing a depressive episode of one sort or another. According to World Health Organization statistics, depression has become the fourth-leading category of disabling disorders worldwide (preceded only by heart disease, cancer and auto accidents). They predict that by 2020, depression will become the second-leading cause of disabling disorders. Depression is increasing in frequency in every age group as well as every demographic group.[1] Little wonder then, that depression has sometimes been called the "common cold" of emotional struggles.[2]

In spite of the complex array of variables that may underlie depression, we are able to identify and confront several basic thinking habits that increase its likelihood. Let's look at three of the most common: *perfectionism, self-deception and fear of rejection.*

EXPECTING PERFECTION IN AN IMPERFECT WORLD

The first and perhaps the most recognizable habit of the mind that sets the stage for depression is the one most familiar to the legalistic believer—*perfectionism*. We've seen this problem as a response to a repressive home where productivity was substituted for feelings. We see this pattern any time someone insists on the faultless outcome—on a life free of any significant setbacks or failures. Such people set their standards of performance unrealistically high and then attack themselves for failing to meet impossible criteria, guaranteeing a sense of inadequacy. They're always anxious about life, even though by any objective measure they're doing well. In spite of their success, they can't shake the conviction that they're bound to fail.

Unremitting perfectionism soon leads to unrelenting depression. Preoccupation with perceived incompetence or fear of ruin crowds out any thought of hope. You'd think the misery this causes would be warning enough to cause a person to reexamine and revise his or her distorted thinking habits. But people often remain stuck, unable to forgive their own mistakes and skeptical of their ability to correct them. The certainty of some failure in every life—the unavoidable reality of life as a trial-and-error process—guarantees a rough ride for the perfectionist.

For the Christian, this is compounded by perpetual guilt for not meeting God's standards. Because of their self-recrimination, many find it impossible to experience God's forgiveness. I remember one woman in her late twenties who dated men who were abusive to her. This was her way of punishing herself for losing her virginity as a teenager. She asked me, "How can you reel back your teenage life?" And then added, "I must be dirt to God...there are so many better people for God to choose from, so why would He bother with me?" Of course, she neglected to mention at the beginning of her "confession" that she had been told by her father that she would go to hell if she failed to remain sexually pure, so she already feared the wrath of God over any indiscretion. She believed that she didn't deserve a man who loved and cherished her, since she had committed the "unforgivable sin" and was now "damaged goods." Her graceless perfectionism led to only one conclusion: Suffering was her inescapable fate.

Whether dealing with common mistakes or moral failures, perfectionists demand a no-win lifestyle that limits spontaneity and freedom. They're convinced of failure and therefore, are unwilling to experiment with new life strategies. Yet without change, life will become one deadening routine after another.

Every day we have a choice either to focus on the assets of life experience or to ruminate on life's real or imagined liabilities. As the apostle Paul advised the Philippians (see 4:8), we're better off reminding ourselves of the truth about God's goodness and what we have in Him. Perfectionism on the other hand, demands a pre-occupation with uncovering every shred of evidence we can find that we're failing in our careers, our marriages or our friendships. We become focused like a laser on proving that without a doubt, we are inadequate.

Life can be painful, even bewildering. But adversity pushes us to invest our emotional capital in thinking that takes us to the next level of personal growth. If we can stop interpreting our struggles as evidence of self-fulfilling prophecies of inadequacy, we will be well on the road to recovery. Author Scott Peck has described it as taking the "road less traveled."

To make sure they remain trapped in misery, perfectionists employ black and white, all-or-nothing thinking that blocks their ability to resolve conflict. They enslave themselves to a labyrinth of rules and unyielding routine, making it impossible to relax. They're desperately hungry for other people's acceptance, yet paradoxically they try to elevate themselves by defeating everyone else around them. When they can't "win," they react with bitter jealousy and a judgmental attitude toward anyone who seems to be doing better than they. To them, everyone else's accomplishments are either superior (and therefore unattainable) or inferior (written off as unimportant and unworthy of their attention).

It's easy to see why perfectionists are so vulnerable to depression. They allow themselves no effective way to adjust to life's unexpected failures and setbacks. Self-reproach and criticism toward others leaves no room for forgiveness. While they may be able to cope when times are smooth, stress and adversity send them into an emotional tailspin. They judge themselves into depression. Their fears and attitudes of condemnation create a looping mental tape that reinforces unchallenged myths that are toxic to a healthy concept of self.

My client, Robert, was like that. His first words to me were almost dictatorial. "I don't know why I'm here, doc…No offense, but you can't fix me—nobody can. You see I've been a screw-up from the git-go. I can't help myself. It's who I am. I could entertain you for hours telling you all the messes I've created. But I'll save you some time by warning you that you are wasting your efforts on me."

In spite of this self-created, defeatist "reality" in which many of us live, God never lets us forget the type of love that turns away no one, that accepts us with all of our darkest secrets. No one is hopeless in God's eyes. Nonetheless, the perfectionist puts up strong resistance to believing in such grace. It just seems too good to be true.

THE LAST WORD ON PERFECTIONISM

The discrepancy between the perfectionist's world and God's is revealed in the wisdom literature of the Old Testament: *God does not expect for us to be perfect here on earth* (see Eccles. 7:20). Instead of seeking perfection, we are instructed to seek God whose standard is perfection, so that we might increase in spiritual maturity and wisdom. The idea is that we might be increasingly influenced by His direction in our lives and less influenced by our own sin nature. Only in heaven will we understand true perfection. In this life, mature believers recognize their limits and place their confidence in the sufficiency of God's power.

In Ecclesiastes, King Solomon describes life based on secular standards for success rather than on God's. He experienced everything the culture offered: enormous wealth, international fame, achievement, adulation, power and sensual pleasure. He had enough wealth and power to realize all of his dreams—but in the end he was left dry and empty. Depressed and unable to dream any more, he realized he was out of touch with life's purpose.

That purpose is found, he concluded, only in a life of obedience to God. Life is worth living, after all! Solomon learned the hard way that existence apart from divine wisdom makes no sense. Theologian Haddon Robinson has likened it to trying to complete a crossword puzzle with a limited vocabulary. He argues that while history can tell us *what* has happened since man's beginning and science can tell us *how* it happened, neither can tell us *why* it happened.[3] Even Friedrich Nietzsche admitted that we can live with almost any *how*, but only if we know the *why*. Nietzsche, however, believed in an atheistic, humanistic why. In truth, only the reality of God's heart satisfies our thirst for meaning.

The Church has the greatest opportunity ever given to man to teach a hope that fulfills its promise. But we endanger this opportunity when we let legalism—our own version of perfectionism—obscure God's message. Legalistic thinking encourages a false security in our efforts to do good, rather than humble confidence in divine grace. Indeed, perfectionism in any guise churns out a depressing array of "shoulds" draining all joy from our faith.

When Solomon observed that there was "not a righteous man on earth who continually does good and who never sins" (Eccles. 7:20), he was making the *righteous* man the standard of *imperfection*. Not the average man or the disreputable man, but the spiritually-mature man, the man after God's own heart—respected men like Billy Graham, who lives in humble acknowledgment that he sins like the rest of us.

You might object; *Aren't good works important?* Yes. But we would respond with another question: Doesn't James 2:14-26 teach that we do good works as *evidence* of our justification, not as the basis for it? In John 15:1-10, Jesus said that the fruit of our lives— our righteous deeds—would flow out of an abiding relationship with Him. We don't earn acceptance from Him by doing good—we do good as a result of drawing from His love out of overwhelming *gratitude*. But when we give in to perfectionism, we have unwittingly perverted God's grace into an insatiable indebtedness.

Jesus viewed grace as a *gift* to be given to sin-laden people who saw their need for transformation. Legalists pay lip service to God's mercy, but they reverse the cause-and-effect connection between grace-based communion with God and the works we do out of gratitude. They blur the distinction between faith's freeing power and conformity's obligatory burden. No wonder this leads to depression.

Cristian Barbosu, a Romanian scholar, observed that decades of totalitarian rule and conformist thinking have infused the Romanian church with an inherited legalism that persists even under the freedoms of democratic reform.[4] He found, as many others before him, that such institutionalization of belief mutates grace into a set of rules. As John Piper writes, "This terrible moment is the birthplace of the 'debtors' ethic."[5]

A Christian client once told me that he felt guilty as a child every time he wanted to watch the Wednesday night television program *The Wonderful World of Disney,* because it conflicted with his church's prayer meeting. It's a toxic spirituality that raises uniformity to the level of worship. Sadly, our own legalistic standards only weaken the importance of those standards, which are ordained by God.

The writer of Ecclesiastes cautioned his readers, "Do not be excessively righteous and do not be overly wise. Why should you ruin yourself?" (Eccles. 7:16, italics added). What a perfect picture of self-destruction and futility this suggests! It's wonderful when my clients finally discover for themselves the bondage inherent in this way of life and begin to let go of their over-regimented thinking, which allows them to find a freedom they never dared to hope existed. Their relief is a reward for accepting their heart's imperfect character and entrusting it to the power of God's grace.

A second habit of the mind that encourages depression is *self-deception.*

UNVEILING THE HARM OF SELF-DECEPTION

When I was a child, an older playmate in the neighborhood used to play a trick on me that was terrifying. If I didn't do what she wanted, she'd take me to nearby "buggy alley" and abandon me to a bunch of deadly spiders. Compliance made a lot of sense to me. One day however, she overplayed her hand and left me in that frightening alley. I panicked at first. But then I realized the place was harmless. Once I realized that she had been perpetrating a hoax, she lost her power over me.

That's what happens when deceptions are exposed. Only *believed* deceptions can frighten us. Many of our most powerful life-governing beliefs are nothing more than self-deceptions. They are hoaxes. But we, of all people, are best at convincing ourselves of untruths. That's why we cringe at confronting our fears—it often means confronting ourselves. What are the "buggy alleys" you inflict on yourself and how do you let them intimidate you into withdrawal or passivity?

Because *self-deception* is such a powerful habit of the mind, it affects many things we do. We find it at the center of almost every painful lifestyle. Scripture issues more warnings *against being deceived* than against any other tactic of the evil one. As the letter of James insists, unless we act in the clarity of the truth, we "delude" ourselves (1:22) and end up "double-minded" and "unstable in all [our] ways" (1:8). Once we forsake truth as the standard for behavior, the Christian walk is compromised by a sense of meaninglessness that can predispose us to sin. We come to rely on momentary feelings to guide our reasoning. Our minds stray from the mind of God, impairing our judgment.

So where does that leave us? For one, it leads us to disillusionment. If we limit our criteria for success to merely feeling good, then we're automatically defining every adversity as a failure. The predictability of suffering in this life then guarantees an unpromising future. But God's criteria for success are based more on *doing* good than on feeling good. In marriage, God commands us to respond to our spouses on the basis of principle (that is, doing what is right), rather than calibrating our response to how we feel at the moment about our spouse's behavior. "Always do what is right," Mark Twain once commented. "It will gratify yourself and astonish all the rest!"[6]

If we want to avoid self-deception and the reasoning that goes with it, should we discount our feelings entirely? No. Feelings are not the measure of truth, but they do perform a vital role. Remember, most negative feelings are alarms that alert us to take some kind of remedial action. On the other hand, positive feelings accompany the fact that our needs and desires have been satisfied.

Feelings were never intended as ends in themselves—they are there to make us aware of needed change and to provide incentive to take action. But they can't be relied upon to evaluate the outcome of our actions. When we trust feelings as the sole criteria for success or failure, we create a self-deception with the potential for a lot of unnecessary pain. It is then that the experience of failure no longer has the ability to teach us what we need to learn. By the same token, we lose the chance to understand the true nature of success. As someone once said, success can be found in experiencing failure without the loss of enthusiasm! The truth is that endurance of adversity often proves to be the *best* teacher we have.

Defining success by emotional reasoning has another unintended result. Since feelings are often related to our relationships with others, we become vulnerable to constant worry about how others see us. Instead of focusing on doing the good God has called us to do, evaluation apprehension sets in and we become more concerned about the visibility of our work. But making our service, not our visibility, our priority is far more fulfilling.

Best-selling author Henri Nouwen demonstrated this. Though a great scholar who had opportunities to stay at several prestigious institutions, he was content to nurture severely impaired patients in a residential care facility. He was satisfied to serve God far from the spotlight of fame and fortune, though it took a while for him to adapt to a life outside of the heady atmosphere of academia. Likewise, long before the press made Mother Teresa a celebrity, she worked anonymously among the poorest of the poor in the slums of Calcutta. God enlists us, not for dramatic results, nor for accolades, but for our willingness to be channels of His sovereign grace.

> **The truth is that endurance of adversity often proves to be the *best* teacher we have.**

Genuine, self-giving service is one of the best therapies for depression because it confronts our deceptions about ourselves and about our ideas of success. If we feel God's good pleasure, it's because it involves our own pleasure as well. In other words, God's pleasure also becomes ours, just as our pleasure becomes His. We see this in His "eternal delights" (Ps. 16:11)—the delights that satisfy the greatest longings of the human heart. According to author John Piper, "The universal biblical mandate to believe is a radical and pervasive call to pursue our own happiness in God."[7]

When we begin conquering our self-deceptions, we are surprised to learn that desire begets desire, that we give pleasure by receiving it. Here we discover our true home, our source of peace. Like the client who said of the woman he loved, "I feel so at home when she's there because there is nothing I can't disclose to her—with her, I have the overwhelming privilege just to be." No more self-sabotaging thought patterns that transform success into imagined failure or contentment into imagined deprivation; only confidence in God's unconditional acceptance and love.

In our most troubled times, we seem to forget these truths. One culprit that sets us up for this amnesia is the cramping ritualization of Christian life. Prayer rituals. Service rituals. Liturgy rituals. Over time it can all become mindlessly habitual or religious without being spiritual. Like singing hymns without thinking about the words. Minds on autopilot, hearts disengaged. Losing our first love, resigned to the mediocrity of mere appearances—these are all sure paths to depression for those designed to walk in intimacy with God. Accepting a stifling, truncated view of God leaves us ripe for a life of terminal inertia—a life that sometimes makes even the shallow pleasures of culture appear better than the best offerings of faith.

Desire is not evil—God created desire as a good thing. It was intended to be fulfilled by His eternal presence in our lives. It's only in our sin that we've deceived ourselves, seeking to fulfill our desire elsewhere thereby corrupting its true purpose.

Now let's take a look at the third habit of the mind, fear, specifically the fear of rejection, which is a common breeding ground for a lot of depression.

THE CASE AGAINST FEAR

Effective families and churches are characterized by unity. But that doesn't mean everyone is the same. In fact, God purposefully made us with an amazing variety of personalities, predispositions, talents and other character-defining traits. God designed these differences to provide richness and texture within families and churches. But many of us find these differences threatening, irritating or even unfair. As when the task-oriented Martha expressed resentment toward her more teachable sister, Mary, for preferring to sit at Jesus' feet rather than help with the chores (see Luke 10:38-42).

Personal insecurity sometimes keeps us from accepting the fact that others can tread paths unfamiliar to us—paths that intimidate us—not merely because they're different, but because we fear they might prove superior to our own. So we envy. We compare. And often we reject. Perhaps that's because earlier in life we were the ones rejected for expressing our uniqueness in the family. We learned that conformity is the ideal and being different is threatening. When we have a history of such pain, our primary concern in life may become self-protection. Our lives become dominated by *fear of rejection*—still another common precondition to depression. Losing anything (or anyone) we consider important for our identity and security is a prominent theme in rendering us vulnerable to emotional struggles.

Defense against rejection is understandable. But we've already seen how a lifestyle of self-preservation becomes destructive. It organizes life around a limited range of options, all focused on relieving anxiety and avoiding unpredictability. It encourages repression rather than the healthy expression that we need. It causes us to frighten ourselves into depression.

Sometimes Christians who regard any emotional battle as a sign of spiritual deficiency, prompt us to go even further underground to hide our depression for fear that we'll be rejected for that too. We saw this happen in the case of my client Denise. When she disclosed her depression, fellow believers' responses, misguided as they were, succeeded only in intensifying her fear. It's hard to overstate how badly this damaged her spirit, contributing to her incessant anxiety about her eternal destiny. Only with professional help did she come to realize that acceptance by God was not dependent on the acceptance of others.

Though fear is one of our God-given alarm systems alerting us to true threats to our safety, its constant activation leads to emotional exhaustion. This can be seen in various physical symptoms that will often develop, sometimes reflecting our compromised immune system. By this time, acute distress has already given way to chronic depression and hopelessness. The sufferer's spiritual life seldom remains unaffected. Because believers with dysfunctional backgrounds rarely view God accurately anyway, their fear of rejection only skews that view still further. They give up any idea of contentment and resign themselves to accepting an "inevitable"—even "God-ordained"—life of frustration. Such deprivation becomes their punishment for past sins. Yet simmering resentment for this wears them down emotionally and spiritually and it sometimes spills over onto others. This leads to even more rejection, merely confirming in a self-fulfilling way their pessimistic outlook on life.

God provides a way of escape and healing from this fear-induced mental trap. But His healing path is not an easy one. After years of self-destructive behavior, both our world view and our understanding of God can be difficult to recognize as false. Confronting this requires taking the risk of trusting God's revelation. There we find the real truth about ourselves, truth that we could never grasp on our own. Truth we may not be prepared to hear. The humility this exploration requires means not only recognition of our limitations but also admission that our lifelong conclusions may be wrong.

To concede our fallibility is an act of courage that seems difficult and for some, nearly impossible. Sometimes it involves acknowledging our unflattering humanness, our tendency to make mistakes and to injure others. But personal growth requires it. Not some kind of self-punishing rumination, mind you, but rather a compassionate review for the sake of change. Without owning up to our offenses and doing something about them, we make little progress toward the life we want. We might be tempted to wait for the "right time" to begin but since the process never feels right, that usually means never pursuing it at all.

To begin, we must believe God's declared interest in us. Jesus referred to our trust when He said that unless we become as little children, we cannot enter the kingdom of heaven (see Matt. 18:1-4). He was describing in experiential terms the kind of faith it takes to enter God's presence. A child naturally trusts in the adults who care for him, for he knows he can't escape danger without their protection and can't feel secure without their love.

Fear of rejection is not innate in humanity. It's learned. Young children don't *initially* hold back from adults, nor do they pull their punches when they're upset or want something. Often their transparency is charming, refreshing and sometimes amusing. At other times, when it catches adults off guard, it can annoy them with its undisguised tone of demand. It's only when caregivers become abusive or neglectful that children learn to fear rejection; like Denise, who learned it while living with her cold, distant and rigid father. This fear later generalized to others, including her peers and even several of her close associates.

Generally speaking, as socialization continues, the increasing divide between the public and private self becomes more and more evident, especially in dysfunctional homes. In the end, the degree of disparity between the two depends on the amount of rejection children have experienced and from whom they've received it.

Patty was an unexpected fourth child; coming ten years after her siblings were born. Her parents, who were active outdoors people, were disappointed that they would have to curtail their plans to go camping for awhile. Actually, they resented having to start over with a new child. These attitudes had an enduring effect on Patty. As she recalled it, "I always felt like I was in the way, that I was some kind of burden to them. They left me in daycare for much of the time and when I wasn't in daycare, I often had babysitters. When I got older, they just left me alone. They came to few of my school activities and showed little interest in my accomplishments.

To this day, I'm convinced no one is interested in me. That's why I rarely go out and also why I almost never go to church. I'm lonely, but still I guess that's better than being snubbed."

Fear of rejection spills over into our relationship with God as well. We can't survive spiritually without the nurturance of God's grace. But for grace to do its work, we must receive it. We must set aside our fear long enough for our risk-taking ability to resurface. Only then can we let God have His healing effect in our lives. That's why Jesus compared the believer's attitude toward God with the transparency and humility of children. We may not be able to approach God without fear, but we can approach Him courageously, trusting His heart and His promise in spite of our fear.

This is true for all of our relationships. Fear of rejection renders honesty and humility difficult and tends to make the world about us. Because of our inward focus, we react out of pain, sometimes becoming desensitized to the damage we do to others.

Our reception of God's truth—and our openness to revisiting our distorted reality—is the means by which we can redeem our damaged relationships.

THE LANGUAGE OF DESPAIR

Language is the engine of our thoughts. It determines both the content and the process of our self-talk. It also determines the way we narrate our unfolding life story. This internal language determines the emotional nature of our thought habits. For people driven by unhealthy thought habits, like perfectionism, self-deception and fear of rejection, their internal language has been cultivated by conditioned reactions to a painful environment. That's the reason it's so necessary to cultivate a new inner language *purposefully,* in order to shape new thought habits and a new world view. Indeed, reforming our self-talk is, perhaps, the first critically important step in response to depression's alarm signal.

Our perception of the world—whether distorted or accurate— is shaped by such internal language. When we rely heavily on "need language" (that is, language related to needs for physical survival), we are likely to over-emotionalize our communication. This, too, often, provokes irrational responses of guilt, fear and anger, which in turn, lead to the experience of depression. Our "need language" reflects the kind of intensity that normally is reserved for experiences involving a real threat to our physical existence. However, such threats are rarely genuine, which means that our words tend to "catastrophize" life events.

We have few true needs in life—food, water, air, shelter and the love required for a child's attachment to a caregiver. If, for example, we are even briefly deprived of air, we panic and flail to regain our air supply. Anyone who has come close to drowning knows this kind of panic.

In contrast to true needs however, most other longings in life would be classed as *desires*. Where we live, who we marry, what career path we follow, what friends we have, what car we drive, how many children we have, what church we attend and so on, are all choices we make based on our preferences. But what happens if we *psychologically* convert a desire into a need and we become fearful that we'll be deprived of that "need"? Precisely. We panic and flail in the emotional sense. For instance, if we convert our desire for someone's approval into a "need" for that approval and that person withholds it for some reason, we either desperately attempt to get it (sometimes compromising our values to do so) or lapse into significant depression over its loss.

If this catastrophizing comes to dominate our thinking, we end up in continual agitation, frustration, anxiety and depression. Such need language terms as "awful," "terrible," "horrible," "I should," "I have to," "I must," "I can't stand it" or "I could just die" take over our vocabulary. This lexicon of need language creates an emotional volatility rarely justified by the circumstances. That's because catastrophes are rare. Our self-talk becomes a consuming liability, constantly prompting us to act upon a lie, an endless trail of worst-case scenarios.

Jesus said, "The truth will set you free" (John 8:32, NIV), by which He meant that the truth of the gospel will set you free from the bondage of sin. As it turns out, this axiom also serves as God's comprehensive litmus test for *all* truth. It's long been known that a nation's exposure to the truth is any dictator's greatest fear. Autocrats tightly control the press, radio and TV stations, private and public gatherings—any means by which truth might be disseminated, thereby undermining what is factually true. The reality is that the truth will always argue for freedom.

When we become our own emotional dictators, we condemn ourselves to imprisonment by our own lies. We must understand just how profoundly our self-talk determines our feelings, perceptions and actions. If we tell ourselves that it would be *horrible* if someone rejects us or that we *can't stand it* if some situation doesn't work out the way we want it to, we will find ourselves in an endless state of emotional turmoil that will leave us exhausted, causing us to respond with feelings of "road rage" or bouts of anxiety that never seem to go away. Even simple things like traffic jams on the freeway can destroy our day. We tell ourselves, "I can't stand this traffic—I've got to get to my appointment—it's terrible, I'm going to be late." As a result, we become upset, gripping the wheel and yelling at the other cars. We're a wreck by the time we get to our destination. But, will we die if we don't make it on time? Of course not! At worst, we will be a little embarrassed. So, it would be far better (and easier on our emotional and physical health) if we told ourselves something like, "While I don't like it, it's not the end of the world."

The apostle Paul spoke about how he and his companions avoided such turmoil by refusing to use the emotionally loaded "need language" to describe setbacks in their ministry. Life was not easy, but neither was it overwhelming. "We are afflicted in every way, but not crushed; perplexed, but *not* despairing; persecuted but *not* forsaken; struck down, but *not* destroyed" (2 Cor. 4:8-9, italics added). Paul described their struggles in realistic terms—they were pushed to the limit of their endurance. But he noted the inaccuracy of catastrophic terms like "crushed," "despairing," "forsaken" and "destroyed."

Paul's inner commentary used more accurate and moderate self-talk—words like "afflicted," "perplexed," "persecuted" and "struck down"(discouraged)—which we refer to as "preference language." It suggests outcomes we'd prefer to avoid, though the world won't end if they happen; words and phrases like "I'm disappointed, but I can handle it," "It's inconvenient, but not the worst thing that can happen," "I'd prefer it to be different, but I'll survive" etc. Such self-talk leads to far less volatile emotions and far more rational responses to adversity. Paul had the wisdom to describe his experiences as events he didn't like rather than as events he couldn't stand. God's mercy operated through this powerful principle, helping Paul weather ongoing persecution without the paralyzing despair.

> **Your thinking habits are not dependent on what others do or say...*you* are fully in charge of your response to adversity.**

Each of these languages has its own distinct footprint, so we can identify which language we're using by tracking backwards from our experience. If we notice that we're upset to a degree that's out of proportion to the cause, chances are we're using need language for our self-talk. But if we're calm, we're likely describing the event to ourselves in preference language.

Take a moment to listen in on your self-talk—you may be surprised how easily you can detect a lie, possibly the very need-language that is the cause for much of your despair. Best of all, you'll find that changing this commentary is one of the quickest means to achieving relief. Your thinking habits are not dependent on what others do or say. To the contrary, you are fully in charge of your response to adversity.

FINDING HOPE

1. Examine your perfectionist tendencies, particularly the negative judgments you make about your mistakes. Remember, *these mistakes are opportunities to learn,* not failures to reject.

2. Emotional reasoning ("if it feels true, it must be true") is challenged by the fact that *feelings are neither true nor false*—and that *strongly negative feelings are most likely suggesting the importance of making positive change.*

3. Whenever you feel guilty about things that don't involve actual moral compromise, remember, they can't serve as legitimate "shoulds." Picture, instead, the freedom you have in God, the *freedom to live without constant guilt.*

4. *Because of your uniqueness in God's design,* whenever you encounter the differences of others, *remember that's their uniqueness too.* This is what *stimulates openness to new ideas.*

5. Substitute *"preference language"* for *"need language"*—every time you catch yourself using the former, notice how *this change alters your emotional reactions to things in a positive direction.*

DEPRESSION AND THE TURBULENT TRIO

To be blind is bad, but worse it is to have eyes and not to see.
—HELEN KELLER—

Julie, a 47 year-old housewife, slumped in her chair in front of me, eyes rimmed with circles of fatigue. She avoided eye contact. Her fingers tapped the arm of the chair—her feet moved constantly. Her lips trembled as she whispered about the latest blow to her crumbling marriage.

She had learned of her husband's sixth affair during their 18 years of marriage. Weary of the roller coaster life with him, she was desperate for even a sliver of stability in her home. Her husband had promised, again, that he wouldn't wander anymore—and that he would somehow make it up to her. She knew of course, that this latest version of the same empty promise was little more than a smoke screen for his denial. "I knew right then, of course, that this would happen again—but I'm stuck. Where am I going to go? Besides, my life is over anyway. I can't see any future worth living for."

You might ask why she hadn't left him long ago to live without worrying about the next nasty surprise. Why, after all, was Julie so tolerant of this compulsive philanderer? Because she was demoralized by the "turbulent trio" of *guilt, rage* and *abandonment*. As a Christian, she was burdened by *guilt* for even thinking of leaving, for she had been convinced that it was her responsibility to stick it out, regardless of his endless lies and betrayals. She struggled too, because she felt ashamed of her rage at the man who had brought her so much pain. Christians, she thought, should never feel that way about anyone, no matter what they've done. But most paralyzing of all were her powerful *abandonment* issues—her intense fear at the thought of living alone.

She came from a religiously-conservative home where, to her shock, her father had left her mother for another woman when Julie was only six. She never saw her dad again until well into adulthood. Having been "daddy's little girl," she felt abandoned, punished by God for somehow failing him. She grew up adopting her mother's strong faith, but always fantasizing about a man who would never forsake her.

Ironically however, she married a man not unlike her father— a man who destroyed her dream of the storybook marriage. Shattered, feeling trapped in a loveless relationship, she became convinced that God was punishing her for a spiritually-substandard life. *Guilty!* Even though she had a Scriptural basis for leaving her husband, she feared that it would nonetheless violate her faith. She had even talked herself into believing that she was "called" to patient endurance, sacrificing her happiness for her husband's compulsions in order to "rescue" him...and maybe herself as well.

It is, of course, essential to guard the sanctity of marriage. God asks no less of us. But this husband was making a mockery of it. He showed no signs of change. Until now, Julie's twisted logic had forced her to tolerate his pathological behavior. Meanwhile, an abiding rage grew inside her—secretly against God, but now openly against her husband. Her fury was tearing her body apart with intestinal disorders, headaches and fatigue. She could no longer keep up her mild-mannered façade. Her anger triggered even more guilt. In fact, she felt guilty about almost everything. By the time she sought help, she was showing intense anxiety, wanting to know just how a believer could feel the way she did and still go to heaven. God *must* reject her.

A surprising number of people like Julie wonder if their secret emotional life has sabotaged their chances with a righteous God.

Even when they've repeatedly had their lights punched out, they believe that God requires them to absorb the blows—if not with a smile, at least with a long-suffering attitude.

It doesn't seem to matter that the Bible speaks at length about God's mercy and compassion. They find it too hard to believe that He understands their pain and the powerful feelings that spring from it—especially their anger. Their view of God is far too limited to see in Him anything beyond the promise of judgment.

They can't comprehend the fact that He cherishes us, in spite of our faithlessness, not because we can offer something to Him but because He delights in offering us His grace. They have missed the point of His sacrifice, which could fire them up to take on life's challenges. Even so, God desires for them to live assertively—as loved kids already accepted by Him. He never expects anyone to merely endure life or to live it riddled with false guilt. He rejoices in our joy, never in the pain of our poor choices.

CONTAINING FALSE GUILT: THE OVER-RESPONSIBILITY TRAP

Assertive living implies that we assume responsibility for our decisions and consequent behaviors. But as with so many things in life, there is wisdom in balance. *It's no surprise then that both under-responsibility and over-responsibility serve as poor blueprints for successful relationships.* In the former, we blame everyone else when things go wrong. In the latter, we assume not merely our own but everyone else's responsibilities as well. It's easy to see why this tendency provides fertile ground for false guilt. After all, when we shoulder the guilt that belongs to others, we become partners in a dance with manipulators who are all too glad to delude themselves and others about their "innocence." But our blurry boundaries can't fool us out of our resentment for taking the blame.

It's our porous boundaries that leave us incapable of distinguishing between our desires and those of others. People pleasers lose contact with what they want and mistake a placating strategy for humility. Underneath, they are wallowing in self-pity and repressed anger. Despite their efforts to please others, placaters continue to be ignored, if not sometimes reviled. They endure the worst of both worlds—overburdened with responsibility yet overlooked by others. No wonder they become livid at the lack of "saviors" to come to their aid when *they* need it.

Why do they keep coming back for more? For starters, it gives them temporary relief from false guilt. It also provides for the momentary reward of the occasional fleeting compliment that calms their fear of rejection. Sooner or later though, depression sets in as their efforts to stay afloat grind to a halt. When others fail to come to their rescue, they sink into an angry despair—yet with little insight into the futility of their placating lifestyle.

Hard core people-pleasers always lack the self-acceptance to set adequate boundaries. Their fear of disappointing others is, in effect, their emotional Mt. Everest. It's only when others recognize their depletion that boundaries are set *for* them.

Christians don't help when they spiritualize this dysfunction by redefining the placating lifestyle as "humble service" before God. What they fail to understand is that boundary setting honors God—it prevents the sins of disrespect, manipulation and exploitation from others. The alternative is a guilt-inspired absence of boundaries that dishonors everyone.

Jesus understood this principle. After many exhausting days of teaching, He escaped the pressing throngs to find rest (see Luke 8:1-4, 19, 22). Doubtlessly disappointing many, but recognizing His need for physical restoration, He set out to sea with His disciples. No apologies. No contorted explanations. Just a graceful exit. The wisdom of this rest was clear when we find Him sleeping through a storm that the disciples feared would sink the boat (see vv. 23-25). By His example, Jesus was teaching the disciples how to deal with the pressures of their own future ministries, preparing them to spread the message of the Messiah without becoming hobbled by guilt or exhausted by the demands of others.

Guilt-produced depression accounts for the convoluted thinking that never saying no is the proper exercise of Christian sacrifice. False guilt strips us of the willingness to acknowledge the longings of our heart. We deny expression to our ideas, our preferences and our opinions. As fatigue builds, we spiral down into a litany of self-condemnation, something we can't stop because we have lost touch with who we are. An exhausted Christian once told me, "Every time I am tempted to say 'no' to somebody in the church who wants me to take on a new responsibility, something which I don't have time or the desire to do anyway, I feel guilty. Why can't I happily do things for the Lord? Is my spiritual life that messed up? Maybe, I'm just tired of being on everybody's list for doing stuff."

There are times when we try to mask this vacuum in our identity—while covering our true sin—with a façade of false righteousness and religious legalism. But the truth is we are still sinners who need to seek God's compassion. The widespread nature of sin, according to author John Piper, results from the misdirected object of our concern. "What does not come *from* satisfaction in God and *through* the guidance of God and *for* the glory of God, is God-less...it is sin."[1]

How much discomfort must depression's alarm signal inflict before we choose to let go of these damaging ideas? When will we realize that where legalistic "shoulds" fail, grace wins? In psychiatrist Paul Tournier's words, "The obliteration of our guilt is free for us because God has paid the price."[2] The cross expresses God's mercy, diverting the justice we deserve onto Jesus. It confronts our history of sin with forgiveness, not condemnation. It opens the way to what our souls hunger for most: intimacy with our Creator.

Our emotional signals remind us that it's up to us to take remedial action, whether that means changing our thinking or changing our behavior. Usually, we will do both. Where guilt is involved, we must first determine the depth of its legitimacy, *and then* consider whether acknowledgment and restitution should be pursued. True guilt is, as we've seen, an emotional indicator of moral compromise—but false guilt is not. We address legitimate guilt by setting things right through confession and contrition. We free ourselves from false guilt by reviewing the mistaken beliefs that have spawned self-hatred and self-punishment. The following chart may help you to distinguish between these two types of guilt so that you can take appropriate action:

TRUE GUILT	FALSE GUILT
is generated by healthy moral conviction	is generated by unhealthy social expectations
reflects disobedience of God's will	reflects violation of internalized legalistic sanctions
is measured by absolute divine standards revealed by God	is measured by relative human standards taught in the home or church
prods us to reach outward (and upward) to repair broken relationships	promotes dysfunctional relationships and self-condemnation
leads to a positive self-concept shaped by the truth	leads to a distorted self-concept shaped by lies
is based on the desirable connection between relationships and the experience of love	is based on the destructive connection between relationships and loss of love
signals the need for spiritual and emotional wholeness	perpetuates spiritual and emotional deformity
is intended to lead to true repentance and genuine healing	leads to more failure and greater dishonesty

With true guilt, the best antidepressant is a clear conscience. But with false guilt, the most effective antidote is a more charitable habit of thinking. Freedom from depression requires us to address both.

FINDING OUR LIMITS WITHOUT GUILT

False guilt ambushed Susan when one of her three children was stricken with a congenital disease that was fatal. The doctor said that her son would begin deteriorating by age five and would die before his eighth birthday. Susan became acutely aware of his every desire, so much so that she had neglected her husband and her other children. As expected, the boy died. Susan suffered severe grief depression, which worsened with time. Her husband brought her in for counseling, fearing she might become suicidal.

During the course of the interview, Susan shared her profound grief. As she did, she was asked if she had any other feelings while caring for her son. She hesitated, and then blurted out, "Once, when I was feeling tired and kind of lonely, I wished my son would go ahead and die so I could get back to normal life with my other children." Then she broke down and sobbed. Between sobs, she asked, "How can any mother worth the name feel that way toward her own son?" In truth, such thoughts are natural and common under these conditions. So her guilt was false. Nevertheless, she had tried to compensate for it by giving her son exaggerated attention, neglecting everyone else. What she was doing was trying to "prove" to herself that she wasn't such a terrible mother after all.

Susan's depression came from more than just the grief of her loss. She was also struggling with what she thought was her gross insensitivity. Once she understood that a normal, loving mother could have such human feelings and reactions, she began to heal. In a short time, her depression, having served its purpose, began to lift. She had taken too much responsibility for something she didn't understand and so had distorted her perception of her own character, assaulting her integrity as a mother.

False guilt often does this, which is why it often results in overcompensating behavior. The compulsion to please everyone serves to silence a fear of rejection and to prevent guilt over disappointing others. But God doesn't want us to depend on acceptance from others for our personal legitimacy. Should we stop caring about others? No. But we must act on internal conviction, not on external approval. It's not easy, but it's the best thing for our mental and spiritual health.

> **The compulsion to please everyone serves to silence a fear of rejection and to prevent guilt over disappointing others.**

Like Moses in the Old Testament, if people-pleasing is our goal we will find ourselves in a constant state of stress. God had asked Moses to be Israel's *leader,* not their *slave*—to bring them *out* of bondage, not to put himself in bondage. But he found himself overburdened with his people's demands. If we want to avoid this error, we are best guided not by popular opinion, but by the freedom of His Spirit. For this is the way we prevent the chronic depression that comes with enslavement to others.

Sometimes we form unrealistic expectations and mistake them for God's direction. We respond to our fear of failure by taking control, trying to create the conditions for these expectations to be fulfilled. But God often teaches us by leading us through the unexpected, sometimes even through our disappointment, forcing us to release control. This can be more than disquieting however, when we are part of the "safety first" crowd.

God wants us, of course, to take appropriate responsibility but never to mistake this desire for meaning that we must take *His* responsibility. He has proven that He can expand our faith with every experience—even our suffering—but we must trust Him with that responsibility. Although we may not always see the pattern, He's weaving these experiences into a beautiful and unique design. We're a work in progress. Nothing can happen to us that escapes His watchful eye. He even protects us from ourselves, finding ways to rein us in when we take on more than our limits can handle. But we can join Him in these efforts by learning to discern where our limits are.

This calls to memory a humorous incident involving former heavyweight champion Muhammad Ali. While flying to a boxing match, the pilot warned of turbulence and asked passengers to fasten their seat belts. Mr. Ali complained to the flight attendant and said, "Superman don't need no seat belt." Whereupon the flight attendant replied, "Yeah and Superman don't need no airplane either!"

Recognizing our boundaries enables us to serve God more effectively. God used Moses for His kingdom, but only *after* convincing Moses of his limits. We resist this lesson, because we think facing our inadequacies threatens our significance. To the contrary, facing them enhances it. For to Him, *our lives really do matter.* How can our significance be any greater than its acknowledgment by the Creator of the universe? Life is all about what we mean to God, not about how we look to others. It's about God's strength displayed through our weakness. God's glory, not ours.

God doesn't accept our weakness as an excuse for failing to serve Him. He takes us as we are and transforms us into what we can become. As someone once said, "What we are is our gift to God, but what we can become is God's gift to us." This gift is our high calling.

The unchurched are repulsed by the Christian's constant anxiety over incurring God's wrath or displeasure. Why would they be drawn to a life tortured by false guilt? The healthy mechanism of guilt signals moral failure, but many misuse it to browbeat themselves—in keeping with their perception of an angry, autocratic God. The picture of dragging our "faith" around as a heavy burden does little else than show how depressing religion can become. Contrary to this picture, it's our responsibility to God, ourselves and the watching world to live the inviting life of both truth and grace.

SWALLOWING ANGER:
THE CASE AGAINST MENTAL INDIGESTION

Closely related to the problem of false guilt is that of unresolved anger. We discussed earlier the way in which pain evokes anger, which in turn, produces guilt for feeling such a "negative" emotion. This guilt tends to stay underneath the surface, as sometimes does the anger as well. Turning these strong emotions inward can trigger a depressive episode that baffles everyone, including your closest friends.

These hidden dynamics became evident in a young man who arrived at my office in a suicidal despair. Tim, a Christian, was distraught over a moral lapse he had promised himself would never happen. He and his fiancée, Elizabeth, had made a pact to avoid sexual involvement before marriage. But one night he stayed too late and the unthinkable happened. Consumed with guilt, he asked Elizabeth to forgive him, to the point that she became concerned about his deepening depression. He could not forgive himself. He felt he'd failed God and his girlfriend and had decided to punish himself by forsaking his most meaningful aspiration—to enter the ministry. He grieved over the apparent death of his dream. "How could I let this happen? I've ruined everything. My dreams are gone. My virginity is gone. My relationship with Elizabeth is forever affected. And, to make things worse, I'm certain that God's done with me. In fact, I'm done with me."

The turning point in his therapy came when he unearthed an emotion he'd denied to his own awareness in the aftermath of the sexual encounter: Anger. He'd felt hurt and angry that Elizabeth hadn't stopped him, but instead accepted his amorous advances. He knew he was responsible for his misbehavior, but he also blamed her. Recognizing his anger spurred a new round of guilt for such an "inappropriate" emotion. But he sat down with Elizabeth and discussed his feelings with her, acknowledging that he was not trying to excuse his sin. He was relieved when she both understood and accepted his anger—she shared responsibility for that evening's events. This watershed moment enabled him at last to forgive himself and thus to accept God's forgiveness. His depression lifted and he once again began to live with hope and optimism.

Tim's depression had been only partially related to guilt about the sexual incident itself. It was when he acknowledged and learned to accept the anger he harbored toward his fiancée that he was able to deal with his feelings appropriately.

Of all our emotions, anger is usually the least well-managed. Some people lament their uncontrolled explosions—others have trouble expressing their anger at all. Many are chronically depressed, unable to handle the reality of their angry feelings or to determine their source. Angry depressives may struggle with inappropriate, hair-trigger rage, often aggravated by their gloomy pessimism about life itself. On the other hand, they may succumb to a stifling withdrawal that looks more like apathy. These are the extremes, between which people experience many variations. But neither extreme is an appropriate way to address life's daily stresses.

Some people—particularly Christians who view anger as a sin—refuse to acknowledge their anger for fear of exposing their unworthiness. Others suppress anger in order to avoid uncomfortable conflict. However, both are dishonest. In fact, we often limit our anger to nonverbal expression so that we can deny that we feel that way. The worst part is that bottling up our anger denies us the only opportunity we have to use our feelings to discover the source of our emotional pain.

In order to avoid the crippling effects of resentment and bitterness, we must talk through our anger with the person toward whom we feel it. Yes, it's possible to privately let go of some anger. But most often we harbor it and as a result, it grows into an emotional cancer, eating away at our relationships and eventually destroying our chances for a happy, meaningful life.

We're not advocating brutal disclosure without tact or kindness, or any kind of retaliatory accusation. It's just as dishonest as denial to verbally hammer someone to a pulp, claiming all the while that we're "just telling the truth." Instead, we're talking about revealing our insides while also acknowledging the other's right to believe and feel differently. The shared experience of considering *both* parties' concerns before reaching mutual resolution will only strengthen a relationship.

Confession and forgiveness should be the tactics of *first* resort whenever we've hurt someone and been hurt by them in return. But many of us resist admitting we're wrong, believing that it weakens our position in the relationship and damages our credibility. To the contrary, it strengthens our believability and softens the other person's heart. Rebuilding trust in a relationship requires a candor that overcomes hidden agendas and ulterior motives. Constructing a better future calls for a climate of emotional safety where integrity can develop in our communications.

Like confession, forgiveness doesn't come easily to many of us. Maybe we fear opening ourselves up to repeated hurt and betrayal. Obsessed with self-protection, we adopt the rule "nothing ventured, nothing lost" as our guiding principle. But we forget that forgiveness and trust are two different things.

Or maybe we think forgiveness is letting the offender off the hook, as though he's free never to feel guilty or suffer consequences for his behavior. But forgiveness is not the same as absolution either. It doesn't excuse wrong behavior or shield the offender from consequences. Rather, it shifts the focus away from retribution as an acceptable response to those who've hurt us.

For some, forgiveness seems foolish, while "defending our honor" feels like the nobler path. But the true ignobility of unforgiveness is revealed by its contrast to Christ's example (and Peter's call that we follow it). "While being reviled, He did not revile in return—while suffering, He uttered no threats, but kept entrusting Himself to Him who judges righteously"(1 Pet. 2:23). Impossible? Not with the healing, character-building power of Christ. Returning injury for injury demeans the self and sacrifices peace of mind—it is stooping to the same deficit of virtue as the other person. Like the aphorism, "Bitterness is like taking poison and expecting the other person to die," a bitter heart is primarily a path to chronic depression.

When we become hardened by an unforgiving spirit, something life-sustaining dies within us. Our empathy and compassion fades—we neglect intimacy in our meaningful relationships. We polarize our world into allies and enemies, most of them oblivious to the original injury. A resident defensiveness settles in, spelling a life of unhappiness, depression and paranoia. Ironically, none of this has much, if any, effect on the original offender. Instead, the sin of bitterness wraps its poisonous fingers around our own soul and squeezes out every drop of tenderness and kindness, leaving an empty shell of cynicism and cruelty.

When Jesus taught about turning the other cheek, He knew that contrary to our expectations, we would lose far more than we would ever gain if we remained secretly resentful or if we lashed out in retaliation. Revenge plays on our natural self-centeredness, but ends in self-destruction. It has killed many marriages and friendships. But humility is a hard-sell to the overindulged and the terribly wronged, who mistakenly equate it with the philosophy of the doormat.

Forgiveness is difficult because it requires an act of grace— a commodity in short supply. Grace is an unconditional decision made in a definable moment, quite unlike trust, which develops with time and experience. Grace depends not on the recipient's merit but on the grantor's benevolence. Trust however is *earned* by the offender over time, not by words but by a discernable change in conduct.

As hard as forgiveness is, it's important for our spiritual character. It means acting with *assertive restraint* that exposes, by contrast, the offender's sin. Equally important, it is likely to foster attitudinal change in both parties. How can we not forgive as God has forgiven us? "How can we speak of God's grace in our lives," a colleague once remarked, "and still bear so little resemblance in character to the One who gave it?" To "turn away from evil and do good" (1 Pet. 3:11) is always challenging, even under the best of circumstances. But God offers His sufficient love and supreme power to strengthen us to do what is foreign to our human nature.

How we conduct ourselves determines our reputation among nonbelievers. It's God's desire to present to the world a body of believers who stand out by their acts of love. An American pastor encountered a man in India who told him that he respected Christians because they were the only ones who compassionately tended to the poor (the so-called "untouchables"), who rescued women from their husbands' funeral pyres (in the Hindu practice of suttee) and who retrieved unwanted female babies thrown into the Ganges River. "How can someone," he asked, "consider such things as anything but noble and courageous in a society whose beliefs and customs have, for centuries, been so brutal and degrading?"

> **It's God's desire to present to the world a body of believers who stand out by their acts of love.**

So far, so good. But the unforgiving attitudes and resulting depression we often find among Christians in this country should serve as a wake-up call to rally the resources we have in a benevolent God, to change the ways we treat each other, both within the church and in the world.

DESERTING ABANDONMENT: REJECTION REVISITED

When I was 12, my grandmother, who had been living with our family for a number of years, became ill and died. She had been close to my sister and me, so it was the first significant loss we experienced. I remember standing by her casket, overwhelmed by the grief that was tearing open a large hole inside me—a chasm that opened still wider when I saw my mother's tears.

This loss was painful, but I was fortunate that I still enjoyed parental nurture and a happy, connected home. Many have suffered losses far more traumatic than mine, including the loss or absence of a loving, intact home. Within them grows a deep and abiding sense of abandonment—the earlier the age at which this happens the more alarming the consequences.

Any traumatizing loss early in life can leave a person more vulnerable to subsequent loss—or even to the perceived threat of loss. Recently, I met with an unstable couple who were dating. The young man insisted on maintaining his friendship with his former fiancée and his girlfriend was jealous. She had a long history of abandonment by the important men in her life beginning with her father and felt threatened by her boyfriend's continued association with this other woman. Her boyfriend's lack of empathy—in fact, outright annoyance over her insecurity—only aggravated the situation, casting serious doubt on the relationship's viability. "Why can't you understand how wrong your relationship with Sheri is? You'd hate it if I started seeing one of my old boyfriends. Why do you have to be like all the rest of the men I've known?" she asked. "You're so unreasonable. Do I have to give up all my friends just because you can't accept them?" he shot back.

Part of the reason that a history of relational loss makes it difficult for many of us to trust is that it suggests that we are somehow unlovable and therefore incapable of holding on to any relationship. Depression is never far away. Some people, in fact, remain in unhealthy and abusive relationships, rationalizing that any relationship is better than none. When failure threatens a current relationship, the abandonment history surfaces and quickly leads to hopeless, sometimes angry despair far deeper than someone without this history would experience. The relationship, if it survives, becomes a lonely one either because each is wary of any further commitment or because there were too many problems from the beginning. To those who question the sustainability of a relationship, emotional safety is always the chief goal, which is one reason why they become so possessive.

Among adults, twice as many women as men seek treatment for depression. That's partly because women tend to more openly admit to their feelings. It is usually the father—the first significant man in a woman's life—who is more likely to leave the home. Men, on the other hand, typically tend to treat problems as a challenge to their adequacy in handling things on their own, so they're more likely to "tough it out" in difficult circumstances. Either that or they bury their emotional distress altogether.

When anyone suffers important childhood loss, it can result in considerable emotional insecurity. A young man might lack confidence in his male role, experience gender confusion or feel intense attachment to his mother. Or he might display aggressive, even criminal behavior that can land him in prison. He could become involved in gangs, in the heavy use of drugs or in promiscuous relationships and father illegitimate children. This is the typical profile of young felons who grow up without fathers—often because their fathers are in jail or involved in criminal behavior of their own.

> **Among adults, twice as many women as men seek treatment for depression.**

Women with abandonment histories may also take drugs and bear illegitimate children, but they're more likely to develop a helplessness that makes them vulnerable to abuse, to become targets for pathological men. They migrate from one transitory relationship to another. They must have a man in the house, but these men rarely stay for long, certainly not long after a baby is born—which of course, starts the cycle all over again.

The common denominator among both men and women who experience loss and trauma is usually depression. By experiencing more of the same, they lose hope for something different. Ultimately, if this hope is to return, they must look not out, but up to find a new meaning to life. As C. S. Lewis put it, "Aim at Heaven and you will get earth 'thrown in': Aim at earth and you get neither."[3]

So it turns out that our hope for salvation becomes one with our hope for intimacy, both in this world and in the next. Conviction is the substance of courage, just as courage is the substance of vulnerability. Although intimacy depends on both, withdrawal is found in neither.

FINDING HOPE

1. Setting appropriate personal boundaries *frees you from false guilt.* It's the best antidote to the passive, placating lifestyle.

2. With *true guilt,* the best antidepressant is *a clear conscience.* But with *false guilt, it is confronting* your mistaken, legalistic, injury inflicting beliefs *with the truth.*

3. When you are no longer guided by the evaluations of others but rather by the Holy Spirit, *life becomes emancipating.*

4. Consider *anger as a valuable emotion* that can expose the source of your emotional pain. Handled appropriately, *hurtful issues can be resolved* before they do further damage.

5. The willingness to *forgive protects your tenderheartedness.* Forgiveness makes certain you don't suffer from the larger injury of bitterness and, later, from the pain of depression.

6. If self-protection has been your chief goal in relationships, challenge yourself to take small incremental steps of interpersonal risk to discover *the pleasure of increasing intimacy.* This is the only real *salve for your fear of abandonment.*

STEREOTYPES OF DEPRESSION: PITFALLS AND PIT STOPS

*A beautiful thing never gives so much pain
as does failing to hear and see it.*

—MICHELANGELO—

Diane tearfully approached her pastor after Sunday service and asked to speak with him for a few minutes. He agreed and led her to his office. For 30 minutes she poured out the story of her endless depression, pleading for help. He promised to connect her with a church counselor. In the meantime, he encouraged her to trust God for His peace. He suggested one of his taped sermons about God's faithfulness.

A few days later he called to inform her that all of the counselors were booked up, but one would call her when an opening became available. He reminded her to continue trusting God, even if she couldn't see His hand at work. And then he hung up after promising to keep in contact. Though three months went by before she got in to see a counselor, this pastor continued to encourage her, even after she had been strung out on drugs and hospitalized. While counseling helped her understand why she had become so self-destructive and what she could do to change it, it was her pastor's compassion and encouraging spiritual instruction that sustained her through her crisis. As she reflected, "My pastor spent more time with me than I could have asked for. He didn't pretend to have all of the answers, but he seemed to care about me...and when it was all said and done, that was probably the most healing thing of all, especially since I never got that from my father."

We naturally turn to our pastors, busy as they are, seeking help for our depression and expecting their wisdom and prayerful insight to lift our spirits and give us direction. And most of the time, this is what happens. The simple hope of connection with someone who cares to alleviate our loneliness promises some measure of relief. But even more, Christians who are unsure of their standing

> **The less people feel validated by their own self-talk, the more they seek validation from others**

before God long to be affirmed by the church as obedient believers, approved and accepted by their leaders and by God. It's an axiom of the counseling profession that the importance of social approval increases in direct proportion to the lack of self-acceptance. The less people feel validated by their own self-talk, the more they seek validation from others. But such validation doesn't always materialize, often because the hurting person's behavior pushes others away. The hurting person soon believes that he or she is not worth *anyone's* attention...even God's.

The harsh self-judgments of depressed people run contrary to the fact of their priceless worth before God, which He has repeated often in His Word and demonstrated throughout history. Their sense of worthlessness robs them of any means of dealing with real rejection from others or imagined rejection from God. Empty and abandoned, they turn to pastoral support, often as a last resort. They come expecting healing, compassion and helpful advice. But, unlike Diane's experience, sometimes they may encounter any number of stereotypes of depression that find their way into the church's thinking. These caricatures of depressed people attribute moral causes to their already profound distress, deepening their depression.

While it's true that moral lapses can trigger depression, most episodes of depression have other causes. To broad-brush the experience as a moral problem intensifies the burden of false guilt already weighing many believers down.

Believers like Bill. He and Sally sought counseling for a marriage that had become organized around his depression. Bill's struggles began a year earlier, shortly after he resigned from his church's deacon board and its heavy requirements. He took this action because he could no longer handle the demands of his job, the responsibilities of his home and the heavy requirements of the deacon board's search for a new youth pastor. This commitment was sapping the time and energy he needed for his job and young family. He was spent and yet he felt guilty. Despite the prudence of resigning from the board to preserve his health and his marriage, the senior pastor reproached him for reneging on his responsibility to the church. "I'm disappointed in you, Bill. I thought you understood that true discipleship required great sacrifice. It's God and His church you're letting down—so, please reconsider what you are doing and get your priorities straight." With that shot across the bow, the pastor, upset at the prospect of losing a good deacon, kept up the pressure on Bill to reverse his decision.

Bill was taken aback and began thinking the pastor might be right. But his angry wife urged her husband to ignore the pastor's so-called "advice." In fact, she wanted to leave the church altogether. Bill was caught between his pastor and his wife, each demanding opposite courses of action. Bill had resisted the notion that church service is the measure of spiritual maturity, but now he spiraled into self-doubt and depression.

In the course of counseling, he began to realize that his vulnerability to self-doubt stemmed from his history with a mother who used guilt to manipulate her children. In time, this insight helped him reaffirm his family as his priority. He became a confident husband and father and learned to combat his passivity and approval dependency. He began to respond with God-guided assertiveness rather than depressed withdrawal and the guilt-inducing manipulations of others.

CARICATURES AND CORRECTIVES

Many Christians are subjected to a variety of stereotypes that tend to flourish in the church. To their credit, the Christian community *intends* to help believers follow a biblically based approach to depression. They have no wish to kick people when they're down. But the unintentional consequences are the same. The stereotypes they believe in end up oversimplifying the complexity of emotional behavior and over-spiritualizing its root causes.

God never intended His Word to provide cookie-cutter approaches to psychological problems. In the New Testament, Jesus always tailored His teaching and responses to fit the unique audience or individual. With the legal scholar, Nicodemus, he used a provocative doctrinal approach—yet with the condemned prostitute or the cohabiting Samaritan woman at the well, He spoke in simple, compassionate terms. He adjusted His presentation of the same redemptive message to the variety of spiritual, intellectual and emotional needs He encountered.

Jesus' practical relevance was so effective that Jewish leaders formed an unlikely coalition of sects, normally hostile toward one another, to silence His message. Their imbalanced instruction of the Scriptures had replaced grace with works and humility with human pride. Indeed, these leaders had committed a "spiritual felony" against their own people in their determination to keep their unquestioned authority.

In one form or another, this legalistic thinking has continued to survive down through the centuries and today is the source of many stereotypes Christians hold about emotional struggles, including depression. Religious platitudes have rarely been useful with the depressed—yet they cause many Christians to struggle with self-doubt because they sound so spiritual. Our purpose in this chapter then, is to replace such thinking with an accurate understanding so that the believer's response to emotional upheaval is appropriate and healing.

The two greatest barriers in the Church to accurate thinking about depression are the rigidity of a closed mind and the misjudgment of an indiscriminately open mind. With the former, the helper's inflexible agenda considers nothing outside of itself and presents a caricature of love. With the latter, the helper is swayed by almost any idea, sometimes compromising his own beliefs and therefore offering a caricature of truth. Neither however, can offer much help to the hurting believer.

What we need in those from whom we seek counsel is patience, insight and, above all, wisdom to sort through all the factors responsible for sounding the alarm bells of depression. To the untrained ear, many of these factors will escape notice, which is why so many well-intentioned Christians fail to reach the hearts of those who are suffering.

Meanwhile, in church, depressed believers sit passively in the pew, half-heartedly singing the choruses and half listening to messages that seem so distant from the devastation they feel inside. To them, nothing seems relevant. Some abandon their faith altogether. Others play the game, inwardly dying while outwardly going through the motions of the Christian life.

The Church is God's institution, yet it is comprised of imperfect people. Righteous people sin, congregations can be misguided and hurting believers can hurt others. But that doesn't excuse us when our most vulnerable members try and fail to get help from their leaders. Conviction and good intentions don't make the stereotypes we promote any more right than did the zeal of medieval crusaders make their cause right. Misguided conviction isn't a virtue.

To our teaching we must add selfless, *empathic* love that understands pain from the inside out, that expresses God's grace to the troubled believer. It means, too, that we abide by sound psychological principles reflected in biblical truth applied by the Truth-giver Himself. Finally it suggests the humility of serving one another without the prejudice of an artificial religious formula.

To capture the power of this argument, we will limit ourselves to four of the many existing stereotypes of depression—the ones we've observed to have the widest influence on suffering believers.

THE STEREOTYPE OF DEPRESSION AS SIN

Perhaps the most harmful of all the stereotypes is the belief that it's sinful to be depressed—that all obedient Christians are happy ones. This implies that depression itself is a moral problem worthy of rebuke. Now, it's true that ongoing, undisclosed sin can be a cause of depression. But even then, depression is not the sin but rather the *emotional consequence* of a sin.

We see this illustrated throughout the Bible. For instance, Saul (later known as the apostle Paul) struggled internally to maintain his rejection of Jesus as the Messiah, despite of all the evidence. He set off on a rampage against Christians to drown out his nagging conscience. When Christ confronted him in person on the road to Damascus, He pointed out the futility of "kicking against the goads" (see Acts 26:14). Immediately, Saul dropped his resistance and offered surrender, overwhelmed by the enormity of his sin. Indeed, in his subsequent depression he refused to eat as he contemplated the evil he had committed against Christ and His followers (see Acts 9:9).

So depression can, in fact, be the result of personal sin. Moral culpability generates real guilt—and when depression is the result, it serves as a built-in signal directing us to confess and repent of our wrongdoing. *But depression can come from many other causes that have nothing to do with the depressed person's sin.*

This point often gets confused because the concept of sin can be considered on two different levels—the general sinfulness of the world in which we live and the sinful acts for which we are responsible. In our fallen world, bad things are going to happen—disease, accidents, natural disaster, suffering caused by the sin of others—that are beyond our personal control. But when we make sinful choices, we bear the burden of culpability. The stereotype of depression as sin fails to make this crucial distinction—it places all causes of depression in the second category (personal sin), when many causes belong in the first (circumstances for which we're not responsible). As a consequence, we fail to appreciate depression as the invaluable signal system that it is. Instead, it's regarded as evidence of the work of the Enemy.

As if that weren't bad enough, many Christians become convinced that because of their depression, they're worthless to God and His kingdom—or worse still, that God sees them as a hindrance to the cause of Christ. When their faith becomes a reminder of their pain, its capacity to give comfort vanishes into the night of despair.

This thinking, of course, has tragic consequences. To believe that God can no longer use us, we must ignore the fact that many prominent figures in the Bible wrestled with profound depression. Yet God's plan of redemption used every one of them as instruments of His glory (as we shall see in a later chapter). What a pity that our theology can so limit what God can do with our brokenness!

Nevertheless, defending the personal worth of the depressed believer is a battle worth fighting. Christians who equate depression with sin are likely to label themselves as hopeless degenerates, crippling their motivation to discover and solve the issues underneath. What's more, false guilt traps them in a prison of counterfeit "shoulds." Little wonder they learn to respond inappropriately to adversity and inflexibly to God. They enslave themselves with rules of their own making and then become their own dictators in enforcing them. Although "shoulds" are always tied in Scripture to God's standard of righteousness and are therefore limited to moral and ethical concerns, we ignore this. Instead, our legalism disengages these "shoulds" from their moral base and applies them to everything we do.

How we interpret God's response to our depression often affects the strength of our faith. If we see Him as judging us for it as if it were willful disobedience, we're destined for deeper depression and weaker faith. But discerning the truth rejuvenates us with a renewed sense of hope. To get there, we must understand that depression is a doorway to new understanding, not a wall trapping us in irresolvable conflict.

This means differentiating cause from effect. Depression is an emotional alarm system (an effect) indicating that something has injured us or that something needs resolution (the cause). The cause (which can involve our ability to choose) may or may not entail sin. But an effect never shares such responsibility because it derives its existence wholly apart from choice. For instance, *how we respond* during the course of our depression can be sinful or not. That's because our response is always a moral decision of our will—on the other hand, our emotional state is, by definition, always *morally neutral.* So, we can determine whether or not we've sinned by *what we do* with depression or by *what choices we made* that led to that depression. But sin can never be determined by the existence of depression itself.

Believing that you're guilty because you're suffering is a false assumption, one that leads to fraudulent self-condemnation. Remember Job's cry. "My heart is broken. Depression haunts my days. My weary nights are filled with pain" (Job 30:16-17, TLB). Yet the Bible reports, "In all of this, Job *did not sin*" (Job 1:22, TLB, emphasis added).

If depression were sin and happiness the only expression of true faith, then repentance would resolve the issue and produce happiness. But that's not what happens. Many depressed Christians fail to find any relief through "repentance." Instead, they see themselves as beyond redemption. As long as no one thinks to question this view of depression, the sufferer's faith will provide no consolation.

Even the father of the Reformation, Martin Luther, suffered most of his life from this vicious cycle. He experienced what he called "Devil sweats" over supposed "forgotten sins." These were nighttime anxiety attacks. He even had nightmares of the Devil dragging him down into hell. These visions prompted him all the more to spend as much as six hours a day in confession. He was never persuaded that he had repented enough, so he never experienced security with God or stopped dreading the fires of hell.

To believe that depression is evidence of sin is to create a classic double bind for believers. Pretending that all is well in order to avoid public stigma only allows the problem to worsen. But openly admitting to depression and seeking help invites suspicion and condemnation. Bad news either way. And that's the problem with this stereotype; it interprets our alarm system as something sinister rather than as something good and necessary for our emotional restoration.

THE STEREOTYPE OF DEPRESSION AS LACK OF FAITH

The belief that depression represents inadequate faith and the failure to trust God is related to the stereotype of depression as sin. It argues that God is sufficient to meet every circumstance of life (true), but assumes that happiness is the necessary evidence of our faith (false). Therefore, the presence of depression means that we're not trusting Him enough. This view minimizes or ignores the emotional effects of the painful circumstances of life in a fallen world—circumstances such as interpersonal misunderstandings—childhood traumas like abuse, neglect or significant loss—adult traumas like rape, divorce and many other circumstances. It also fails to account for the overwhelming nature of "cluster stress"—several stressors taxing our coping system at the same time, any one of which could push us to the breaking point. If you lose your job, encounter marital problems and suffer the loss of a parent all within a short time, your coping skills can prove inadequate to the task and you will lapse into depression.

That doesn't mean, however, that a lack of faith in God's ability or desire to intervene in some way can't trigger depression. It can—if for no other reason than to add to the burden of helpless-ness. But to assume that depression is automatically an expression of faithlessness leads to a lot of false guilt about our emotional responses to traumas—many over which we have no control.

Yet in spite of these considerations, someone who equates depression with weak faith sees no reason for a Christian with strong faith ever to be depressed. Belief in God's promises is assumed to be the sole source of power for strength and coping. The problem is that it reduces every human experience to spiritual explanations, a position that defies the multi-layered nature of the divine image. We call this position "Christian reductionism." It rarely does justice to the complicated character of depression and, frankly, it's out of step with biblical teaching.

In Scripture, time after time, God responded to depression not by reproaching His servants for lack of faith but by bring-ing His compassion to bear on their struggles. He provided new perspectives and timely strategies for change that helped them resolve their dilemmas and encouraged them in their walk with Him. That's because *something other than their trust in God* was the problem.

The prophet Samuel despaired because the Israelites wanted a king and he interpreted their demand as a personal rebuke of his ministry. God reminded him not to take it personally. He wasn't confronting sin in Samuel, but correcting a misunderstanding. In the New Testament, we read that God eased the apostle Paul's distress in one of his darkest times. "For even when we came into Macedonia our flesh had no rest, but we were afflicted on every side: conflicts without, fears within. But God, who comforts the depressed, comforted us by the coming of Titus" (2 Cor. 7:5-6). The problem was one of insufficient respite from affliction, not of insufficient trust in God.

How many times has God sent a Titus to comfort you, some-one who ministered to you in your darkest hour? Time and again, God's gentle touch is evident in His covenant of intimacy with us—especially in our episodes of depression. God, in His mercy, remains forever vigilant to the adversities we encounter and always stands ready to grow us through our experience of them. What a contrast with our own tendency of being judgmental toward others and shooting our wounded in the church.

Author Philip Yancey once described an elderly man who had spent his life pursuing godly character—reading the Bible, praying, devoting himself to his family and others. But when he lost his wife, whose faithful companionship had been life-giving, his behavior changed. Speaking of this change in his grandfather's state, his grandson observed, "Since the death of his wife, he has lived alone in a state of near paranoia, anxious about heating bills and lights left on—when I look at him...I don't see a joyful saint in communion with God—I see a tired, lonely old man just sitting around waiting to go to heaven."[1] This grandson's harsh judgment implied criticism that, for all his grandfather's pursuit of godliness, there was little evidence of it in his final days. What this grandson failed to acknowledge was that profound depression was his grandfather's grief reaction to his life's greatest loss. His apparent inability to cope with a loss of such magnitude bore no reflection on his faith in God. More than anything, this man needed a Titus to comfort him and renew his sense of meaning.

Those of us who object to the stereotype of depression as a lack of faith are sometimes accused of psychologizing away the importance of the spiritual life. On the contrary, we do *not* dismiss spiritual problems in depression. But limiting causal explanations to matters of faith alone ignores what years of clinical experience and biblical study have taught us. Scripture reveals a God whose response to our emotional conflicts—though sometimes paradoxical and sometimes confrontational—is always tender and compassionate and always effective. Above all, He knows that depression occurs because our alarm systems are working according to His design.

In rebuttal, you might cite the fact that the Bible teaches we should take joy in our trials and tribulations (e.g., James 1: 2-3). But, if you look closely, James is speaking about our response to what God is doing to strengthen our ability to endure tough times, not about enjoying the circumstances themselves. We are not asked to become masochistic, cheering every occasion when financial setbacks, assaults by others, accidents or physical disease may occur. Instead, we are to take heart in the fact that God can and will use these painful experiences to make us more like Christ.

> **As Christians, we're not merely in the business of informing minds. We're in the business of changing hearts.**

If the church is to be a healing community, Christians must be honest with themselves and each other about their emotional experience. As Christians, we're not merely in the business of informing minds. We're in the business of changing hearts. Our preaching and the values we live out must be relevant to people's pain.

THE STEREOTYPE OF DEPRESSION AS GOD'S PUNISHMENT

The third stereotype of depression is a grotesque example of the ability to turn truth into a lie. It's based on the idea that since God is our judge, our depression must represent His judgment. Our depression becomes the personal price we pay for displeasing God. This view differs from the others in that depression is not the display of sin or the proof of inadequate faith, but the penalty itself. This view fits with the concept of God as a feared dictator. It produces a Christian who is always looking over his shoulder for some visitation of divine wrath—perhaps a personal loss or physical illness. Repentance is accompanied by dread of retribution, not the freeing anticipation of forgiveness.

This view of depression is damaging—it breeds fear in people who are pessimistic to begin with. With this twisted logic any self-destructive act, including self-mutilation and suicide, could be justified in the sufferer's mind as carrying out God's judgment. One middle-aged woman who had been hospitalized over the years many times for self-inflicted injury revealed, "I only feel good when I am cutting. I'm not worth anything anyway. Besides, I deserve to be punished and God is pleased when I am. Why should He want me to be happy? All I have done is let Him down a million times." These thought patterns are difficult to break. A person's fear-based beliefs about God are similar to a child's expectations of an abusive father. God becomes someone not to love but to avoid or to placate.

Yet we read in 1 John 4:18 that "perfect love drives out fear, *because fear has to do with punishment"*(NIV, italics added). By "punishment," John meant the eternal punishment of unbelievers, not the discipline of believers. Discipline involves fatherly lessons for our good. In contrast, punishment is meted out as the consequences of the sin of one who refuses

> **The Bible says *God is teaching His children to love Him, not to dread Him.***

God's forgiveness. The Bible says *God is teaching His children to love Him, not to dread Him.* He sometimes teaches us through adversity, but then adversity is transformed into a good tool to a loving end, not a retributive end in itself.

Believers who already hate themselves accept this stereotype, understanding their depression not as an alarm system but as a "deserved" instrument of wrath. They deflect the solace of others and the grace of God as carrots meant for the spiritually acceptable. They however, should only get the stick. God becomes the avenging enforcer, not the protective Good Shepherd.

It's difficult for such people to accept God's affirmation of their worth. But challenge them, we must. That's why author Henri Nouwen dared them to, "change from living life as a painful task to prove that you deserve to be loved to living it as an unceasing 'yes' to the truth of that belovedness."[2] He refers to God as "a lover who wants to be loved."[3] As bearers of His image, we too, are meant to be lovers in search of someone to love. This is the reason for our existence, the point of our creation.

But self-hatred sabotages our quest for love, poisoning our relationships in multiple directions. In our anger for feeling badly about ourselves, we may punish others—especially those closest to us. We may even blame them. Most people however, do not understand how despair drives this pattern.

Years of profound depression were evident in Edith, a Christian who sat limply in her chair. Her controlling husband, Dan, directed every activity in the home, punishing Edith with silence if she tried to help. She spent most of her time in bed, unable to take a shower or even get dressed. Dan had tried many times to get her out of the house but to no avail.

One day she came alone to her counseling appointment, smiling and energetic. I had noted the remarkable change in her behavior and asked her what had happened. She replied, "My husband is sick and is flat on his back in bed. And he hardly ever gets sick. So, I had no choice—I had to get up and get going. By the way, I've got a thousand errands to do, so I need to leave a little early!" By the next session a month later, Dan had recovered and Edith had relapsed. It turned out that she was outraged at Dan's control but felt helpless to do anything about it. To a large extent, she retaliated by sabotaging his efforts to cheer her up and by using her depression to avoid sex with him. Only when he was down did she allow herself a normal life.

Punishment can cut both ways. When we mislabel depression as God's punishment, we open Pandora's box and every relationship can become punitive—all because we're so good at punishing ourselves.

THE STEREOTYPE OF DEPRESSION AS DEMON POSSESSION

One of the most controversial stereotypes of depression is the notion that it's the result of demonic possession or at least oppression. This stereotype assumes that satanic influence invades by way of weaknesses in our character, slowly and subtly destroying our spiritual health. Like previous stereotypes, this one also views psychological issues as only a spiritual problem. In this case, the problem is demonic activity and the best treatment for depression is some form of exorcism.

Whole orders of Christian clergy have been devoted to the task of exorcism. Treatments were sometimes harsh, even fatal, designed to make the body unfit for an evil spirit. Today, exorcism techniques are far more humane, tied to rituals and prayers. Studies have shown, nonetheless, that many such people have seen their depression return weeks or months later, sometimes with greater severity. Several Hollywood films have raised both fear and curiosity about the paranormal, spurring a fascination with demon activity.

Few Christians would deny that demon possession can occur, although the community is divided over whether it can happen to a Christian. Instances of demon possession are well-documented in the Bible, throughout history and today, especially in cultures where the practice of the occult arts is popular. While we're not sure how prevalent true demonism is in American culture, we see an alarming increase in evil practices in general and the number of satanic cults and occult practices in particular.

By challenging the demon possession concept of depression, we're in no way questioning the reality of Satan and his dominion over the world. He exerts a powerful influence and we must guard against him. Even our Lord, before beginning His earthly ministry, had to defeat satanic power on the battleground of His own humanity. But the Bible makes one point clear: Satanic power at its pinnacle of strength is but a sputtering candle flame that God can puff out with His slightest breath.

When Jesus came into the world as the light of life, He faced accelerated demonic activity. We know, likewise, that the Christian message will not go supernaturally unopposed today. But we must be careful about labeling a specific emotional struggle as a case of demon possession, an accusation that can only further defeat the despairing. In a case widely reported several years ago, a woman was told by her therapist that her depression was the result of demonic activity and that her parents had, in all likelihood, subjected her to a satanic cult when she was a child. The result? She alienated her parents and divorced her husband. By the time she discovered that none of this was true, it was too late. She sued her counselor, though her court victory could never recoup her relational losses.

It's risky business to brand an emotional alarm system intended for a person's benefit, as the work of an evil spirit. At the very least, before making judgments of this sort, we must review pertinent Scriptures. The New Testament, for instance, describes three major characteristics of demon-possessed behavior that are relevant to our discussion. First, the behavior was violent and aggressive. Second, the evil spirits acknowledged Christ's divinity—they knew they were subordinate to His power (e.g. Matt. 8:28; Mark 1:23-26; Luke 4:41). And third, demon possession always incorporated common physical and psychological symptoms—like blindness, inability to speak, uncontrolled violence toward self or others and convulsive attacks—but these same symptoms were also documented in cases that did *not* involve demon possession (e.g. Matt. 4:24). If the Gospels make these distinctions, then we should do so as well.

It is interesting to note that all of these accounts in the New Testament occurred during a time of scientific awakening in the ancient world. The Jews had in fact become quite sophisticated in their thinking about mental illness as a result of their contacts with Babylon, Greece and Rome. They cultivated philosophy, law and medicine, accounting for the large number of physicians practicing among them (e.g. Mark 5:26). Luke, one of the Gospel writers, was himself a physician of note and would have been well aware of the recognized differences between demon possession and mental disorders.

While depression might accompany some genuine cases of demon possession, it does not follow that depression is itself an expression of demon possession. The biblical and psychological evidence speaks to the contrary. Those who stigmatize depression as demonic activity have caused much heartache among hurting people who can conceive of few things worse than falling prey to the forces of evil.

We are, by design, psychological as well as spiritual beings. One dimension can affect the other, but that doesn't allow us to interchange them in our causal explanations. Doing that only blurs the differences we need to understand in order to effectively treat depression.

FINDING HOPE

1. While religious platitudes create a caricature of love and truth, *addressing one another's emotional struggles* without the prejudice of an artificial religious formula *reflects both biblical principle and sound psychological practice.*

2. Depression is not sin, but can be the *emotional consequence* of sin. Yet it can also come from *many other causes* that have nothing to do with a depressed person's sin.

3. In Scripture, we read that *God responded to depression,* not with rebuke for lack of faith, but *with compassion, instruction and grace-filled intervention.*

4. *Good things,* like encountering a "Titus" in your life, *can come from difficult events.* It is in this context that *your pain can be an occasion for lasting gratitude.*

5. God is in the business of *teaching us to love Him,* not to dread Him or resent Him. *God is a lover who forever delights in your love.*

6. *Satanic power,* at its pinnacle of strength, is *still far weaker than God's* power in its most minimal demonstration.

THE GOD WHO DEFIES STEREOTYPING

When can I go and meet with God?
My tears have been my food day and night...
Put your hope in God, for I will yet praise him,
my Savior and my God.

—PSALM 42:2B-3A, 5B. NIV—

O ver the course of history, many religious movements have aimed at controlling our natural appetite for evil. The monastic movement attempts to curb our excesses in mind and body by exercises in "purity," practice in meditation and engagement in self-restraint. But discipline alone has never been successful in conquering these appetites. At best, we deceive ourselves into *thinking* we've achieved righteousness, much as the rich young ruler's legalistic zeal concealed, even from himself, his secret love of wealth (Matt. 19:16-22).

Most people simply do not want to hear that they are by nature, imprisoned by their own sin. They want to believe that man is essentially good and that peace—personal and global—can be achieved by collective determination. Their repeated failure to accomplish these things on their own however, has led to despair and disillusionment. But God has a better way. The way of His love. It is the freedom we have through His grace. Best of all, it allows us to acknowledge our sin without feeling hopeless. This life of humility is the most effective antidote to the impoverishment at the core of our misplaced utopian ideas.

Changing belief systems always creates a crisis—whether at the level of the culture or in the life of the individual or in both.

As troubling as this crisis might seem, in God's hand it can be the doorway to the unchanging truth that liberates our thinking. The life of personal healing and growth involves many such crises, opening many such doors. We'll never live perfectly or attain complete understanding this side of heaven. After all, we are human. That's why our spiritual maturity is measured not by knowledge alone but by the strength of our faith. God desires our wholeness rather than demanding our perfection. And it is the quality of our connection with Him and with one another that determines that wholeness.

AUTHENTICITY: A GIFT BELIEVERS RESIST

"Know thyself" is one of the oldest principles of life. It is also part of God's design. Perhaps that's the reason we have a natural curiosity to discover why we do what we do. But scientific interest and personal insight are two different things. While the former is stimulating, the latter can at times be threatening. Yet living in denial carries a heavy price—including inability to learn from our mistakes, insensitivity to others without knowing why we injure them, damage to our view of God, our world and ourselves and loneliness and depression. Nonetheless, we persist in denial thinking it's much safer that way.

The healthy alternative—*authenticity* in our relationships to self and others—will change our thinking about the past, our experience of the present and our expectations for the future. Authenticity involves honest self-examination. It becomes godly when it means examining our pain through our Lord's redemptive lens and revealing ways to avoid compounding it. Authenticity invites good theology to drive our experience rather than letting experience determine our theology. Whenever we allow denial to distort either, the likelihood of depression increases.

Christians have their own 'sanctified' forms of dishonesty.

Christians have their own "sanctified" forms of dishonesty. When we attempt to help the despairing with well-intended but pointless spiritual platitudes, we make things worse. Our denial keeps us uncomfortable around those who are struggling, so we try our best to spiritualize their depression away. (Notice how it becomes more about our discomfort than about their pain.) Little wonder we are not helpful. Here's one pastor's testimony from his depression experience:

> *"I'll never forget the well-meaning but painful platitudes offered by uninformed friends during those gloomiest days of depression...but those 'platitudes' always hurt much more than they helped. In fact, they* never *helped! So I apologize to anyone who is shaken by the assertion that God might want to use things as painful as depression to do good or that depression could be a 'companion' that enriches or helps us in any way."*[1]

This pastor had possessed a forceful personality that intimidated some people, but he became softer, more humble and more approachable after his depression. He identified this newfound empathy as God's gift to him and to his church. "Depression has often been the only thing," he said, "that could pin my nose to the carpet in search of the Lord's feet."[2]

The tipping point for almost every imbalance is found in how we see ourselves. Inside, we feel worthless and inadequate. Weaklings who can't resist temptation. Damaged goods. Failures God could never use.

Publicly we wear a protective disguise. We ourselves may even come to believe the false face we've assumed. Our dishonesty leads us not to healing but to despair. What's more, our misconceptions of God and our stereotypes of depression keep both the hurting individual and the Christian community from discovering what is healing.

In the last chapter, we looked at a few of these misperceptions of the way God deals with depression. They all involved denial and inauthenticity in some form or another. We've examined the counterfeits—now let's take a good look at the real thing. Once we understand God's perspective, we can devise better strategies for changing our own.

In order to get a better picture of how God works in our down times, it's useful to introduce the conditions under which His servants in the Bible walked through episodes of depression. Prophets, judges, kings and commoners, all of them served God in extraordinary ways—sometimes changing the course of history to enact God's redemptive purpose. Yet they did these things in spite of—sometimes *because of*—their depression. Some suffered turmoil because of self-injury through sin—others suffered despite their righteousness. Still, the common theme was the important role their depression played in highlighting something God wanted to teach them or the people they served.

When we stare into the mirror of Scripture, we find a familiar face. But we're also startled to find there a radically different outcome, one that forces us to rethink our choices—to realize that there's a different way to live.

WHEN DISOBEDIENCE GETS YOU DOWN

We may think we're too broken to find our way back or too lost to ever serve God again. Likewise, we may read the Bible and tell ourselves that we are too destitute, that we sin far too much to ever aspire to do great things for our Lord. As a result, many of us give up and withdraw into mediocrity.

But what made the Bible heroes heroic? Did they have unusual strength to resist temptation and sin? Let's examine the record and see.

First, we might cast a glance at the father of the Israelites, the enigmatic Abraham. Twice he lied about his marriage to his wife, Sarah, so that pagan leaders wouldn't kill him in their lust for her (see Gen. 12:10-20; Gen. 20). It was God, not Abraham, who protected Sarah from these men. How would you wives feel if your husbands shoved you in front of them to protect themselves from a potential assailant, shouting, "Here, take her, she's not my wife"? I don't think you would feel very safe with your husband. Most likely you would be livid with him. So Abraham didn't exactly burnish his image with that gambit. Later on, we find him discouraged by the infighting in his own home. Not wanting to hear any more complaints, he gave Sarah carte blanche to do what she wanted to defend herself against the attacks of Hagar, his proxy wife. Anything to quiet her. Of course, that made things worse, compounding Abraham's problems.

Then there was his son Isaac who, like his father, lied about his marriage to protect his own skin in fear of the Philistine king Abimelech (see Gen. 26:1-11). The apple did not fall far from the tree. And because of his dysfunctional parenting, Isaac encountered the depressing reality that his beloved son, Esau, was cheated not once, but twice out of the family inheritance by his other son, Jacob (see Gen. 25:29-34; 27:1-40). Not surprisingly, Jacob incurred the wrath of his brother, who threatened to kill him, forcing him to flee the family (see Gen. 27:41-45). Sadly, everyone lost. It's ironic that Jacob, later in his life, suffered the loss of his own son, Joseph, when his jealous brothers sold the young boy to traders (see Gen. 37). The sins of our fathers do indeed reach across generations.

Centuries later, despite the privileges of the royal court, Moses became a murderer and an exile (see Exod. 2:11-15). When God commanded him to deliver His people from slavery in Egypt, Moses used every possible excuse to avoid obedience (see Exod. 3–4). And as Israel's leader, he struggled to set proper boundaries, became overextended and, in moments of despair, accused God of retribution against him (see Num. 11).

Then there was Samson, a judge of Israel, with his own checkered history. He made special vows of separation unto God and then proceeded to violate every stipulation of these vows (see Judges 13–16). He violated God's prohibition against marrying women from the idolatrous nations neighboring Israel. He was promiscuous, even taking up with at least one prostitute. It was with Delilah that his sin caught up with him, landing him in the depressing confines of a Philistine prison (see Judges 16:1-22). Yet despite the fact that Samson sinned often, God used his gift of unusual strength to protect His people from the oppressive Philistines (see Judges 16:23-31).

And, of course, there was Rahab, who was even granted a privileged role in the lineage of Christ and yet she was a harlot in Jericho, regarded as an occupation of disgrace (see Josh. 2; 6:25).

Perhaps, most famous of all was King David's sexual encounter with Bathsheba, a married woman (see 2 Sam. 11). He proceeded to compound his sin by having her husband, Uriah, murdered in an attempt to cover up his adultery. It was a terrible moment David had to live with for the rest of his life. Indeed, this reflected later in his readiness to accept another's cursing as a sign of God's judgment (see 2 Sam.16:5-12). The cracks in David's character were seen too, in his responsibilities as a father, raising sons so out of control that they committed rape, murder and treason (see 2 Sam. 13–15). Still, God's inspired Word describes David as a *man after God's own heart* (see 1 Sam. 13:14, italics added). In fact, God established the Davidic throne forever among His people and designated David's ancestral line to produce the coming Messiah (see 2 Sam. 7:11-16; Luke 20:41-44).

Though incomplete, we have a sufficient sample of flawed, sinful men and women whom God nevertheless loved and used to accomplish great things for the Kingdom. The Bible even says that, *"the world was not worthy of them"* (see Heb. 11:17-40, NIV, italics mine). Imagine that! These servants of God did things most of us would regard as reprehensible. It's doubtful that with their backgrounds, any of them would have even qualified to become an elder or deacon in our churches today. Yet God didn't consider them beyond His forgiveness and restoration. Rather, He gave them the highest accolades and we call them *heroes of the faith!*

If they were so considered by God, then perhaps we can see that, despite our own frailties and flaws, we are also honored by God if we have faith in Him. We as well, are invited to become heroes of the faith. God presents the major players in redemptive history that we might understand it is not our sin that defines us. Rather, it is His love and His power through our faith.

DOWN EVEN WHEN DOING RIGHT

Just as we find encouragement from those whose battle with sin has been overcome by faith, we also find an uplifting message in those who struggle with circumstances not of their own making. Let's look at some of these.

We all know that life can be cruel at times. And no circumstances seem crueler than what happened to Naomi as recorded in the book of Ruth. Due to a drought in Judah, Naomi and her family moved to the land of Moab. There she endured the tragic deaths of her husband and both of her sons. In her deep grief, she wept as she bid good-bye to her daughters-in-law, telling them to "Return, my daughters! Go, for I am too old to have a husband" (Ruth 1:12). Her crushing losses left her alone—but God in His mercy placed in Ruth's heart the desire to go back to Judah with Naomi so that she might serve Naomi and dispel her loneliness.

In another narrative, we find the story of Hannah who, like Sarah before her, could not bear a child—humiliating for a woman in her time (see 1 Samuel 1). For a long time, Hannah wept and even refused to eat. But in the midst of her depression, she cried out to God, making a vow that, if she were given a child, she would dedicate him to God's service. God granted her petition through the word of Eli, the priest, after which her depression lifted. "Then the woman went to her quarters, ate and drank with her husband and her countenance was sad no longer" (1 Sam. 1:18, NRSV). That child's name was Samuel.

We know of Samuel in his later years, who though faithful in his mission, was devastated by his people's rejection of God's rule (see 1 Sam. 8:5). But such rejection was recorded as well in the New Testament, where we read that the apostle Paul also struggled against opposition. "We are under great pressure," he said, *"far beyond our ability to endure, so that we despaired even of life"* (2 Cor. 1:8, NIV, italics added). Whatever these hardships were at the time, he appears to have suffered physically and psychologically. But God, the "Father of compassion," comforted him in his depression, an experience that enabled him to comfort others in their trials (see 2 Cor. 1:3-4, NIV).

Most of the Old Testament prophets suffered similar episodes of depression. For they felt the weight of their messages of condemnation, even as their fellow countrymen continued to resist God's call to repentance. Men like Amos, a shepherd from Tekoa, Ezekiel and Jeremiah, both of whom were priests, were called away from their own vocations to address the crisis of their nation's sin. Though they did so with heavy hearts, God never failed to console them with the truth of His righteousness. But they kept on preaching with the knowledge of God's good purpose on their side.

Again, there was David: Icon, warrior, musician and composer. His poetic descriptions of depression are exquisite in their detail (see Ps. 22, 42, 130).

His episodic despair was most often prompted by his weariness of fighting a never-ending parade of enemies. "For dogs are all around me," he cried, "a company of evildoers encircles me" (Ps. 22:16, NRSV). Yet he spoke of God's faithfulness: "For he did not despise or abhor the affliction of the afflicted—he did not hide his face from me, but heard when I cried to him" (Ps. 22:24, NRSV).

We cannot conclude this discussion without mentioning Job, whose experience of depression we will discuss in greater detail in the next chapter. For now, it's enough to point out that here was a man who had, by all accounts, lived a laudable life. Yet when adversity struck, he disintegrated to the point of wishing death. Was that because he was a spiritual fraud? No. Rather, he was a follower of God caught up in the disastrous events that can happen in a person's life. He was also a man who was open to learning new things and indeed, with God's help, he did.

Though this is but a small sample, we can see that Scripture provides ample evidence of God's understanding that even when we are doing things right, we cannot avoid the occasional struggle with depression. Knowing this gives us courage to confront the issues that may have paralyzed us. By encouraging others to do the same, we make our victories contagious to the Body of believers. This is, in its deepest sense, what it means to love one another.

> ...Scripture provides ample evidence...that, even when we are doing things right, we cannot avoid the occasional struggle with depression.

To know God's heart, we must allow Him to transform our cheerless expectations into joyful anticipation of His goodness. Never does He condemn or scold us for being depressed. In every instance we see Him as wise and gentle, what we would expect of the Wonderful Counselor He is (see Isa. 9:6).

CHANGED LIVES CHANGE MINDS

A skilled counselor will always respect his client's faith. It's his professional and ethical responsibility. But a Christian counselor can take it one step further. As a fellow believer, he integrates his therapeutic work with matters of faith so that clients can more clearly understand how their spiritual life is connected to their emotional life. Far from "leading them astray," the Christian counselor is interested in helping clients value even more the relevancy of faith to everyday life.

It's with sadness then, that we encounter opposition in the church. Many assume that the humanistic arguments of some outspoken secular psychologists speak for the entire field of psychotherapy—and that Christian clinicians draw from the same well of metaphysical ideas. The real losers in this tug of war are our hurting brethren—God's own children—who need the help that Christian therapists can give them.

A surprising number of our clients are pastors who once regarded and taught that psychology was a tool of the devil. But the actual experience of deep depression often changes these opinions. When a pastor finds relief from psychotherapy or medication, (or both), he discovers that God has worked through a trained fellow believer to help strengthen his faith. Listen to the comments of one pastor:

> *Some pastors struggle with the appropriateness of receiving help that isn't exclusively theological or specifically Scriptural in approach. Others are so used to being the ones giving help that they find it difficult to receive any. And of course, some question the ministry of Christian therapy altogether. I was a member of the second and third groups, especially the third. "The Scriptures are my therapist," I would say, "and they don't charge me a hundred dollars per hour for the service."*
>
> *Certainly the Bible contributed much to my recovery. Its comforts were amazing. Its instructions of insight incredible. But being forced by my circumstances to ask for help from an able counselor changed my entire outlook. Without that wonderful man's prayer, honest questioning and practical help, I don't know how long it would have taken me to heal or if I ever would have. I continue to find strength and guidance from the Word of God but in it I read about the importance of Christian community in discerning the deep things of the Spirit. In my experience with depression, the Bible was good, even excellent. But it was the Bible in partnership with a gifted, discerning therapist that God used to loosen me from the hands of this unrelenting monster called "depression."*[3]

Since God created the emotional as well as the spiritual dimension in man, it's no surprise that He speaks to us through both. God's tenderness toward us when we're in pain teaches us this principle.

Years ago, a pastor experienced depression that rendered him unable to get out of bed and preach on Sunday mornings. The congregation was told that he was "sick." After receiving urgent professional care, one Sunday morning the pastor revealed the nature of his problems and apologized for his misguided preaching against psychotherapy and his depression-as-sin dogma. He acknowledged that he may have discouraged some from seeking professional help, causing needless suffering.

The Christian community is called to lead dying hearts to living intimacy with God. That means that we must be honest about our pain and willing to engage in open dialogue that can bring healing to the Church. The Bible's honesty about the struggles of God's servants testifies to His high regard for authenticity. As we have seen, He can accomplish great things as easily through our weaknesses as through our strengths. From the wellsprings of His love, God transforms broken lives into whole people eager to serve Him.

ADVERSITY: A NEW OPPORTUNITY

By now, you know that depression is not a monopoly of the unfaithful or disobedient. But even though many of life's hardships don't stem from spiritual causes, we know, nonetheless, that God can still use them for spiritual purposes. You may remember Corrie ten Boom's cruel imprisonment in a Nazi concentration camp. She saw it as an opportunity to see God at work and as an occasion for her to serve God by ministering to others. Because of her confidence that a purpose was being served in her suffering, her life remained meaningful and she experienced a quiet inner contentment that seemed strange to those around her. Yes, she walked the valleys of depression—the inevitable human response to such horrific circumstances—but she didn't give up. Instead, she developed new coping skills and continued to make a difference among her fellow death camp inmates.

Many believers find such joy and contentment elusive. But that doesn't mean it's not available. Life may deal its depressing blows, but we lose sight of our destiny because of all the added emotional baggage we bring into every situation. We are too busy questioning God's plan—maybe even questioning our salvation—to enjoy what He has given us. Instead of asking what we can learn on the journey, we react with the disillusionment of a cheated tourist.

In Ecclesiastes 3:1-11, we read that the bad times, like the good, are seasons that shall pass. They may seem endless, but with purpose and God's provision, we can endure them to their conclusion. The writer of Ecclesiastes reveals a world view that sees beyond our horizon through lenses of hope and wisdom. As Ecclesiastes puts it, those who follow Him are in the hand of God (see Eccles. 9:1). What better place to be when earthly life seems so cruel and unfair! No matter how bleak things may look, the end game remains the same: God's goodness and justice will prevail.

When depression strikes, we may not find all of our questions answered. But wisdom gives us the advantage of living more comfortably with paradox and mystery. Life can be so complex that we can't understand every circumstance or avoid every pitfall. But this need not distract us from the reality that God is in charge. Strengthening our intimate confidence in Him means establishing a secure beachhead against emotional paralysis. That's why we must have the wisdom to know the difference between what we can change and what we must accept.

God offers this wisdom to every believer for the asking (Jas. 1:5). But wisdom means change in our thinking and behavior, which at first may be difficult. This difficulty can be eased, however, if a therapist works in collaboration with a pastor where together they can provide an effective combination of strengths to help burdened people heal. But both the pastor and the psychologist must value the collaborative effort.

A client asked her pastor to work with me to help her through her depression. To her surprise, he declined. He doubted that such consultation would be of much value. Disappointed at first, she knew she needed more than her church's counseling, so she pressed on. She achieved success in therapy, in part by recognizing how her rigid ideas about spiritual things was getting in the way of identifying the issues causing her depression. It's a pity that her pastor missed out on the joy of seeing how her unfolding freedom contributed to the reemergence of optimism in her faith.

THE WISDOM OF LOVE

Several years ago, I spoke with a friend who had taken his nine year-old son deep-sea fishing. A violent storm developed on the open sea. Huge whitecaps crashed over the bow of the boat, rocking it viciously. When the father saw his boy throwing up and reduced to dry heaves, he implored the captain to turn back. Once in port, he helped his son out of the boat and onto the dock where the boy laid down, unable to walk. The father bent down and began stroking his stricken son. Then the young boy looked up, managed a weak grin and blurted out, "Wasn't that a great trip?"

Later, the boy recounted his experience to his family as a stirring, memorable adventure, not as a miserable disaster to be forgotten. Why? Because he prized every moment he spent with his father. And no mere circumstance could blur this reality. He even talked enthusiastically about going again!

When we experience the fulfillment of our deepest desires, it consumes us and sustains our focus in spite of our painful distractions. This is the kind of fulfillment the Bible means when it speaks of the abundant life. It's the uninterrupted time spent with our heavenly Father. Here we find wisdom, the secret of hope and peace in the midst of suffering.

The book of James speaks of this wisdom—not just knowledge, but also a transformation that the world can't explain (see Jas. 1:2-5; 2:14-18; 3:13, 18; 4:4-6; 5:17-18). It means accepting difficulties that the Holy Spirit can use to shape our character, finding purpose in the synergy of faith and adversity and working out our faith in service to others who need our help. But this involves a personal investment in our belief. Although it's possible to believe in something you don't have much commitment to, it's not possible to be committed to something you don't really believe in. That's why James speaks of serving widows and orphans as the natural and necessary outworking of true faith.

So we come full circle. Responding to the alarm system of depression, we seek professional help and pastoral care. We experience psychological and spiritual growth. We discover wisdom and richness in intimacy with God. And our deepening intimacy with Him stirs us to share hope and vision with others who are depressed—one desert survivor showing another where to find the life-giving oasis. In these ways we authenticate our transformation.

> **We have a choice: To be hearers only, who forget and do not act—or to be doers who enact the unforgettable.**

At last, we've established a virtuous cycle to replace the vicious cycles—an elegant, pragmatic pattern of Christian witness and multiplication—freely offered to a world helpless to provide its own meaning to pain.

James invites us to be *doers* of the Word and not merely hearers (see Jas. 1:22-25). Intimacy with God is active, not passive. Real faith is demonstrated in real works (see Jas. 2:18). We have a choice: To be hearers only, who forget and do not act—or to be doers who enact the unforgettable. Healing from depression is the destiny of doers. What's more, "they will be blessed in their doing" (Jas. 1:25, NRSV).

AN ABNORMAL LOVE

Few of us connect love and suffering because few of us experience loving feelings while we are suffering. Yet implicit in genuine love is the risk of suffering. God made Himself vulnerable to this risk when He created man.

Jesus' love and mercy for us led to the cross. Our invitation to His eternal wedding banquet is printed in His blood. What other evidence do we need to know that His goodness and compassion are real?

So why do people resist this invitation to love? Inside, they believe that something is wrong with who they are—their shame prevents the vulnerability of self-revelation.

In the Sermon on the Mount, Jesus invited us to place our trust in a love that prompts behavior that runs counter to everything we've learned. Who in his right mind would turn his cheek for a second slap? Or respond to coercion by walking twice as far? Or give everything to someone taking him to court? Or loan without promise of repayment? Or, most bizarre of all, lay down his life for someone who hates him (see Matt. 5:38-48)? Picture today's fanatical, genocidal terrorists who would murder someone you love. Would you love them in return? Yet these are the things our Lord did (see Matt. 26:36-27:56). He stood on the Mount of Olives on that Sunday before His crucifixion, looking across the Kidron Valley to Mount Zion on which stood Jerusalem and the magnificent Temple complex glinting in the sun, a city filled with scribes and Pharisees who hated Him and were plotting to kill Him. And what did He do? He wept for the lost souls of His beloved Jerusalem!

He did what we find impossible. He fulfilled every admonition He gave in that memorable Sermon, the ones that seemed absurd to His audience. He was beaten but didn't fight back. He was accused in court without defending Himself. He carried the cross that was forced upon Him. He allowed His clothes to be taken and distributed among the soldiers, even when He could have stepped down off the cross to reclaim them. And He died because He loved His persecutors (see 1 Pet. 2:23-24).

Crazy, right? Only from our human perspective. On our own, we could never imagine loving like that. But because God does love that way, we can receive healing for our wounds. But we must trust Him enough to open our wounds to His inspection. And we must allow His appointed doctors of the soul to nurture us back to spiritual and emotional health.

Jesus came to heal the sick, not to congratulate the self-righteous. He responds to those who know they need Him, not to those who want Him to need them. What better Counselor do we have to entrust with our pain, to welcome into our lives healers of the mind that He has commissioned for His service?

FINDING HOPE

1. Depression can help you *become gentler, more humble and more empathic,* which in turn, can make you *more approachable to others.*

2. In biblical history, *God did great things through His servants*—sometimes in spite of and sometimes *because of—their depression.*

3. The fact that God uses flawed people to accomplish His purposes demonstrates how *each of you are defined not by your sin but by His love and power, through your faith.*

4. Because depression occurred among God's most trusted servants, *you can know that depression is no respecter of persons.* Indeed, it is in *periods of depression that God sometimes most powerfully manifests His wisdom.*

5. *The advantage of living with God is to more comfortably live with paradox and mystery.* It's characteristic of the abundant life.

6. *We have a choice:* To be hearers only, who forget and do not act—or *to be doers who enact the unforgettable.*

UNFINISHED VIEWS OF GOD

No nation, no people has ever risen above its religion and no religion has ever risen above its concept of God.

—A. W. TOZER—

"I feel all alone in the universe," she wrote, reflecting our last session. "If only I could just lie down on the wind and let it bear me up and away just to let go and stop trying to understand the mind of God. How do people find belief when nothing makes sense?" Her words were tense and her mood anxious. There was a pause as if she were studying my face for some kind of reaction. She continued, "I feel like a kid with my nose pressed against the glass. The people I see on the other side struggle over the details but they always have their faith as a firm foundation in the darkest time." Tears were beginning to fill the pages now. With tight pen strokes she blurted, "I seem to be spinning through space unable to hold on to a sense of meaning and purpose and yet I do believe that there is Someone in charge." And then after another, still more pensive reflection, she added, "Maybe the longing to just be held and loved is at bottom a sign of the depression I'm experiencing as the healing process continues."

This lovely divorced woman wanted nothing more than to be important to someone else. She couldn't let go of her belief that God was out there someplace giving comfort and meaning, at least to others. But she couldn't apply this truth to her life. In the midst of her agonizing conflict, she ached for someone to see her pain, to respond with a little nurture. Her despair had not only driven her to the emotional edge, but also to a crisis of faith.

183

We might wonder what kind of God would have the idea of creating a person whose longings for intimacy could be so frustrated. A person whose soul is crafted for love, but whose life seems so empty of it. We find the answer to this question in God's response to Adam and Eve when they squandered their opportunity for companionship with Him. He did not revile them. Nor did he condemn them to their own endless futility. Instead, He wasted no time inaugurating a plan to redeem His most precious creation.

So, rather than wondering whether He cares, it might be better to ask, who is this God who would give man freedom and then pursue his heart after he had turned against Him? Why would He purpose to create human life with the capacity to reject Him and then enter the brutal world of human brokenness and suffering to set things right again?

This is the story of God's response to fallen man's struggle with his unrighteous character. There is a momentous beginning, a tragic middle and a glorious end to this story. While it has captured the imagination of people around the globe, it has also been reviled by many as threatening to their way of life, as a dangerous book that prompts reactionary thinking.

In truth, it is a simple love story. It reveals the force of God's grace and the final triumph of His love.

We are still in the middle part of this story, though we are drawing ever closer to its conclusion. In the meantime though, we must deal with life in the trenches. That's where faith always has its greatest impact.

We see this impact in the gripping accounts of men whose crises served as a backdrop for God's great lessons of living. We have alluded to some of them earlier, but now we turn to them in more detail to see what more we can learn.

SAUL: A LESSON FOR ALL SEASONS

While Saul was no hero of the faith, he was nevertheless Israel's first king who, by a predicament of his own making, fulfilled God's purpose in teaching his people the errors of their ways. It came about because the Israelite people demanded to have a warrior king "like all the other nations," a dramatic moment in their capitulation to pagan values (see 1 Sam. 8:4-5).

In a surprising move, God then instructed His servant, Samuel, to grant the people what they wanted. Saul was tall and muscular and a courageous warrior. In short, he was the popular image of the perfect king to protect them from their enemies. Like their pagan neighbors, they were persuaded by external appearances, something not unfamiliar to the television age today. But Saul was flawed as a king. His feelings of inadequacy clouded his judgment and perverted his behavior as he swung from intense fear and anger to depressed mood states in which he was incapable of any intelligent action (see 1 Sam. 16–18). About the only relief he found came from the music of the young man David, who played a stringed instrument for him to soothe his darkened spirit.

Driven by unrestrained jealousy over David's growing popularity, Saul turned against him. In his delusions of persecution, he saw David as a self-styled pretender to the throne and was convinced that David was trying to usurp his authority and take over the reins of power. As we have

> **He gave the Israelites what they wanted in order to teach them what they needed**

sometimes seen in ourselves, Saul personified in his behavior that moral contradiction in which people are drawn to a course of action that in their more sober thinking, they would otherwise recognize as self-destructive.

In the end, Saul's distraction compromised his military judgment and led him into a suicidal engagement with the Philistines that ended his life and left Israel once again helpless against her enemies. While the judges who preceded Saul had only to perform a single feat of military glory to fulfill the promise of leadership, as king, Saul was required to perform such feats continuously. He was always on stage. It was too much for his fragile state and forced him to exhibit the darkest element of his personality.

Why then, did God provide a king who was so long on appearances but so short on stability? The biblical story underlines God's intention: *He gave the Israelites what they wanted in order to teach them what they needed.*

Have you ever gained something you wanted only to discover that something else would have been much better for you? This is an important way that God teaches us His wisdom. This would be useful to think about the next time you are upset that God doesn't seem to be answering your prayers.

JONAH: WHAT WOULD OTHERS THINK?

Anger was no stranger to someone like Jonah. God had asked him to take the message of forgiveness to the people of the Assyrian capital of Nineveh. He refused the mission and in fact, tried to escape by boarding a ship sailing in the opposite direction. But God had other ideas. Through His unusual use of a large fish, He brought the unwilling Jonah to Nineveh to do His bidding. When Jonah began to preach, there was an awakening among the Ninevites such as had never been seen before. With great remorse, they repented of their sin and covered themselves with sackcloth and ashes. As a consequence, God withdrew the calamity that was about to befall them as judgment for their sin.

This outcome was what Jonah had feared all along would happen and it angered him. Why? Because the Assyrians were Israel's mortal enemy and nothing would have pleased Jonah more than to see them destroyed. But alas, that was not going to happen, at least not anytime soon.

Jonah became depressed because he had played a pivotal part in these events. He was convinced that this news would not play well back home. It appears that Jonah cared too much about what his fellow Israelites thought. Of course, he also wanted to indulge his own hatred of the Assyrian people. As a consequence, Jonah was willing to disobey God's command.

It might surprise you that God responded to Jonah's anger and depression with tolerance, not rebuke. Twice he asked Jonah if he had good reason to be angry and Jonah replied that he had. He then proceeded to win Jonah's heart by giving him the reason for His compassion and forgiveness of the Ninevites whom He described as blind to their sinful ways. Contrary to Jonah's heart, it was God's desire to forgive every contrite heart, whether Jew or Gentile, friend or foe. To withhold His mercy from a repentant sinner would have violated His loving character.

It's hard to confront our own pettiness. But that was what Jonah had to do. If God had allowed him to circumvent the chance for the Assyrians to repent, God would have proven Himself to be unworthy of worship. Even Jonah himself would have had a diminished view of Him.

Jonah demonstrated what happens when we compromise our virtue for the sake of the crowd. He showed us, too, how remorseless revenge can be. These are important lessons to learn if we wish to avoid traps that trigger depression.

JOB: THE ABUNDANT LIFE REVISITED

We bestow honor on those who serve as models of inspiration. But let them fall from their pedestal of success and we can be merciless in our criticism. This is what happened to Job. He had everything: wealth, social status, great family, strong faith and the good health to enjoy it all. His friends agreed that Job was blessed of God for living righteously before Him. All this changed when Job lost everything, including his health. When even his friends challenged the purity of his faith and the righteous character of his life, his spirit sank into the hopeless anguish of a broken heart.

It was in this depressed state that God met Job with compassion. He challenged him, enlarged his vision and restored his soul. Above all, he opened Job's eyes with such astounding self-disclosure that he was moved to declare God's goodness as never before. Listen to some excerpts of the concluding conversation between them:

Then the LORD *answered Job out of the storm... "Would you discredit my justice? Would you condemn me to justify yourself... (If so) Then adorn yourself with glory and splendor and clothe yourself in honor and majesty. Unleash the fury of your wrath."...Following this God proceeded, not to explain His ways to Job, but rather to reveal His majesty and power through a series of penetrating questions. Unable to answer God's questions, Job then replied to the Lord... "Surely, I spoke of things I did not understand, things too wonderful for me to know... My ears had heard of you but now my eyes have seen you" (Job 40:6,8,10-11; 42:1,3,5, NIV).*

Notice that God challenged Job to re-examine his anger. He knew that if Job bottled up his anger and failed to understand what it was telling him, he would never learn anything from it. Instead, he would only languish in depression. Then God taught Job about His eternal power and purpose by pointing to what could be seen in all of creation. That God would consider Job important enough to disclose His glory revealed His desire to open Job's eyes to the meaning and purpose of creation.

Everything else paled in comparison to the revelation of the God of the universe. How could Job remain depressed when exposed to such grandeur? Listen again to Job's response to all that he had seen and heard—but this time, I will state it in contemporary terms and interpret it in the first person:

God has shown that he cared enough to uplift my troubled spirit and clouded mind with teaching too astonishing for words. I used to be terrified of Him, but now I stand in awe of His grace. Although I was instructed in the faith of my fathers, as every Jew has been, I know now that I only knew the words but didn't grasp the full meaning. I had always operated by the book, but now I see God for who He is. Oh, I had the God-talk down all right, but now I know Him, not just know about Him. Before, it was more of an intellectual thing; but now it is experiential. I never understood how love and power could be displayed together like that. I learned, too, that my circumstances are not an adequate criterion of His caring. I will never doubt Him again.

Job was never the same after that experience. Because he was told by his friends that the cruelty of his circumstances was God's punishment for his sin, he lost his ability to trust. He saw God as harsh, as one who would inflict deep wounds, even for sins Job wasn't aware of. Now however, Job's fear was erased by the perfect love of God who desired to have a relationship with him. Above all, Job learned that God had blessed him by an act of His own free grace, not as a payoff for a meritorious life. For Job, on that day, legalism died.

In all of this, though he was mistaken, even presumptuous in his accusations, Job was honest to the way he was feeling as he questioned God. He was able to ask the hard questions, even though he admitted that he was fearful of God's power. Instead of cutting Job off or punishing him because of his challenging questions, God used those questions to confront him about his misconceptions, especially those concerning his right to cross-examine God's righteous purpose. Most importantly though, God took the opportunity to teach Job new things about the majesty of His person, to enlarge Job's vision concerning the limitless scope of His eternal nature.

The problem with us today is that we've stopped asking the difficult questions. Too often we back away from examining the tough dilemmas, the ones that open up uncomfortable issues that are not easily resolved. We are often left without any answers that are credible to the crowds of young skeptics who are looking for something to believe in. Nonetheless, as with His servant Job, God invites us to question Him so that we too, might be strengthened in our faith.

AHITHOPHEL: THE GAMBLER WHO LOST

The desire for social approval characterizes almost every human relationship. It is the driving force behind our constant search for something that we can offer others. When approval is denied, the consequences can be severe. Anyone, great or small, can fall to the frustration of this powerful social impulse.

In the Old Testament, Ahithophel gave clear testimony to this truth. He sat on the inner council of Absalom after Absalom had ousted his father, King David, from the throne. This coup had forced David and the troops loyal to him to flee to the east side of the Jordan in order to regroup and prepare for the battle to take his throne back. Meanwhile, Absalom was soliciting counsel from his closest advisors about what to do next.

Ahithophel had been a counselor of David, one whose wisdom was heralded throughout the kingdom. It was once said that, "the advice of Ahithophel, which he gave in those days, was as if one inquired of the word of God" (2 Sam. 16:23). Not only did he enjoy great prestige, but he also was related to the royal court through the marriage of his granddaughter, Bathsheba, to David.

Though Ahithophel was a man of great reputation, as well as a man who had far-reaching family connections, it turns out that he had placed all of his personal worth in his accomplishments. As long as the events in his life were going well and his advice was esteemed, this did not appear to pose much of a problem. But when those events took a sudden downturn, as they did when Absalom rejected Ahithophel's advice to pursue David, then it was a different story.

Ahithophel was devastated that his advice was overruled in such an important matter of state. To him it was the supreme humiliation, something that meant a fall from grace. He knew, too, that Absalom's foolish decision to allow a veteran warrior like King David time to regroup with his men spelled disaster and that he, Ahithophel, would be executed or exiled as a traitor once David returned to power. Any way he looked at it, the prospects for his future seemed grim. As he saw it, the best he could hope for was a life of obscurity, one that forever carried with it the stigma of betrayal.

The result of these conclusions was a reactive depression so severe that it prompted a suicidal course of action. Ahithophel, driven by the shame of public rejection, did not have the emotional stamina to withstand such a major blow to his social and political position.

His advice was his stock-in-trade. Since it was now no longer accepted, he felt he had nothing left for which he could lay claim to respect and honor. He knew his career was over figuring that David, whom he had betrayed, would see it the same way.

With hopelessness having run its course, Ahithophel took his life. "Now when Ahithophel saw that his counsel was not followed, he saddled his donkey and arose and went to his home, to his city and set his house in order and strangled himself—thus he died and was buried in the grave of his father" (2 Sam. 17:23). When his life's work was gone, so was his desire to live any longer. That's the *danger of emotionally investing everything in your career.*

Thinking himself wise, Ahithophel became a fool. He had taken the ultimate gamble, thinking he would come out on top. But his choice left him linked as a conspirator to the fate of the rebel Absalom. As a consequence, Ahithophel became as ignominious in death as he had been acclaimed in life. That was the price he paid for turning his strength into a weakness.

MOSES: OVERWORKED AND UNDERAPPRECIATED

We have seen brief glimpses of the two great Old Testament prophets, Moses and Elijah, in earlier discussion. Now let's revisit each of them to explore in more detail God's particular response to their depressions.

For Moses, answering God's call was no easy matter. That's because it required him to return to the land from which he had escaped as a fugitive. Moses feared the dangers posed by the mission, but he also worried that his own people would reject him as their leader. After all, he reasoned he had neither the poise nor the courage to be their leader, nor was he good with words. "O, Lord, I have never been eloquent, neither in the past nor since you have spoken to your servant. I am slow of speech and tongue" (Exod. 4:10, NIV).

Understanding that his fear was greater than his desire to obey, God nevertheless pressed Moses into service because He knew the enterprise rested on His own sovereign power, not on Moses' confidence to do the job. Yet He was compassionate in responding to Moses' needs, providing him with the support of Aaron, a proven leader.

Despite the success of the exodus however, Moses struggled with his people-pleasing tendencies. While he tried to accommodate the people's many demands on his time, he failed to protect himself from the exhaustion that comes from trying to be the jack-of-all-trades. Even his father-in-law, Jethro, recognized this problem. And so Jethro advised Moses to *delegate* some of his responsibilities. In reality, this was God's timely guidance through the words of a concerned family member—guidance that was as merciful as it was sensible.

Unfortunately, this helpful advice didn't last long. Later we find Moses again assuming responsibility for solving every problem and consequently, becoming exhausted (see Num. 11).

Moses routinely ignored his own limits until it was too late. Worse still, the people complained to Moses about almost everything. So Moses was not only exhausted, but he was frustrated as well. No matter how hard he tried to satisfy them, his leadership never seemed to be appreciated. It was a nightmare scenario for any people-pleaser. In the throes of his depression, he took his frustration out on God, not on the people who were always whining. Moses accused God of "punishing" him because He had burdened him with such people (see Num. 11:10-15). But of course it was

Moses, not God, who had abdicated his responsibility to protect his boundaries.

Instead of taking Moses to the woodshed for his unfounded charges however, God instructed him a second time to delegate his responsibilities to lighten the load. Once more, God intervened on behalf of his beleaguered servant. Moses' depression lifted and he returned to his post having learned that listening to God instead of placating others was the best way to manage his stress.

ELIJAH: THE DISCONNECT OF OVER-RESPONSIBILITY

Unlike Moses, Elijah had a problem knowing when his responsibility ended and God's began. After he had defeated the prophets of Baal, he expected a great awakening among his people—but instead he saw little change in their behavior. With the Israelites still loyal to the idolatry of Ahab and Jezebel, Elijah became depressed. Jezebel herself, having pledged to kill Elijah before the day was out, compounded his troubles. He was now convinced that he had failed in his mission as a prophet of God.

By assuming blame for the results, he had concluded that he was the failure. "It is enough; now, O Lord, take away my life, for I am no better than my ancestors" (1 Kings 19:4, NRSV). In other words, he had failed just like those who had gone before him. He believed it was his job to bring the people to repentance and that didn't happen. Now he was a fugitive with a bounty on his head.

God was moved with compassion at the sight of his wounded but obedient servant sitting there, fearful for his life and in despair over what he believed to be a useless mission. Instead of rebuking him for wanting to quit, God challenged Elijah to rethink his response. He did this by using a demonstration of His power as a means of teaching Elijah that it was the small quiet voice of the Spirit that called people to repentance (see 1 Kings 19:11-13).

While great displays of supernatural force are impressive, the real work of renewal comes from God's gentle but persuasive "whisper." Elijah's error had been to attribute his people's resistance to the ineffectiveness of the messenger rather than to their insensitivity to the quiet presence of God.

To prepare Elijah for this teaching, God knew that Elijah first needed to regain his physical strength. It had, after all, been a long ordeal. Once he had gotten some rest, God fed him not once, but twice, to give him the energy necessary to complete the journey to Mount Horeb. No one who is exhausted and hungry is going to be ready to rethink his response to anything.

Once Elijah understood the work of the Spirit, he had a better grasp of how God works in the souls of men and whose responsibility that is. And with that understanding, he was ready to serve God again, but this time with a more humane perspective.

In the book of James we read that Elijah had been an ordinary man doing extraordinary things, "Elijah was a man just like us. He prayed earnestly that it would not rain and it did not rain on the land for three and a half years. Again he prayed and the heavens gave rain and the earth produced its crops" (Jas. 5:17-18, NIV).

> **Unregenerate people need to see something in our lives that they don't see in their own lives, or otherwise they will no longer be interested in what we have.**

Just like us? That doesn't sound like most of us. What could James mean? What he seems to be saying here is that Elijah had suffered adversity like everyone else. But what stood out about him was that "he prayed earnestly" about big things, not halfheartedly about small things. He *believed* in what he prayed for. A great deal is said about the power of prayer, but much less about the power of conviction behind it. Most of us are such timid souls, asking for so little, always afraid to dream big dreams. "You do not have because you do not ask," James observed (Jas. 4:2).

God has called us to have a vision, one that's irresistible to others. Unregenerate people need to see something in our lives that they don't see in their owner otherwise they will no longer be interested in what we have. This "something" could be seen in Elijah and great things happened.

PICKING UP THE MISSING PIECES

Many of the biblical stories recounted in this chapter have been about people with damaged concepts of self and unfinished concepts of God. Like believers of old, many today see God as an *accountant* who "audits" their performance to determine their worthiness for the kingdom. Every behavior is entered on a sort of divine ledger as a credit or a debit, depending on its moral character. The prevailing "balance" of their "spiritual bank account" then determines the position they have before God. In this system, suffering is seen as borrowing from God's judgment to cover the deficit left by sin. On the other hand, blessings are viewed as the interest paid on the investment in good works. They spend much of their time in this debtor's ethic, plagued by guilt, most of it false guilt. And when they aren't feeling guilty, they're often feeling anxious—afraid they won't measure up.

Others see God more like a *dictator* who is pictured as a kind of celestial policeman, ever mindful of the believer's shortcomings and always alert to pounce on that spiritual miscue. This idea is similar to the unpredictable bully who prefers to intimidate people and dole out punishment at the drop of a hat. These people live in constant fear of God's punishment.

Still others view God's actions as those of someone who is *detached.* God is seen as aloof and disengaged, His attention difficult to capture. This view does not so much question God's sovereign power in our lives as it does his basic interest in our person. With a detached God, it is up to man to run his own life as best he can rather than wasting his time with appeals for divine intervention. Underlying this thinking is the idea that if God cared, He wouldn't let things happen the way they do.

Then there is the *peer* concept of God. With this approach, God is viewed more as a friend who is obligated by the relationship to use His divine power to ease a person around the rough spots of life. In effect, the relationship is a unilateral one wherein most of the expectations flow God-ward and most of the benefits flow man-ward. There is no sense of awe and little sensitivity to His transcendence.

Finally, there is the *rescuer* concept. People who think of God as a rescuer usually marginalize Him in their daily lives. They cry out to God for help when adversity strikes, promising renewed dedication if He does. But once the crisis passes, the promises are forgotten and God recedes into the background again. The Israelites were notorious for this. And so, too, are many of us.

Each of these concepts denies some important attribute of God. The *accountant* concept denies the grace of God, so that He is someone to impress. The *dictator* concept denies the mercy of God, so that He is someone to fear. The *detached* concept denies the love of God, so that He is someone to convince. The *peer* concept denies the holiness of God, so that He is someone to manipulate. And the *rescuer* concept denies the sovereign purposefulness of God, so that He is someone to ignore outside of crisis.

The result of these denials is a truncated image of who God is, which breeds unrealistic expectations, anxiety and a lack of attachment.

Come to think of it, that sounds a lot like the grounds for depression.

PETER: FINDING THE WHOLE GOD

To find the remedy, we must visit the apostle Peter, that fiery disciple of Jesus who, in his darkest hour, discovered the freedom of God's love. Though he was a bit rough around the edges, Peter felt deeply about things. Right after he declared that he would never betray his Messiah, he denied knowing Him at all. He did this not once but three times to a crowd gathered to watch the proceedings of Jesus' trial. Each denial became more emphatic than the last until Peter swore that he had nothing to do with Jesus. At that moment the cock crowed and the crushing reality of what he had just done sank in. Peter left quickly, walking out of the city in despair, weeping over having done the unthinkable. He was bewildered, too, that he had so easily caved in to the pressure of the crowd. He had *underestimated the power of fear to silence even his firmest conviction.*

Nothing had prepared Peter to handle the mob mentality with its narrow focus on conformity to the group. Still, at that moment, he hated himself for betraying the one Person who had given him meaning and purpose. Indeed, as one Bible teacher pointed out, so disconsolate was Peter that after the crucifixion it seems that he separated himself from the company of the other disciples—for when the angel at the tomb told Mary Magdalene and her companions to go tell the disciples that Jesus had risen, he mentioned Peter by name (using the phrase "and Peter") as though he was not with the other disciples (see Mark 16:7).

Jesus yearned for Peter to know that He *wanted* him there with the others, that He still saw Peter as His trustworthy disciple. Later at the Sea of Galilee, He made a point to ask Peter to "feed His sheep." Think of that. He was entrusting Peter with the task of teaching others how liberating it is to embrace the Gospel message. He was saying in effect, "I love you and forgive you and know that you love Me in return; and now, I want you to do something great for the kingdom." What a welcome message from someone whom Peter had betrayed in His greatest hour of travail!

We can now understand, perhaps, why Peter spoke with such power and conviction on the Day of Pentecost. He had been relieved of his despair and burden of guilt by the Messiah Himself. Unlike many, Peter understood grace. He knew firsthand what it meant to serve a master who never stopped loving nor ceased forgiving. He knew the whole God, the One who was at once just and merciful, sovereign and benevolent. He wanted to shout this message of hope from the rooftops.

And, indeed, he did.

FINDING HOPE

1. The *Bible is a love story* that reveals the *unstoppable force of God's redemptive purpose.*

2. God sometimes gives you what you want in order to *teach you what you need.* The goal? To understand the *superiority of His wisdom.*

3. No matter how momentarily satisfying revenge can be, *mercy and forgiveness yield better outcomes.*

4. Asking the *tough questions* not only *strengthens your own faith, but it also gives honest skeptics something to think about.*

5. Investing everything in your career carries with it the danger of emptiness when it's over. *Better to invest in intimate relationships* for the long term.

6. *God understands your limits* even better than you do. That's why *He encourages healthy boundaries.*

7. You are called to *believe in what you pray for.* God bids us to *pray earnestly about big things,* not halfheartedly about small things.

8. While you may be limited by an unfinished concept of God, *you are more likely to challenge your fears when you understand God in His wholeness.*

THE BIOLOGY OF DEPRESSION: A BODY OF EVIDENCE

*So in my brain my body comes together,
every part knows that it is not alone.*

—DR. PAUL BRAND—

One of the best things about being a family doctor is the opportunity to develop long-term relationships with a wide variety of people in the community. Because I (Dr. Knopf) am outspoken about my faith, many Christian people are referred to me for a variety of medical conditions. That Christians and non-Christians alike would trust me to share the sacred space of the intimate issues regarding their person and body, is humbling and kept in utmost confidence.

As I glanced over the list of people I was to see one afternoon, I recognized a familiar name of someone who is a marriage and family counselor in the community. I assumed that I would be seeing him for some type of medical problem like back pain, sore neck or indigestion. As I entered the room, John and I exchanged a warm greeting before I opened his chart to begin the office visit. To my surprise, John began describing a long history (lasting multiple years) of severe mood swings. Recently, they had become so bad that he was having thoughts of suicide. He expressed frustration in the fact that in his role as counselor he had helped innumerable people in similar situations achieve relief from their sense of hopelessness. "I know all the right answers and have studied all the books and yet I find myself incapable of experiencing relief," John said.

His medical history revealed a man who had been in excellent physical health his entire life. He had never taken any long-term medications, had grown up in a Christian family, was successful in his career and was enjoying a strong relationship with his wife and children. It wasn't until we began discussing his mother's health that the pieces of the puzzle began to fit. John's mother had suffered a "nervous breakdown" after the birth of her fifth child and for the rest of her life, suffered severe bouts of depression, to the point of needing hospitalization several times and receiving ECT (Electroconvulsive Therapy).

Reserved for only the most severe and resistant cases of depression, ECT consists of causing a person to have a grand mal seizure by passing electrical shock waves through the brain while the person is under general anesthesia. In some cases, for still undiscovered reasons, this procedure results in a lessening of depressive mood states although such improvement is often temporary. There are risks involved in this type of treatment. It poses for instance, the danger of some short-term memory loss (and perhaps other damage to the central nervous system), particularly with repeated use. As a consequence, this method should remain one of last resort.

Given his background, I thought to myself what courage it has taken for John to step forward and disclose the problem with which he had so long been privately struggling. There has been a tendency in the Christian community to embrace a set of assumptions that can be damaging. There is an implicit assumption that if you live a life obedient to God, you will be shielded from emotional pain or severe hopelessness. Likewise, reminiscent of the counsel of Job's friends, there is the implied contract that you will have God's continued protection only if you are obedient in confessing every sin.

We read in Psalm 32:3-5 that God desires, for our sake, our unhindered disclosure of sin to Him:

"When I kept silent, my bones wasted away through my groaning all day long. For day and night your hand was

heavy upon me; my strength was sapped as in the heat
of summer. Then I acknowledged my sin to you and did
not cover up my iniquity. I said, "I will confess my trans-
gressions to the LORD" and you forgave the guilt of my
sin (NIV)."

Here we see an example of a spiritual reason why people can
become depressed and "their bones waste away."

King David, the author of this psalm, spoke of his own personal experience in his sin with Bathsheba. Thus, if we violate
God's clear commands and refuse to repent, there will be physical
and psychological consequences emanating from true guilt. *But the*
reverse is not necessarily true. Not all hopelessness or feelings of
despondency can be traced to issues of moral compromise; something that we have discussed at length in this book.

Such rigid thinking can often lead to compartmentalization of
a person's life where no connection is seen between the physical,
spiritual and emotional realms. We have argued throughout our
discussion of depression that we are complex creatures and our
thoughts cannot be reduced to nice, neat categories. Our emotions
can affect our spiritual life. Physical illness like low thyroid can
affect our emotional life. Each area affects the other. Therefore,
conducting an accurate assessment of each of the areas optimizes
any intervention.

The purpose of this chapter is to focus attention on the physical aspects of depression. One of the hardest questions to answer
is "When should medical treatment be considered?" When has the
line been crossed from human emotion to medical disorder? Dr.
Stephen Stahl, M.D., one of the world's leading authorities on the
functions of brain chemistry, has said:

"Depression is an emotion that is universally experienced
by virtually everyone at some time in life. Distinguishing
the "normal" emotion of depression from an illness
requiring medical treatment is often problematic for those

who are not trained in the mental health sciences. Stigma and misinformation in our culture create the widespread, popular misconception that...depression is...a deficiency of character, which can be overcome with effort. For example, a survey in the early 1990s of the general population revealed that 71% thought that mental illness was due to emotional weakness; 65% thought it was caused by bad parenting; 45% thought it was the victim's fault and could be willed away; 43% thought that mental illness was incurable; 35% thought it was the consequence of sinful behavior; and only 10% thought it had a biological basis or involved the brain." [1]

Dr. Stahl's point that stereotypes of depression abound in our culture is well taken. Contrary to the dichotomies that exist in the public mind, there is abundant evidence of a complex mind-body interaction. This interaction makes it challenging to sort out the origins of change even at the physiological level. We know that emotional and behavioral changes made in therapy—changes that involve making different choices in life—can prompt changes in brain chemistry just as much as changes in brain chemistry can prompt corresponding changes in emotions and behavior. In other words, psychological causes and brain chemistry are linked to one another.

Notwithstanding the "chicken and egg" issues that we discussed earlier in the book, the fact that depression involves the biochemistry of the brain is central to our consideration of the biology of any mood disorder. We have already noted that in addition to the many psychogenic depressions, there are some predominantly biological depressions, such as bipolar affective disorder, that can be treated with a combination psychotherapy and medication.

Before we get into some of the more specific medical issues, I thought it would be helpful to try and explain in a simplified manner how the brain works.

NEUROTRANSMITTER RECEPTOR HYPOTHESIS

Neurotransmitters are hormones or chemicals that "hand off" or "transmit" the signal from one nerve to another across a gap called the "synapse." There are many neurotransmitters, some of which have not yet been fully identified. They include: Serotonin, Norepinephrine, Acetylcholine and Dopamine.

In order to function normally, you need to have a full reservoir or "tank" of these hormones in the nerve cell ready to be released and thus communicate the "message" to the next nerve. The synapse is the space between the ending of one nerve and the beginning of another nerve that must be "bridged" by the movement of these hormones. The concentration of these hormones must be sufficient enough to stimulate or "heat up" the "receptors" at the next nerve to create a chain reaction and "transmit" the message to the next nerve. This is not unlike getting up in the morning and standing outside your shower and turning on the hot water spigot, waiting for the cold water to be flushed from the pipes before you step in to take your shower with warm water.

> **...depression becomes synonymous with 'depletion' of the neurotransmitter hormones, like running out of hot water**

Therefore, for our purposes, depression becomes synonymous with "depletion" of the neurotransmitter hormones, like running out of hot water. If the brain does not have an adequate amount of these hormones, it begins to malfunction. Some people have inherited a tendency to have low hormone levels because their nerve cells either break down more of the hormones than other people's do or they do not make enough, leaving them in a deficit situation. In either of these processes going on in the brain, these levels can be depleted either through increased demand and overuse or from inadequate production or replacement.

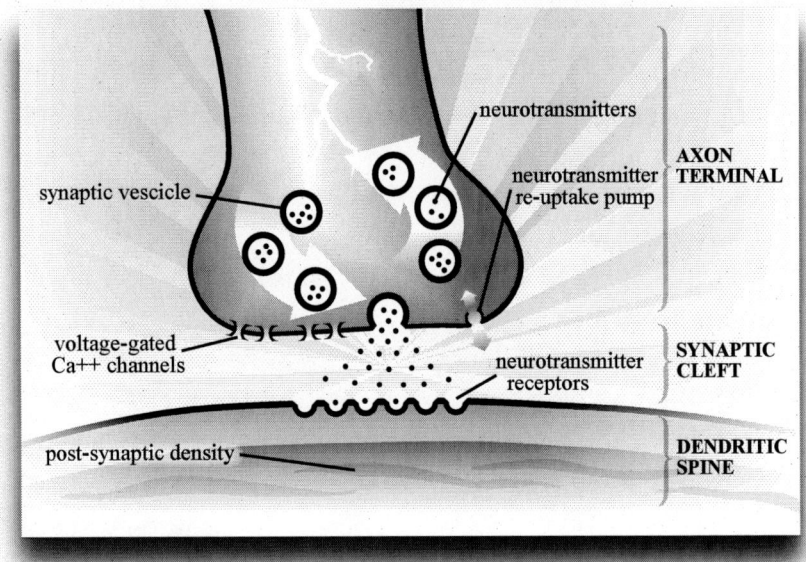

Figure 1. Neurotransmitters at the Synapse

The brain "fills up" the tanks of serotonin, norepinephrine and dopamine during sleep. Consequently, if you do not get adequate sleep for some reason, you will be starting the next day without a normal reservoir of neurotransmitters, putting you at risk for sub-optimal functioning.

When people experience significant loss like a divorce or the death of a child, or experience physical or emotional burnout or a number of other factors that create severe stress, the brain works overtime in anticipation of the worst possible situation. In this "full combat alert state," the mind plays the what-if game, expending energy trying to anticipate the worst possible scenario and make early preparation for all of the likely or unlikely possibilities. This leads to a vicious cycle because the more stressed you are, the less capable you are of functioning at your optimum level, which creates even more stress.

The spiral of anxiety, sleep problems, fatigue, poor performance and depressed mood can become progressively more severe until the person becomes incapacitated. With this entire process going on in the brain, it is hard to pull yourself up by your own bootstraps and reverse this cycle. This is where medication comes in to lend assistance to raise the level of neurotransmitter hormones by blocking their re-uptake into the sending nerve, which will metabolize and breakdown a significant share of these hormones. This allows the levels of hormones to be sufficient enough at the synapse so the "message" can be sent from one nerve to the next in a more normal fashion (like having instant hot water). Antidepressant medications are not addicting like Valium, narcotics or cocaine that act by directly stimulating various nerves at the synapse in certain areas of the brain and provide an altered state of consciousness or euphoria.

Some of the confusion as to why certain people struggle with adversity more than others can be answered in the concept of individual variability. Each person is unique and so we have to individually assess the potential for significant depression. Some people can go through divorce, lose their job and seem to manage just fine, while others seem to collapse into depression if they get disappointed by not getting a new car. Just like the color of your eyes and hair, there is individual variability in your body's ability to manufacture or metabolize (break down) the brain hormones. If you inherited a tendency to have low levels of these hormones, you will be more vulnerable to experiencing a chain of events that leads to depletion and therefore, it is more likely that medication will be necessary to provide relief.

Can significant depletion be caused by long-term emotional stress? Yes. Can significant depletion be caused by an environmental stressor? Yes. Can significant depletion be caused by family genetics? Yes. Therefore, how should the issue of using medications be viewed? As a necessary evil? As something to avoid at all costs? Is medication a panacea that should be given to everyone?

The good news is that 90 percent of people can be helped significantly with their depression once they have found a suitable medication. And with this help, they are much more amenable to the work of psychotherapy, which is more likely to bring about lasting change.

COMMON QUESTIONS ABOUT DEPRESSION

When is depression severe enough to consider medication?

In chapter 1, we outlined the basic symptoms diagnostic of clinical depression and some of their implications. If you recall, these included the following: (1) depressed mood and feeling of hopelessness; (2) loss of interest in daily activities and pleasures; (3) inappropriate guilt and feelings of worthlessness; (4) appetite changes causing either weight gain or weight loss; (5) sleep problems, especially early morning awakening; (6) agitation and restlessness; (7) concentration difficulties and inability to make decisions; (8) fatigue and lack of energy; (9) recurring thoughts of suicide, in which life seems empty and not worth living; 10) irritability and feeling "stressed out." If a person has at least four of these symptoms nearly every day for at least two weeks, significant depression is likely.

It is estimated that only 30 percent of people who experience biological depression are adequately treated.

There are of course, assessment tools (e.g., questionnaires, personality inventories, various other paper and pencil tests and clinical interviews) that increase our accuracy in confirming the diagnosis of depression. (See Appendix A for an example of the Hamilton Depression Scale; see also Appendix B for Dr. Lovejoy's summary of the 10 most common irrational beliefs that contribute to depression.)

What are the factors in under-diagnosis and under-treatment?

It is estimated that only 30 percent of people who experience biological depression are being adequately treated. Some of the major contributing factors include: (1) stigma—it is not "okay" for some people to take antidepressant medications because it is considered "drug abuse"; (2) lack of public knowledge as to what depression is, its various subtypes and how it can be treated; (3) lack of reporting of depressed mood—only 17 percent of people who are eventually diagnosed with depression actually go to their doctor for their depressed mood; (4) depressive symptoms are often masked by physical symptoms like fatigue or associated medical illnesses, including low thyroid, heart attacks and sleep apnea; (5) poor medication prescribing and follow-through on the part of physicians who are not fully knowledgeable and skilled in using the newer and more effective medications.

Should non-medication treatments be tried first?

It's useful to do an assessment of a person's current lifestyle. Are they simply exhausted and need more sleep? Are they experiencing loneliness through death or loss of a relationship? Are they angry or bitter over an injustice? Are they physically depleted and in need of proper nutrition and exercise? Have they taken steps to nurture their spiritual life? If people have done all these things and are still experiencing significant problems in mood, I believe it is time to see their family doctor.

What about St. John's Wort?

St. John's Wort is an herb that does have an effect on the brain hormones although its effect is considered to be milder than prescription medications. Simply because it is nonprescription does not mean it is safe. Many people can experience elevations of blood pressure if they eat certain foods like cheese, beans or wine. St. John's Wort should not be taken with other prescription medications and there may be some evidence of early cataract formation with exposure to sunlight. In my experience, taking St. John's Wort has not been all that helpful for most people and does pose some risks to a person's health.

What does an episode of depression look like?

The course of treated depression follows some clearly definable stages. The following is a graphic representation of a depressive episode with the various possible outcomes.

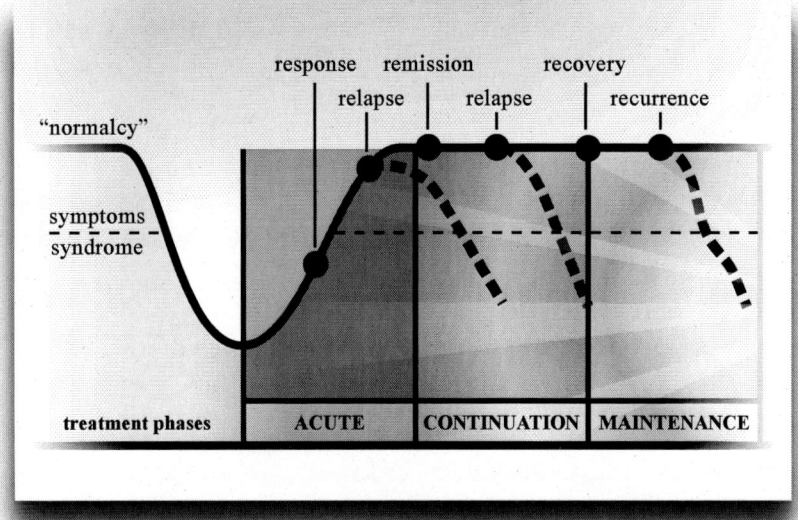

Figure 2. Kupfer Curve[2]

The term "response" generally means that a depressed patient has experienced at least a 50 percent reduction in symptoms as assessed by the Hamilton Depression Rating Scale. "Relapse" is the term used when a person gets worse after treatment began to work but the person had not "gotten well." "Remission" is the term used when essentially all symptoms have gone away and the person is feeling totally normal. "Recovery" means that the remission has lasted for at least 6 to 12 months. "Recurrence" means the symptoms of depression have returned, causing significant problems in functioning and mood.

Are depression and weight problems connected?

Depression can cause cravings and overeating behavior in some people because food is actually a "mild antidepressant" since food actually raises our brain serotonin levels. Therefore, some people are "treating" their depression by overeating without knowing it. There is a medication called Meridia, which is in the same class of certain antidepressant medications like Prozac, which has been helpful in curbing the appetite in some people. If you are taking Meridia, you cannot take other antidepressant medications at the same time.

How long should a person take medication?

Rule of thirds: Approximately one-third of people will experience a single episode of significant depression usually precipitated by a major traumatic event. Treatment is usually required for at least six months and then the medication can be phased out. This is somewhat similar to a physician using a cast to hold the broken bone of the leg in proper alignment so the bone can develop a strong union. Approximately one-third of people will experience relapses of depression. If you have had more than one episode of depression requiring medication, your chances are greater than 80 percent that you will require medication at some time in the future to treat another episode. Approximately one-third of people have a more prolonged type of depression called "chronic dysthymic disorder," which is best treated with long-term medication.

What medication should I take?

Just like trying on a pair of shoes, there is no one medication that is perfect for everyone. Not only are there differences in a person's susceptibility to depression, but also there is also individual variability in a person's response to medications. This makes the prescribing of antidepressants closer to "trial and error" than "one size fits all." In most people, Prozac will stimulate and energize those who are depressed or sluggish, but in a minority of people, they will be sedated. If the medication causes significant side effects, it should be stopped and a different medication tried. Most likely, one of the medications available today will significantly help you feel good without creating significant side effects.

If a person is having mood problems as well as problems with memory, with ability to concentrate and with maintaining attention and experiencing fatigue, they should be considered for a medication that would boost their levels of the norepinephrine neurotransmitter. If they are having mood problems associated with anxiety, panic disorder or phobias of multiple types, including social phobias as well as obsessive-compulsive problems, they should be considered for medication that would primarily increase the levels of serotonin.

Some of the latest scientific evidence indicates that using medications that increase both serotonin and norepinephrine levels are superior in helping a person improve their mood state as compared to medications that work on either serotonin or norepineph-rine alone. Medications like Effexor XR, Remeron and Serzone raise the levels of both serotonin and norepinephrine. Many times physicians will use combinations of antidepressants to obtain full remission and lower the amount of side effects. In essence, one plus one equals three in providing greater effectiveness while reducing the overall number of side effects. (See Appendix C for a list of the major medications currently available with my assessment of the advantages, disadvantages and personal recommendations as to the situations in which they are most likely to work best. See also Appendix D for treatment guidelines regarding medication priori-ties that increase the chance for a successful outcome on the first try rather than a more random choice process).

After learning of John's family history and his struggles with suicide, I had John take a Hamilton Depression Scale. His score revealed significant depression. Because John was having associ-ated symptoms of agitation and fidgeting as well as irritability, I elected to try John on the duo-acting antidepressant Effexor XR which enhances both the serotonin and norepinephrine neurotrans-mitter systems. I gave him some samples to try and asked him to return in three weeks. John's experience was somewhat unusual but not rare. He described such a dramatic change in his symptoms that he said, "It was like the clouds parted and the sun began to shine on me." It was an entirely new experience for him after he started taking the medication.

This kind of response is the exception rather than the rule but does illustrate the point that some people do have an inherited tendency that can only be adequately treated with medical intervention. John's prognosis is excellent, but he will probably always require a maintenance dose of medication.

Even with biological depressions, the message is the same: We are exquisitely designed with emotional alarm systems to tell us when it is time to take action so that we might be restored to the fulfillment of our God-given desires. There is no greater upside to the experience of depression than to meaningfully grow through our pain. In the end, is this not what Jesus meant when He spoke of living in the kingdom of God now? The abundant life He promised is not the easy life or necessarily the prosperous life as the world measures prosperity. It is the fulfilling life, the life of wisdom that understands the importance of what makes the difference for eternity.

FINDING HOPE

1. Your emotional experience affects your theology just as theology affects your emotional experience. *Reassessing both can lead to surprising spiritual benefits.*

2. Emotional and behavioral changes that involve making *different choices in life can produce corresponding changes in brain chemistry and vice versa.*

3. Because we know that depression can result from a "depletion" of neurotransmitter hormones, *we have medications that can "re-supply" them* at the synapse.

4. The good news is that *90 percent of people who are depressed can be helped with medication.* This makes possible much *greater gains in psychotherapy.*

5. While *relapses* during or after treatment often occur, *knowing this enables us to better prepare for (or prevent) them.* Sustained remission is always the goal.

6. Medication decisions are tailored to the particular symptoms that predominate and the overall number of side effects.

THE PROMISE OF TRANSFORMATION: CHANGING THE FUTURE

*The real voyage of discovery consists not in
seeking new landscapes but in having new eyes.*

—MARCEL PROUST—

The best news about depression is that you can change your future. Although simply trying to will yourself out of depression is not realistic, don't be misled into thinking you're without options. *We are continuously making choices in life that will determine our future, even if we feel helpless and are paralyzed by indecision.* Whether we recognize the truth of it or not, choices made by default are just as real as those made by deliberation. We can make passive choices that reflect a life of withdrawn despair as well as active choices that reflect the passionate desires of the heart.

Passivity leads to the path of least resistance. Sadly, many choose this path by accommodating to a life of silent surrender to the ordinary. You can see it in their lack of intentionality and in their vacant faraway look that betrays any words of false cheer. It's evident in nearly every choice they make.

Once we have decided to drop anchor inside the protective breakwater of resignation, the ship of our human spirit loses its seaworthiness. The dry rot of apathy and despair that follows soon reduces our vessel to a shadow of what it once was. Gone is the means of travel on the high seas of adventure in personal growth.

213

Gone too, is the joy of our redemption or even the appreciation of the sacrifice that made it possible. God never intended our lives to be this way though He understands, of course, how we got there. From the beginning, His intentions for us were almost breathtaking. "What are human beings that you [God] are mindful of them, mortals that you care for them? Yet you have made them a little lower than God and crowned them with glory and honor" (Psalm 8:4-5, NRSV).

Benevolence on this scale reveals the splendor of God's love and the full sweep of His commitment to give us an unforgettable life. Although we may be marred by the Fall, we have this love and commitment from Him no less now than when we were first conceived. Nowhere is this more evident than in His Son's sacrifice on the cross. Nonetheless, this love can be obscured, even sabotaged, by the depressing pessimism of our pain.

After many years in the pastorate listening to church members pour out their heartaches, one minister came to the conclusion that if we touch any heart it will bleed a little. This is no doubt true. We have said that suffering is a part of every life—man or woman, rich or poor, sophisticated or untutored.

Although we may feel the ravages of such suffering, we often don't want others to know about it. So we disguise what we feel by telling others, "everything is just fine." We are convinced this disguise is necessary to avoid the attention we don't want for a state of mind we can't accept. The irony is that this dishonesty is itself an occasion for still further isolation and only guarantees the loneliness that comes from a lack of connection.

> **We are convinced this disguise is necessary to avoid the attention we don't want for a state of mind we cannot accept**

Part of the genius of divine creation is that we remain malleable throughout life if given the guidance that is necessary. But all too frequently we have exchanged this malleability for a rigid compulsion to keep doing the same things over and over again. We mesmerize ourselves with the same debilitating irrational beliefs (See Appendix B). We engage the same distorted thoughts, such as all-or-nothing thinking, overgeneralization, jumping to conclusions, emotional reasoning and self- blame. Yet despite this endless repetition, we are always surprised and disappointed that life doesn't seem to change.

Psychiatrist Viktor Frankl pointed out that because life experience is transitory, we have a responsibility to make the most of it while we can. And what we make of it will either reduce or enlarge our options for growth.

In this chapter we will discuss practical strategies for altering the way we live, which in combination present hope for real change.

CHANGE THE UNCHANGING

Consider any book you have read. How did the author communicate his meaning? Which word pictures set a peaceful tone and which established a dark, oppressive mood? Which produced feelings of excitement or fear and despair? In a similar fashion, you are the author of the stories you are writing in your mind. The words you use and the assumptions you make about events in your life are important in determining their impact on you. We saw this in our earlier discussion on "need language."

What if you assumed that you (or others) were "guilty until proven innocent"? Would you not become the unwitting victim of your own injustice? Certainly it would not be an acceptable premise on which to base society's legal system. You would not hesitate to protest such a miscarriage of justice. Yet you are more than ready to accept this premise in the courtroom of self-evaluation. Many people are surprised to discover how often they allow such prejudicial thinking, which they would never accept in a court of law, to propel them into a state of rage or plunge them into despair.

To challenge this thinking, we must first realize its habitual nature. We accept it without review. Yet without accountability to reality, our thought life can become stereotyped, leaving negative footprints on every conclusion we draw. So when we ruminate on pessimistic "what ifs " or obsess over every injury, we end up feeling helpless and depressed. In effect, we become compulsive stenographers of "tragedy," victimizing ourselves and, by implication, suggesting that our self-hatred is justified.

This mindset is sometimes called "learned helplessness." People who have not experienced much mastery of outcomes in their early life are vulnerable to believing they are powerless to influence life events. As children, if bad things happened to them, they had little ability to do anything about it. For some, this results in the belief that experiences in life are beyond their control and it is foolish to try to change them. Instead of taking the initiative to carve out a different path, they cede this power to other people. When I asked one woman why she always turned to look at her husband before she answered a question, she became flustered and said, "Oh, I was just seeing how he was reacting to the question." When I asked her what she was looking for, she replied, "Oh, nothing I guess." In reality, she was checking to see if it was all right to answer the question or to defer to him. In fact, he often tried to answer for her or to "clarify" her statements by substituting his own. His controlling influence was noticeable from the beginning. So was her sense of helplessness.

Meanwhile, others who feel helpless are so busy replaying history in their mind that they fail to see the opportunities to take charge of the present. Their past becomes, in effect, the altar on which they are sacrificing any chance for lasting happiness. But never forget, this focus is a choice.

Actively challenging our distorted thinking patterns is necessary for reducing their credibility. Suppose you went to hear a noted speaker and when he was about five or ten minutes into his speech, someone who was knowledgeable stood up and questioned the accuracy of what he was saying, citing compelling evidence for his view? You might cross out that part of the speech before resuming your note taking. Suppose further that this happened many times with others in the audience who were also knowledgeable in their fields. The likelihood is that you would quit taking notes, since you could no longer trust anything the speaker was saying. In fact, you would likely get up and leave, believing the meeting was a waste of your time. That's what happens when false ideas are challenged. Without such challenges, you would continue believing everything you heard was true. You would do well then, if the next time you are in turmoil you remember that the distorted, often irrational ideas underlying it need to be challenged with the truth. You can check the list in Appendix B to help you identify which beliefs most dominate your thinking and the best arguments that challenge them.

Most people think that their reactions are the direct result of the events that seem to give rise to them. For instance, say that you went for a job interview and were turned down for the job. By the time you get home, your disappointment has left you depressed. If I were to ask you why you are depressed, you would tell me that it was because you failed to get the job you wanted. But that would not be why you are depressed. You're depressed because of your *beliefs* about being turned down for the job. You would be saying to yourself that *it's awful you didn't get the job, proving that you'll never get the job you want.* Now that thought, if you believed it, *would* be depressing.

Some people might have the same experience you did, but respond differently. That's because they would be thinking that, while disappointing, there are other good jobs for which they could apply and they'll get one of them—all they have to do is keep trying. The difference in emotional response is attributed to the difference in beliefs, not the activating event, which is the same in each case. Think of this as the ABC analysis of your response: The *activating* event (A), triggers a *belief* (B), about that event, which

217

produces certain emotional and behavioral *consequences* (C). Only by challenging the beliefs will you change the consequences.

Another way for change-resistant people to realize how self-defeating they have become is to first experiment around the edges of their disabling ideology. That means altering what they do just enough to provide a different picture of what's possible. Glimpsing what it would be like if things were different often emboldens them to try a little more. Eventually, the neurotic beliefs protected by their pathological defense system can be countered by the whole truth.

This is not an easy task since depressed people are constrained by the straitjacket of routine. As we have said, this is due to the conviction that if they attempt something new, they *must* succeed. Otherwise, they will see themselves as utter failures. Which, of course, means to them that they are somehow defective. Breaking new ground increases the anxiety they already feel.

To overcome this fear requires minimizing the degree of threat while, at the same time, opening up opportunities to achieve some success. Because changing behavior first sometimes best alters attitudes, *doing* something different can sometimes be more effective than trying to think something different.

If you want to change your behavior, begin by identifying what you are most fearful of doing and then work backward to some *approximation* of this activity, to something you're willing to try altering. This is less likely to induce the level of anxiety that inhibits trying at all.

Remember, it is in the nature of experimentation that the results are not preordained. When a scientist carries out a study, regardless of the outcome (whether it supports his hypothesis or not) he has generated valuable data for the body of science. No well-run experiment proves the experimenter a failure—it can only fail to confirm the experimenter's hypothesis. Studies that produce negative results are just as important as studies that produce positive ones, because they direct the researcher's future study.

Likewise, personal experiments yield valuable feedback *both about what works and about what doesn't*—feedback that is crucial for making effective adjustments in your behavior. Such experiments are never failures. The important thing is that the new behaviors are ones *you* engage in, ones that have originated from strategies *you* have devised. This fact alone speaks volumes about your ability to participate in your own growth.

Though you may not always achieve the outcomes you want, you will at least be able to define the boundaries of what is possible. But wherever those boundaries are, they can never define you as a failure or your actions as experiences in futility. They can only provide invaluable information on which actions to do more and which to do less. It's this information that makes your experiments successful.

The anxiety that accompanies depression and experimentation is based on false conclusions that complicate a person's efforts to grow. What's more, misplaced fears create symptoms of their own. These symptoms are sometimes so terrifying to people that they will go to great lengths to avoid any situation that might evoke them. They may refuse to go to certain places or drive their car beyond a certain limited range. When that's the case, I often point out to my clients that such anxiety attacks tend to duplicate the physical characteristics of exercise, which we *choose* to engage in for the sake of our health. Think about that for a moment. Such symptoms as rapid breathing, elevated heart rate and increased sweating, which we also describe as signs of anxiety, are the same things we try to achieve when we work out in the gym.

Since we seek these experiences to improve our physical conditioning, which is good for us, why should we think that calling them "symptoms of anxiety" makes them somehow dangerous, even indicators that we are going to die? How can such physical symptoms appear so ominous when under other circumstances, we welcome them as signs of a good workout?

Try to think of such experiences then, as aerobic moments. In fact, I challenge you to try to *increase* these symptoms when you have them. Try to sweat more, to make your heart beat even faster and to breathe more deeply. When the episode is over, remind yourself that it was a valuable aerobic moment and that you feel even more fit because of it. (If these aerobic moments decrease in frequency, you can always begin supplementing them by visiting an athletic gym of your choice!)

EFFICIENT WORRY

Another way to overcome negative thoughts is to defer them to a designated time by scheduling a "worry hour." Instead of spreading your worry inefficiently throughout the day, you can consolidate it into one hour of your choosing. During this daily period, sit at a table and write down all of your self-rejecting worries—your guilt-inducing, depression-generating thoughts and your obsessive concerns about social approval. If you complete the list in less than the hour allotted—and you usually will—write them over again until the hour is up.

When the hour is over, burn the list and toss the ashes away. If you start to experience worry or guilt or some other depressogenic thought before the next day's worry hour, remind yourself that you have set aside a time for this and will write it down then. You can then let the thought go, with the promise that you will pick it up later. In this fashion, you can condense all your debilitating ruminations into one 60-minute time period.

If a given day is free of anxiety-inducing thoughts, you may skip the worry hour, but only for that day. Daily consistency is necessary—even when it feels like an ordeal—if you wish to gain the greatest benefit from this exercise.

WHAT ABOUT GRUDGES?

Griping about someone else's mistakes in the past demands perpetual "penance" for something that has long since ceased to be relevant in the present. I counseled a couple where the wife spoke vehemently about some mistake her husband had made. She spoke as if it had happened only a few days before. But I discovered it had happened more than 20 years ago! She just could not let go of any perceived injustice.

Not only did bitterness destroy this woman's ability to affirm her husband, but also just as important, it blocked her ability to encourage the best in herself. Since childhood, she had retreated into a fortress mentality. In her thinking, the only way she could protect herself from getting hurt was *to attack first.* Her grudges displayed her intense fear and insecurity.

When you hold a grudge against someone, you're shackled to that person. You're trapped in a powerful, unhealthy bond that robs you of even the pretense of independent thinking. On the other hand, the ability to lay aside bitterness provides an unimaginable freedom. In fact, it's the freedom that only love can give. "[Love] is not rude, it is not self-seeking, it is not easily angered, it *keeps no record of wrongs"* (1 Cor. 13:5, italics added). When

...what didn't destroy us then cannot harm us now.

we are released from the past and free ourselves from the silent slavery of our hidden secrets and lack of forgiveness, we realize, perhaps for the first time, that those past experiences didn't destroy us after all. And what didn't destroy us then cannot harm us now. That we survived these experiences is a monumental conquest. In remembering and grieving the pain of our personal histories, it's also important to honor the triumphs so that triumph rather than defeat can become our new theme for living.

This shift in thinking allows us to let go of those who were responsible for our pain. It is one thing to have suffered by their hand in some way when we were children or adolescents, but it is quite another to allow the memory of that suffering to control us as adults. We didn't deserve that treatment in the past and we don't deserve the shame and self-rejection that results from it in the present.

Most people who have been wounded don't understand that forgiveness is what will keep them from using their bitterness as an excuse for their own destructive behavior. Plainly, forgiveness without God's help is impossible, particularly when the sins against us are great. But with His help, faith becomes the gateway to freedom from further injury that we would otherwise inflict on ourselves in the name of our resentment.

Unless we are honest with ourselves, there is little chance that the anger underneath will ever be processed. There are of course, certain cultures (and certain groups within our culture) where privately "letting go" is viewed as an important family virtue. But still, it's useful to ask, *what happens when we become more transparent?*

CHANGE YOUR APPROACH

Jim hated his job, even though he was good at what he did. The workplace had become a war zone with his sales manager, Bill, who often pressed his authority. In Jim's view, Bill made poor decisions. Sensing something wrong in Jim's demeanor, his boss was always on edge around him.

When Jim resisted some directive, Bill started making strident demands. It appeared that the only reason Jim had not been fired was because he was the company's top salesman.

For his part, Jim had not resigned from his position because he was paid well and he knew he would take a substantial pay cut to work with one of his company's competitors. But he went home every night feeling hopeless about ever enjoying his job again. He sought professional counseling to help him determine what to do.

During one counseling session, Jim's eyebrows arched in surprise when it was suggested that his manager might feel insecure about his position and threatened by a subordinate as competent and knowledgeable as Jim. This insecurity could contribute to his poor decision making. "I never thought of that," Jim responded. "Do you suppose Bill would be open to a gentler approach, maybe if I took him out to lunch and showed some personal interest in him?" I told him that sounded like a good idea to try. "Who knows, you might get some fruitful conversation going that might lead to actual change."

When Jim returned for a counseling session a month later, he recounted his astonishment at his manager's positive response to his invitation to discuss their differences. When it was apparent that Jim was making an effort to find some middle ground, Bill proved gracious. As a result, they were able to hammer out a workable solution that eased the sense of threat to the manager while granting greater freedom to Jim to exercise his professional judgment.

Shortly afterward, Jim's depression lifted and he began to approach his work with renewed energy. The important point was not whether Jim's manager had been experiencing insecurity but that Jim needed to find another way to look at the problem, which nudged him to try a different means of solving it.

> **By introducing the unexpected, we make our relationships more interesting, even intriguing....**

When we assume the worst about others, it's because we are protecting ourselves from disappointment and rejection. Sometimes we compensate for that fear by becoming overbearing. By making ourselves as indispensable as we can, we are trying to satisfy our guilt for "being less than what we should be." But in attempting to alleviate our fear of being rejected by others, we end up rejecting ourselves. It's ironic that while we are trying to be all things to all people, we are withholding all things from ourselves.

Making changes in the way we approach problems—changes that relieve a stressful situation—can alter our mood. That's why it's so important to find ways to break up an entrenched but negative pattern of interaction. We can often be successful at this by changing our behavior in a way that *surprises* the other person. By introducing the unexpected, we make our relationships more interesting, even intriguing and create a new and different context for stimulating change.

Keeping that in mind, try the following approach the next time someone is angry with you. Instead of getting defensive and counterattacking as most people do, excuse yourself for a moment, go to the next room and reduce your hyper-aroused state (taking deep breaths, etc.). This buys you time to cool off. Then ask yourself what the other person would *least expect* in response. When you have the answer, return to the room and carry out the course of action you have determined would take that person by surprise.

You will find that most people when caught off guard respond with the hesitation that the unfamiliar produces and then a reaction of increased curiosity. Sooner or later, they are likely to change their behavior to accommodate your new, innovative response. You may well discover, too, that the challenge of generating surprise reawakens your spirit of creativity, something that can lie dormant when a relationship has become too predictable.

WHEN YOU DON'T FEEL LIKE IT

Depressed clients will often recite with resignation many activities they used to enjoy, such as going to movies, cycling, hiking, engaging in sports or playing cards with friends. They add that they no longer do these things because they "just *don't* feel like it anymore."

To counter this tendency to withdraw, ask yourself, "What would I do if I felt good about myself and were content with my world?" If you don't know, think of a person you perceive to have high self-regard and base your response on the way you imagine that person would respond. Once you have determined what you would do under these circumstances, carry it out.

You may object that you can't do this because you don't feel that way about yourself. However, there are many things you do that you don't feel like doing. Even though you don't always feel like getting out of bed and going to work in the morning, you do it anyway. In the past, you haven't allowed your feelings to stop you from carrying out many activities or responsibilities you believed were important.

THIS DIRECTIVE IS NO DIFFERENT.

Healthy self-esteem comes from the pledge to treat yourself in a valuing, tenderhearted way, regardless of how you feel. It means behaving in a way that gives you the message that you count for something, that you are worth the effort. Otherwise, your internalized messages of self-hatred will continue to flourish unopposed. By being a friend to yourself, then you, not others, are in charge of changing your self-concept.

Try this experiment (doing what you would do if you felt good about yourself) for at least a month and record the changes you experience as a result. It is important to do these things on a *daily* basis, rather than occasionally or only when you want to. Doing them when you *don't particularly feel like it* demonstrates a higher level of commitment and results in greater empowerment. You will learn to revise your reasons for doing or not doing things to align more clearly with a proactive lifestyle instead of resigning yourself to a reactive coping pattern. In time, you will discover the truth of author Paul Watzlawick's observation that, "what the world does not hold it cannot withhold...we cannot find out there in the world and thus can never *have* what we already *are.*"[1] And what we are has already been determined by God's loving, creative hand.

MAKING SENSE OUT OF NONSENSE

To 18 year-old Suzanne, who had gone to private Christian schools all of her life, college experience proved to be a shock. Overwhelmed by the "scholarly" arguments of agnostic professors, she concluded that her faith must be little more than self-delusion. Thereafter, she drifted into the college party scene and began living a life of self-indulgence. Without her faith as a compass, Suzanne's world was drained of all meaning and she became depressed.

Later, trying to sort out how she got where she was, she wondered why life had become so pointless. "I'm doing all the things that are supposed to make me happy, you know, all the stuff you were never allowed to do; what one of my teachers called *freedom*. But it isn't what it's cracked up to be. I mean, where's the real fun?" Somehow her happiness had been kidnapped. Underneath, she yearned for a God who was personal and for a future she could believe in. In time, Suzanne discovered that the empty secularism she had encountered was just that—flat. It offered nothing more than momentary gratification.

Without the context of her faith, the world no longer made sense. The pain she experienced made no sense either. When we are stripped of our answers to life, we tend to fill in the blanks ourselves, like Suzanne did, with the assistance of those who are as just as lost as we are.

God loves us in spite of the flaws in our character—but He does not ignore them. He wants us to mature and know Him more intimately. Although suffering does not originate with God, it can serve as the backdrop for personal growth. Even with faith, it is sometimes difficult to see and appreciate God's love and purposefulness in hardships. But without faith, it is impossible.

We must understand that our distress is not His goal—it is the prelude to something better. If we want to grow, we must become patient in His love and flexible in our adversity. It means asking God *how* rather than *why*. Using hardship as a springboard to meaning rather than as a reason for helplessness. One client said it best, "It seems...like a window of opportunity to understand things that the mind can never know, only the heart." She was right to say that it is primarily an issue of the heart—both our heart and God's heart. It is an intimate connection with God, which enables us to cope with difficult realities, including depression.

If God is to be our source of hope, we must trust that He always acts in our best interest and that He is not limited to a specific timetable. And we must be willing to slow down long enough to hear His voice. Remember, God's aim is not instant relief from suffering, but a process of transformation that brings joy even in the midst of suffering. The end goal is to make us more like Him.

STEPPING OUT BY WORKING OUT

One of the ways of tackling depression is also one of the simplest: Physical exercise. When we become depressed, we tend to withdraw into a protracted state of lethargy. We just don't feel like doing anything—in a word, we vegetate. Even the simplest of tasks seem to require a herculean effort to do. So, of course, the last thing we are likely to pursue is physical exercise. Yet this is precisely one of the best things we can do to alleviate depressive symptoms.

In keeping with what we know about mind-body interaction, there is now considerable evidence that physical exercise has a significant impact on the biochemistry of the brain—in particular, on those chemicals in the brain responsible for changes in mood states. Exercise boosts the production of endorphins, those mood-elevating hormones that are part of the so-called "opiate system" in the brain.

Exercise also affects the supply of certain neurotransmitters, the biochemical messengers between nerve cells in the brain, which we talked about in the last chapter. It just so happens that the ones affected by exercise are the same ones targeted by antidepressant medications. Author and psychiatrist John Ratey cites an impressive number of studies suggesting that physical exercise elevates the levels of norepinephrine, long known for its involvement in feelings of well-being, primes the dopamine pump which improves mood and helps the attention span and increases serotonin which, as we have already discussed, is understood to be critical to the regulation of mood as well. It's not surprising then, that the neural pathways where all three of these brain chemicals can be found also run through the "reward centers" of the brain. These are areas that are activated during experiences of personal pleasure.

Perhaps even more important though, is the fact that exercise encourages the production of BDNF or "brain-derived neurotrophic factor," reversing the inhibitory effect of long-term depression on this brain protein. We have already discussed the fact that any increase in BDNF is significant because of its role in renewing and restoring brain function and stimulating cell production in those parts of the brain responsible for learning, memory and higher thinking. But we also know that it counteracts the effects of cortisol, a natural steroid (a corticosteroid hormone) released during stress which if found in excess, can be detrimental to the health of the body.

If you want to avoid a deteriorating brain and a declining body, avoid the tendency to merely adapt to depression as a way of life. One way to do this is to begin exercising. It's best to start slowly and then work up to 30 or more minutes a day. Studies have shown that for some people, such exercise is just as effective as medication in reducing depressive symptoms. And when, for some reason, medication doesn't seem to be effective, exercise still is.

You don't have to know how the brain works to know what works for your brain.

Though not a panacea, what a simple, inexpensive way to begin addressing your depression! You don't have to know how the brain works to know what works for your brain. The bottom line is if you condition your body, you will be doing one of the fastest things you can do to alter your mood and get back on track with a more proactive lifestyle. When people say, "It's the simple things that count," they couldn't be more accurate than when they are talking about the importance of getting the body active again.

THE CONTEMPLATIVE LIFE

Aside from isolated monastic communities in some Catholic and Eastern traditions, meditation has all but disappeared from the religious culture of America. But did you know that the Bible encourages it? A busy culture like our own leaves little time for inner reflection. But meditation was and is an important strategy for keeping our spiritual eyes on God.

Biblical meditation is *the act of silently reflecting on the truths of God's nature and mentally acknowledging His loving presence.* It is the conscious reminder of the life we have in Him now and of the life we will have with Him in eternity. When I was in college, I used to drop by a church nearby the campus that was open during the day. With soft choir music playing in the background, it was a serene environment where I could catch my breath from my busy schedule and contemplate God and my life with Him. I found those times rejuvenating to both the mind and the soul. With the prompting of the Holy Spirit, meditation inspires us to love more, give more and serve more. Our relationships with others become our primary focus and ministering to others becomes our highest priority.

Meditation also inspires a deeper kind of contentment. King David said it best: "The Lord is my shepherd, I shall not be in want. He makes me lie down in green pastures, he leads me beside still waters, he restores my soul." (Psa. 23:1-3a). Think about that. As a friend, a missionary to Austria, pointed out, He emotionally nourishes us ("green pastures"), provides refreshment and a sense of well-being ("quiet or restful waters") and spiritually revives us ("restores my soul")—if only we stop long enough to fully drink in His presence.

Part of this spiritually contemplative life is the communion of prayer. When we sense the nearness of God, we find that it reveals the truth about us—about things we need to learn. It also provides healing for our painful memories and losses. Personal, purifying change becomes internalized in the presence of the Person whom we love. It is a bond that makes our faith an experiential fellowship. To pray is to linger in the presence of the Author of our worth and lovability. And prayer is the instrument of a growing life attachment to His heart.

Jesus told us to come to Him with our requests—not to inform Him but to sift out the supplications we make on a whim from those made from honest, lasting desire. Jesus promised that what we ask in the Spirit will be given us—what we seek for the sake of righteousness we will find—and when we take the risk to knock with intention, He will open the door of his direction (see Matt. 7:7). These verbs have tremendous significance. Our Lord was telling His listeners to keep on doing those things that are basic to knowing His will. Exercising our privilege of prayer gives us the spiritual preparation for a durable faith in hard times. Such times may be our chance to learn from God about things made significant only by our pain.

We often look up at the sky on a crisp, clear night and say, "The stars are out tonight." Although we say that they "come out" at night, they are there all the time. But we only see them after the sun "goes down" and the sky grows dark.

In the same way, people who suffer in the darkness of adversity have a greater opportunity to see and appreciate the good things in life. It was reported that an aged Jewish man was found living alone in dreadful squalor on the back streets of a small town in the north part of Iraq. The compassionate relief worker who found him brought him out of the indescribable place he had called home for more than 20 years and took him to live in a modern assisted living complex in Israel. Later, he spoke of his overwhelming happiness and his eternal gratitude for his rescue—things he felt so deeply because of how lonely and depressing his conditions had been for so long. The contrast was so dramatic that he wept tears of joy over every precious day of freedom.

If we are free enough and willing enough to see it, there is an upside that either accompanies or follows every downside—a light that penetrates every darkness. And just as there is a responsibility that comes with every freedom, there is a challenge that comes with every insight. The challenge is to trust God's heart. It is not a call to blind trust, but to a trust informed by His gracious acts in history. Our faith depends on it. Our personal healing must likewise stem from it.

MAKING A DIFFERENCE

Reaching out to those in need is both an extension of faith and a practical means of combating depression. There is nothing quite like helping other people rise above their adversities in life to revive your own spirit. And there is nothing quite like intimacy with God to inspire love for other people.

Two things can happen when we give of ourselves in this way. First, we discover the principle that both the helper and the helped tend to stimulate growth in each other, provided they are receptive to it. It reflects the importance of true gratitude in relationships. We also find that serving others reminds us that we can still create outcomes that make a difference. Both results challenge the depressing belief that we are helpless to achieve anything worthwhile.

It's the gift of our uniqueness—freely given—that elegantly sets the framework for the possibilities ahead for ourselves and for those we touch. Author Andrew Solomon, who struggled with depression, wrote, "the unexamined life is unavailable to the depressed—that is perhaps the greatest revelation I have had: not that depression is compelling but that people who suffer from it may be compelling because of it."[2]

People who have struggled with depression are often led to make changes that make them more patient, more empathic and more thoughtful. This is why they become more compelling and more healing in the lives of others. The lesson of depression invites us to cherish life more, to value greater wisdom and to enlarge our appreciation for the deeper concerns of the human soul.

FINDING HOPE

1. If you want to change the stories being written in your mind, *change your behavior first. Doing* something different can sometimes be more effective than trying to *think* something different.

2. Try to view your anxiety attacks as *"aerobic moments."* Then try to paradoxically increase your symptoms when you have them. *Discover the usefulness of behavioral experiments.*

3. Increase the *efficiency* of your worrying: Each day, *condense all your anxiety-inducing thoughts into a single hour.* Use the rest of the time for more enjoyable activities.

4. Think of *forgiveness as the gateway to freedom* from the toxic burden of bitterness.

5. *Doing the unexpected* in a relationship increases its *interest value* and provides the *context for change.*

6. Emotional distress is never God's goal—*maturation* is.

7. By practicing God's loving presence in *meditation,* you initiate a *growing life attachment* to Him and a *more durable faith.*

HAMILTON SURVEY FOR EMOTIONAL AND PHYSICAL WELLNESS

DR. GREGORY KNOPF MD

INSTRUCTIONS: Think over the past two weeks and rate yourself for each question as you identify with the phrases, symptoms and feelings.

Rating Scale: **0=None, 1=Mild, 2=Moderate, 3=Severe, 4=Extreme**

_____**1) Depressed Mood:** I find myself feeling very sad and helpless, either because of the present circumstances or for no reason at all. I feel a sense of hopelessness that things will never get better. I find myself crying more frequently and am not able to "hold it together." I often feel worthless.

_____**2) Guilt Feelings:** I sometimes feel like I should be punished. I really do not like myself right now and maybe I deserve some of the things that are happening to me. Even though I can't think of specific examples, I feel guilty much of the time.

_____**3) Suicide:** I often find myself thinking about death and sometimes wish that I didn't have to live anymore. My life seems empty and not worth the effort it is taking. I find myself wanting to avoid other people and be alone. I've told at least one other person that it would be better if I were dead or gone. Sometimes I find myself wanting to cut myself or think about taking a lot of pills.

_____**4) Initial Insomnia:** I have difficulty falling asleep after I get into bed at night.

_____**5) Middle Insomnia:** I have difficulty sleeping all night long without interruption. I wake up for no reason several times During the night. I sometimes get back to sleep and sometimes not.

_____**6) Delayed Insomnia:** I find myself waking up 2-3 hours before I want to, for no reason, and cannot get back to sleep.

_____**7) Work and interest:** My job and family are no longer enjoyable. I often find myself not caring about my job or home responsibilities. I rarely do any of the hobbies that I used to enjoy. My friends invite me to do things, but I often find reasons to say no. The things that I use to enjoy don't seem to lift my spirits. People at work are noticing that the quality of my work has deteriorated. My family members are beginning to complain that I don't do the usual things around the house that I did in the past.

_____**8) Alertness:** I find myself feeling sluggish in my ability to think, communicate my ideas, and sometimes just moving around.

_____**9) Agitation:** I find myself fidgeting and feeling very restless. Often I will pace back and forth or sometimes clench my fists. Sometimes I will tap my feet or hands for no reasons or bite my lips. I often find myself wringing my hands. Sometimes I will pull at my hair or pick at my fingernails or clothes.

_____**10) Anxiety (Psychological):** I often feel tense and unable to relax. I find myself irritable with family or coworkers. I am easily startled. Even though I try not to, I often worry over trivial matters. Often, I am fearful for no reason. I have a sense that things are going to get worse and I will be unable to do anything to change it. I feel out of control and that I could have a panic attack.

_____**11) Anxiety (Physical):** I often times have "butterflies" in my stomach. Many times my stomach will cramp or I will have indigestion. Recently I have noted more belching or diarrhea. My heart has begun to beat much faster that it used to. I often find myself feeling like I can't get enough air. Sometimes I have noted tingling in my fingers or around my mouth. I am sweating more than I used to or feel flushed. I have noticed that my hands have begun to shake slightly. I have recently started having headaches for no reason. I find that I have to go to the bathroom and urinate more frequently, and often smaller amounts.

_____**12) Loss of Appetite:** Food no longer seems appealing to me. I just don't feel like eating as much as I used to. My friends have expressed concern about my eating habits.

_____**13) Fatigue:** I feel exhausted almost all the time. I no longer have the kind of energy to function like I used to. I often feel like my arms or legs are heavy. I have wondered if I have "chronic fatigue syndrome."

_____**14) Sexual:** I have lost my desire for sexual intimacy that I used to have. I am finding that it is not worth the effort to be involved in sex.

_____**15) Fear:** I am afraid that I might have cancer or something really bad affecting my health. I think a lot about many kinds of symptoms which I have never had before, and it upsets me.

_____**16) Weight Loss:** I am now losing weight, even though I am not trying to lose weight.

_____**17) Unexplained Pains:** I have pain in my muscles and around my joints and along my spine. Doctors have not given me a clear reason for the pains because they consider the symptoms too vague. I wonder if I could have " fibromyalgia." I often have headaches and low back pains.

_____**18) Mood Swings:** I find that my moods can range from high to low, often for no reason, and even on the same day. It upsets me to think that I cannot control my emotions when I am down.

_____**19) Oversleeping:** I am finding that it is harder to get up in the morning, even though I go to bed on time. I don't get the kind of sleep I would like, and stay in bed for hours at a time.

_____**20) Oversleeping:** I am sleeping more than ever before. It seems that all I want to do is sleep.

_____**21) Napping:** It is difficult for me to get through the day without taking a nap or wanting to take a nap. I am so tired by the afternoon that when I come home I can hardly function.

_____**22) Increased Appetite:** I am finding myself eating more even if I am not hungry. I am having more cravings than ever for certain foods like chocolate. I am eating more during my regular meals and having snacks between meals. My friends have expressed concern about my eating habits. I sometimes binge on junk food.

_____**23) Weight Gain:** I have gained weight recently. It seems like I am gaining weight even though I am not eating enough to explain the increase.

_____**24) Sluggishness:** I oftentimes feel almost paralyzed in my ability to process my thoughts and feelings. I am unable to find the will power to do the things I need to do. I just can't think as quickly as I used to.

_____**25) Physical Movement:** I feel sluggish physically. People ask me if there is something wrong because they say I look sad.

_____ **ITEM TOTAL** .

Guide to interpretation of total score:
0-7 Normal
8-19 Mild "dysthymia" or "sub-clinical depression"
20-29 "mild to moderate" major depressive disorder (MDD)
30-39 "moderately severe" major depressive disorder (MDD)
Greater than 40 is consistent with "severe" major depressive disorder (MDD)

Note: A downloadable version of the *Hamilton Survey For Emotional and Physical Wellness* is available at our website, ITLCommunications.com.

MORE ONLINE RESOURCES

To access other, easy to take, alternative depression scales (such as the Zung Self Rated Depression Scale, the Beck Self Rated Scale, or the PHQ-9 Scale), which you may wish to review, you can go to each of the following internet links:

Zung Self Rated Scale:
http://healthnet.umassmed.edu/mhealth/
ZungSelfRatedDepressionScale.pdf

Beck Self Rated Scale:
http://www.ibogaine.desk.nl/graphics/3639b1c_23.pdf

PHQ-9 Depression Questionnaire:
http://www.mhqp.org/mhqp_attachments/PHQ-9%20
depression%20screening%20tool.pdf

APPENDIX B

IRRATIONAL BELIEFS: RESULTS AND COUNTER BELIEFS

The following are the most common irrational beliefs and their rational counter beliefs as measured by the *Irrational Beliefs Test* (IBT). The IBT is an independently scored inventory containing a hundred statements. The test taker is asked to agree or disagree with each statement on a 5 point scale to determine the strength of their beliefs. It is useful for identifying the dysfunctional ideologies of those suffering from depression and anxiety.

These irrational beliefs lead to a variety of agitated feelings and behaviors that block a more adaptive lifestyle. As you will notice, most of them support a life of self-victimization. The following is a breakdown of the effects specific to each irrational belief along with their corresponding rational counter beliefs.

IRRATIONAL BELIEF and WHAT IT LEADS TO	RATIONAL BELIEF
① It is a dire necessity for me to be loved and approved of by virtually every person who is significant to me in any way. **RESULT:** Leads to a *desperate search for social approval* as a criterion for self-acceptance. It often reflects an underlying self-hatred.	While it is nice to be loved and approved of by certain select people, it is not necessary. My self-worth does not depend on the approval of others.
② I should be thoroughly competent, adequate and achieving in every respect if I am to consider myself worthwhile. **RESULT:** Leads to a *paralyzing fear of failure* where performance becomes the basis for all personal worth.	Being competent and achieving in some areas certainly has its rewards, but my self-worth has nothing to do with my level of performance.
③ Certain people are bad, wicked or villainous and they should be severely blamed and punished for their villainy. **RESULT:** Leads to a lot of *blaming behavior* where fault finding and accusations are the major preoccupation.	While certain people may do bad, wicked or villainous things, they still have personal worth. Negative consequences are used to correct the bad behavior, not to punish.

239

IRRATIONAL BELIEF and WHAT IT LEADS TO	RATIONAL BELIEF
4 It is awful and catastrophic when things are not the way I very much want them to be. **RESULT:** Leads to a lot of *frustration, anger and even rage* because life is deemed unfair and people are seen as cruel or hurtful.	It is unfortunate and disappointing when things are not the way I would like them to be, but that is not the end of the world.
5 Human unhappiness is externally caused and I have little or no ability to control my sorrows and disturbances. **RESULT:** Leads to *overwhelming sense of helplessness* where passive resignation is the rule.	Unfortunate events may happen to me that are beyond my control, but I do have control over the degree to which these negative events will upset me.
6 If something is or may be dangerous or fearsome, I should be terribly concerned about it and should keep dwelling on the possibility of its occurring. **RESULT:** Leads to *crippling anxiety* where worst-case scenarios dominate one's thinking.	If something is or may be dangerous or fearsome, I will take whatever precautions are reasonable and then forget about what I cannot control.
7 It is easier to avoid than to face certain life difficulties and self-responsibilities. **RESULT:** Leads to a life of *avoidance and irresponsibility* where there is little self-discipline to be proactive.	In the long run, it is easier to face than avoid certain life difficulties and self-responsibilities.
8 I should be dependent on others to give me support and make decisions for me. **RESULT:** Leads to a life of *childlike overdependency* where searching for others to lean on is the primary motive.	Although gathering information from experts and support from friends is quite acceptable, I am the one who makes the final decision and deals with the unpleasant situations of life.
9 My past history is an all-important determinant of my present behavior and because something once strongly affected my life, it should indefinitely have a similar effect. **RESULT:** Leads to *living perpetually in the past* where all rationales are found for passive inaction.	My past history can have an important effect on my present behavior. However, just because something once strongly affected my life, there is no reason it should continue to have a similar effect.
10 There is invariably a right, precise and perfect solution to human problems and it is catastrophic if this perfect solution is not found. **RESULT:** Leads to *inflexible perfectionism* where rigid compartmentalization is the norm. It's the refusal to accept imperfect reality.	There is seldom a right, precise and perfect solution to human problems. It is better to choose the best of the available alternatives than to search for a nonexistent perfect solution.

MEDICATION OVERVIEW

Note: Not mentioned in the following table are medications used to treat BIPOLAR MANIA, which include the following: Lithium, Depakote, Atypical Anti-psychotics (Zyprexa, Seroquel, Risperdal, Abilify, Geodon). Medications that can more generally treat BIPOLAR DISORDER include Seroquel and Lamictal. If you have been diagnosed with this disorder, discuss with your doctor which one would be best for you.

SEROTONIN AND NOREPINEPHRINE REUPTAKE INHIBITORS—(SNRI)

MEDICATION	DOSAGE	ADVANTAGES	DISADVANTAGES	NICHE
EFFEXOR XR (Venlafaxine) extended release capsules	37.5 mg to 375 mg	Raises serotonin and norepinephrine. Few side effects; Very effective; Minimal sexual dysfunction; Also effective in anxiety	Initially causes nausea Can cause sweats, constipation, and tremor Withdrawal/Rebound problems; Increase BP in some people at high doses	Excellent broad spectrum; Few side effects; Can be used in combination; Improves cognitive dysfunction Low sexual dysfunction
CYMBALTA (Duloxetine)	30 mg to 120 mg	"Balanced" elevation of serotonin and norepinephrine; Minimal sexual dysfunction; also approved for diabetic peripheral neuropathic pain and fibromyalgia	Some nausea for the first 6 days when starting medicine	Some advantages in reducing musculoskeletal pain from depression and "fibromyalgia." Good for people with diabetic neuropathic pain. Low sexual dysfunction.
PRISTIQ	50mg, one a day for most people, 100mg once a day for some people	Cleanest of all antidepressants because it is not metabolized in the liver. Few side effects. Less rebound and BP problems with less sexual problems.	Some nausea first 6 days when starting the medication.	Fewer side effects than Effexor XR. Very effective and predictable in people who may be either rapid or poor metabolizers.

SELECTIVE SEROTONIN REUPTAKE INHIBITORS—(SSRI)

MEDICATION	DOSAGE	ADVANTAGES	DISADVANTAGES	NICHE
PROZAC (Fluoxetine) (Sarafem)	10 mg to 80 mg	May increase energy initially, approved for PMS syndrome, longest lasting (half life of med)	Slower onset of action; Sexual dysfunction; Long residual May cause fatigue after long-term use	Minimizes problems of noncompliance, (people forgetting to take pill) Good for PMS and anxiety, available as generic.

SELECTIVE SEROTONIN REUPTAKE INHIBITORS—CONTINUED

MEDICATION	DOSAGE	ADVANTAGES	DISADVANTAGES	NICHE
PAXIL (Paroxetine)	10 mg to 50 mg	Approved for depression, OCD, and panic disorder	Side effects; nausea and sedation; Sexual dysfunction	For social anxiety, OCD/panic, available as generic
ZOLOFT (Sertraline)	25 mg to 200 mg	Increases mood "middle of road" SSRI; OCD approved	Side effects; Some sedation; Sexual dysfunction	"Middle of the road SSRI" available as generic
CELEXA (Citalopram)	20 mg to 40 mg	Increase mood; Good for anxiety	Possibly less potent; Sexual dysfunction	Try when other SSRIs cause side effects or in combination, available as generic.
LEXAPRO (Escitalopram)	10 mg to 20 mg	Less side effects than CELEXA, "pure SSRI"	Some sexual dysfunction	Try when other SSRIs cause side effects or in combination

OTHER ANTIDEPRESSANT MEDICATIONS

MEDICATION	DOSAGE	ADVANTAGES	DISADVANTAGES	NICHE
WELLBUTRIN SR WELLBUTRIN XL APLENZIN (Bupropion)	100 mg to 300 mg 348 mg and 522 mg	Lifts mood; approved for addictions (smoking); used for ADHD; Least sexual dysfunction of all anti-depressants	May cause seizures in high doses or in people with eating disorders; Inconsistent response	Depression with fatigue, and ADHD, Addictions (smoking, overeating)
DESYREL (Trazodone)	50 mg to 400 mg	Most sedating antidepressant	Weaker at lifting mood Some morning sedation Priapism	Used in combination with other antidepressants for people with severe sleep difficulty
REMERON (Mirtazapine)	15 mg to 45 mg	Helps with insomnia Minimal sexual dysfunction	Sedation in >50% Weight gain with lower dose	Depression with insomnia; Patients with needed weight gain -(Anorexia/ wt loss)
EFFEXOR Venlafaxine immediate release tablets	37.5 mg to 375 mg	Fast acting in crisis situations	Significant side effects, particularly nausea, withdrawal rebound problems, 2 X/day dosing	Used only when a person can not afford Effexor XR. Available in generic
TRICYCLICS: Amitryptyline Doxepin Nortryptyline Imipramine others	Variable	Help with sleep Stabilize mood Help with musculoskeletal pain and headaches	Side effects including dry mouth (60%) Lethal in overdose Weight gain; Drug Interaction Orthostatic BP changes	No longer "first line" agents Good for patients with fibromyalgia and chronic pain
TRIMONOAMINE MODULATOR: Deplin	7.5mg	NO side effects	Will not work for everyone	Very safe medication to add on to an antidepressant. Also good to use in those who are taking Lamictal for Bipolar disorder.

SYMPTOMS, DIAGNOSIS AND TREATMENT OF DEPRESSION

SYMPTOMS OF DEPRESSION

- ✔ Depressed Mood
- ✔ Loss of interest
- ✔ Guilt/Feelings of Worthlessness
- ✔ Weight Gain/ Weight Loss
- ✔ Insomnia/ Oversleeping
- ✔ Agitation/Restlessness
- ✔ Lack of Concentration
- ✔ Fatigue
- ✔ Recurrent Thoughts of Suicide
- ✔ Irritability/ "Stressed Out"

DIAGNOSIS OF DEPRESSION

A person must have a total of at least 5 of the above symptoms, (one of which must be depressed mood or loss of interest) for a minimum of two weeks, or a total score of >20 on the Hamilton Survey for Emotional and Physical Wellness.

TREATMENT OF DEPRESSION

Depression with fatigue no anxiety	Depression with anxiety no sleep disturbance	Depression with anxiety and sleep disturbance
FIRST CHOICE	**FIRST CHOICE**	**FIRST CHOICE**
Wellbutrin Pristiq Effexor XR Cymbalta	Pristiq Effexor XR Cymbalta Zoloft + Wellbutrin	Zoloft *(also for short-term use: add* Pristiq *Sonata, Ambien,* Lexapro *Lunesta, Rozerem)* Cymbalta Effexor XR Trazodone + 1 of the above

Psychotherapy as appropriate with all medications

Schedule for follow-up appointment in 3 weeks or call if symptoms worsen, there are increased thoughts of suicide, or side effects are intolerable.

UNSUCCESSFUL RESPONSE
Assess medication follow-through and dosage. (Side effects can be reduced by slower dose increases.) Consider adding Deplin or Abilify. Consider alternative diagnoses including Bi-polar Disorder or concomitant Attention Deficit Disorder. Switch to different medication in the same or different class (SSRI or SNRI). Consider prescribing a combination of medications. Consider psychiatric referral for evaluation.

SUCCESSFUL RESPONSE OR FULL REMISION
Goal is Hamilton Scale < 7. Monitor dosage and side effects. Office visits every 2–6 months.

OTHER CONTRIBUTING MEDICAL FACTORS TO DEPRESSION

Many, including family members and even the patients themselves, are often unaware of the fact that some of the symptoms they observe or experience in their illness are due to depression. It is not uncommon for people who suffer from a chronic illness or medical condition to also suffer from depression. But it is easily concealed by other medical problems and so, as a result, frequently goes undetected and untreated. Nonetheless, it is one of the most prevalent emotional consequences of physical illness. Typically, it reflects the stress of coping with disease; but the disease itself can also cause it.

Some studies suggest that as many as one-third of all patients with some kind of chronic medical condition also suffer from depression. This is partly due to the limitations imposed by the illness or condition on their mobility, on their ability to engage in activities they once enjoyed, and on their expectations of the future. The severity of the depression is often proportional to the severity of the illness and the limitations it imposes.

Depression can actually further complicate the medical condition (e.g., increase the risk of coronary heart disease) as well as increase the patient's fatigue and immobility. What's more, it often causes people to become isolated, further amplifying their loneliness and hopelessness. Partly because this can likewise enhance the risk of suicide, it is important to diagnose the presence of depression as early as possible.

DEPRESSION RATES ASSOCIATED WITH CHRONIC CONDITIONS

Sometimes, the combination of chronic illness and depression can make things considerably worse by giving rise to a destructive loop: The chronic condition can trigger depression which, in turn, can hamper effective treatment of the illness, which, as a consequence of continued (and, perhaps, increased) pain and disability, leads to even more depression. Add to that the fact that some medications used to treat the medical condition can, themselves, cause depression, and you can have a rapidly deteriorating situation. That's why it is important to seek therapeutic help as soon as possible. It is wise, too, for friends and family to make every effort to keep the chronically ill person actively engaged with life to prevent their withdrawal—something that can otherwise likely happen.

CHRONIC CONDITION	% EXPERIENCING DEPRESSION
Heart attack	40–65%
Coronary artery disease (without heart attack)	18–20%
Parkinson's disease	40%
Multiple sclerosis	40%
Stroke	15–20%
Cancer	25% (up to 45-50% with cancer of the pancreas)
Diabetes	25%
Chronic pain syndrome	30–54%

MEDICAL CONDITIONS RELATED TO DEPRESSION

There are a number of general Medical conditions that can cause or, at least can be associated with depression. The following is a list of medical conditions as adapted from a compilation of medical sources.

GENERAL CONDITION	SPECIFIC CONDITION
Cancer	Breast cancer, Leukemia, Lymphoma, Prostate cancer
Cardiovascular	Heart attack, Congestive heart failure, Stroke
Gynecological	Perimenopausal (Involutional Melancolia), Pregnancy/Post-partum depression, Premenstral Syndrome (PMS)
Musculoskeletal	Back pain, Chronic pain, Chronic fatigue syndrome, Fibromyalgia, Rheumatoid Arthritis, Systemic lupus
Endrocrine	Diabetes (Hyperglycemia), Hypoglycemia, Hypothyroidism, Hyperthyroidism, Adrenal Dysfunction (Addison's Disease), Cushing Syndrome (adrenal tumor), Anemia, Hyperparathyroidism
Neurologic	Dementia, Epilepsy, Migraines, Multiple Sclerosis, Parkinson's Disease, Lewy Body Disease, Traumatic Brain Injury
Infections	HIV-Positive-AIDS, Infectious hepatitis A, B, C, Syphilis

MEDICATIONS ASSOCIATED WITH DEPRESSION

These medications are known either to have possible depressive side effects or cause depression with rapid withdrawal.*

CATEGORY	MEDICATION or TREATMENT
Blood pressure (Antihypertensives)	Reserpine (Brand name: Serpasil), Beta Blockers (e.g., Brand name: Inderal), Calcium Channel Blockers, Methyldopa (Brand name: Aldomet), Guanethidine sulfate (Brand name: Ismelin sulfate), Clonidine hydrochloride (Brand name: Catapres)
Contraceptives	Progestin-Estrogen combination (various brands), Norplant (discontinued distribution after 2002,but some still have implant)
Hormone	Estrogen (e.g., Premarin, Ogen, Estrace, Estraderm), Progesterone and derivatives (e.g., Provera, DepoProvera)
Antiparkinsons disease agents	Levodopa carbidopa (Brand name: Sinemet), Amantadine hydrochloride (Brand names: Dopar, Larodopa, Symmetrel)
Antianxiety agents-Benzodiazapines (especially withdrawal after addiction)	Diazepam (Brand name: Valium), Chlordiazepoxide (Brand name: Librium)
Psychoactive substances	Alcohol (tends to have a masking effect with depression), Opiates (e.g., Opium, Heroin, Codeine, Hydrocone, Methodone, Morphine, Oxycodone, Darvocet, Percocet, Percodan, Vicodon, to name some of the more common ones), Amphetamines, Cocaine, Anabolic steroids
Chemotherapy agents	Vincristine, vinblastine, procarbazine, Interferon.
Glucosteroids	Cortisone acetate
First Generation Antipsychotic medications	Phenothiazines (e.g., Thorazine, Mellaril, Stelazine, Trilafon, Phenergan), Haloperidol (Brand name: Haldol)

Adopted and modified from "Practical Pharmacology", professional seminars by Dr. Gollapudi Shankar, PharmD, MS., PH-C, BCPP, CGP.

ENDNOTES

CHAPTER 1

1. Name changed.

2. A. W. Tozer, *The Attributes of God* (Camp Hill, PA: Christian Publications, 1997), pp. 42-43.

3. *Chariots of Fire.* Warner Studios, 1981.

4. Kenneth Blanchard, author of *The One Minute Apology,* in an interview on the Laura Ingraham radio show, January 21, 2003.

CHAPTER 2

1. Andrew Solomon, *The Noonday Demon: An Atlas of Depression* (NY: Simon & Schuster, 2002), pp. 435, 441, 443.

2. Edith Schaeffer, *The Art of Life* (Wheaton, IL: Crossway Books, 1987).

3. Paul Brand, *Pain: The Gift Nobody Wants* (New York: HarperCollins, 1993).

4. Robert Frost, quoted in the *Quotidian* (Portland and Corvallis, Oregon: Telesis, 1978).

5. Viktor E. Frankl, *Man's Search for Meaning* (New York: Washington Square Press, 1963).

6. Jack Reimer, article in the *Houston Chronicle* (September 15, 2001). Used with permission.

CHAPTER 3

1. Andrew Solomon, *The Noonday Demon: An Atlas of Depression* (NY: Simon & Schuster, 2002), p. 81.

2. Louis Pasteur, in *Quotidian,* (Portland and Corvallis, Oregon: Telesis 1978).

3. John Eldridge, *Journey of Desire: Searching for the Life We've Only Dreamed Of* (Nashville: Thomas Nelson Publishers, 2000), p. 9.

CHAPTER 4

1. Andrew Solomon, *The Noonday Demon: An Atlas of Depression* (NY: Simon & Schuster, 2002), p. 432.

2. Richard E. Byrd, *Alone* (G.P. Putnam's Sons, 1938), chapter 5 (May 11, 10:00 p.m.).

CHAPTER 5

1. A. W. Tozer, *The Pursuit of God* (Camp Hill, PA: Christian Publications, 1982), p. 112.

2. Theodore Isaac Rubin, *Compassion and Self-Hate: An Alternative to Despair* (NY: Simon & Schuster, 1975), p. 62.

CHAPTER 6

1. Michael D. Yapko, "Breaking the Patterns of Depression: Affective Treatment and Skill-building Interventions," presented at the Therapeutic and Alcohol/Drug Interventions Conference, May 2-4, 2007.

2. Arthur Freeman, "Self-directed Negative Behavior: Cognitive Behavioral Treatment of Depression Spectrum Disorders," presented at the Therapeutic and Alcohol/Drug Interventions Conference, May 2-4, 2007.

3. Haddon Robinson, in a message delivered in Vancouver, Washington, April 1994.

4. Cristian Barbosu, report in *The Church Around the World,* vol. 35, no. 1 (Carol Stream, IL: Tyndale House Publishers, 2004).

5. John Piper, *Future Grace* (Sisters, OR: Multnomah Books, 1995), p. 32.

6. Mark Twain, in *Quotidian* (Portland and Corvallis, Oregon: Telesis, 1978).

7. John Piper, *Future Grace*, pp. 386-387.

CHAPTER 7

1. John Piper, *Future Grace* (Sisters, OR: Multnomah Books, 1995), p. 324.

2. Paul Tournier, *Guilt and Grace* (NY: Harper & Row Publishing, 1962), p. 185.

3. C. S. Lewis, *Mere Christianity* (Grand Rapids, MI: Zondervan Publishing, 1980), p. 118.

CHAPTER 8

1. A. W. Tozer, *The Attributes of God* (Camp Hill, PA: Christian Publications, 1997).

2. Paul Tournier, *Guilt and Grace* (NY: Harper & Row Publishers, 1962), p. 174.

3. C. S. Lewis, *The Weight of Glory* (NY: HarperCollins Publishing, 2001), pp. 1-2. (Originally published in 1949).

4. This discussion and C. S. Lewis's quote were taken from Armand M. Nicholi, Jr., *The Question of God: C.S. Lewis and Sigmund Freud Debate God, Love, Sex and the Meaning of Life* (NY: Simon & Schuster, 2002), p. 106.

5. Lindsay Lee Johnson, *Soul Moon Soup* (Asheville, NC: Front Street, 2002), pp. 106-107.

CHAPTER 9

1. Philip Yancey, *Reaching for the Invisible God* (Grand Rapids, MI: Zondervan, 2000), p. 16.

2. Henri J. M, Nouwen, *Life of the Beloved: Spiritual Living in a Secular World* (NY: Crossroad Publishing Co., 1992), p. 106.

3. Ibid., p. 106.

CHAPTER 10

1. Art Greco, "The Monster in My Closet: A Story of Depression," *The Covenant Companion* (Covenant Publications, Sept. 2004), pp. 9, 21.

2. Ibid., p. 21.

3. Ibid., p. 9.

CHAPTER 12

1. Stephen M. Stahl, *Essential Psychopharmacology of Depression and Bipolar Disorder* (Cambridge, UK: Cambridge University Press, 2000), p. 2.

2. Developed by Dr. David Kupfer, M. D.

CHAPTER 13

1. Paul Watzlawick, *Ultra-Solutions: How to Fail Most Successfully* (New York: W.W. Norton and Co. Publishers, 1988), p. 107.

2. Andrew Solomon, *The Noonday Demon: An Atlas of Depression* (NewYork: Simon & Schuster), 2002, p. 438.

THE AUTHORS

GARY H. LOVEJOY, PH.D.

Gary H. Lovejoy, Ph.D., has had a private practice in counseling psychology for over 30 years, working with individuals, couples and families dealing with depression, anxiety, conflict resolution, marital issues, parenting and teenager problems and a host of other issues. He continues an active practice with Valley View Counseling Services, LLC in Portland, Oregon. He was also a professor of psychology and a professor of religion at Mt. Hood Community College for 32 years, teaching courses in World Religions and the Old and New Testament in addition to his core load of Psychology courses. He earned a master's degree in religious education from Fuller Theological Seminary as well as a master's in psychology from California State University, Los Angeles, and his doctorate in psychology from United States International University. Dr. Lovejoy has spoken at many family camps, couple's retreats, college conferences and the like, as well as conducting seminars on depression. Dr. Lovejoy and his wife, Sue, have two adult children.

Valley View Counseling Services, LLC
PO Box 66176 | Portland, OR 97290
1 (877) ITL-3762 or 1 (877) 485-3762

GREGORY M. KNOPF, M.D.

Gregory M. Knopf, M.D., has been a family practice physician for 30 years and is the founder and medical director of the Gresham-Troutdale Family Medical Center. He is a graduate and Clinical Associate Professor of Family Medicine at Oregon Health Sciences University. Dr. Knopf is Board Certified in Family Medicine but has a special interest in the treatment of anxiety and depression. He speaks across the country on these topics, principally for professional audiences, and for churches and the general public as well. He has been involved in clinical research and is a member of the national primary care advisory board for Wyeth Pharmaceuticals. He enjoys tennis, gardening, and is on the leadership team of Radiant Church in Gresham, Oregon. Dr. Knopf and his wife, Bonnie, live on a 26 acre farm and have three adult children.

Gresham-Troutdale Family Medical Center
1700 SW 257th Avenue | Troutdale, OR 97060
(503) 669-6800 Fax (503) 492-1352